Humanizing Grief in Higher Education

By showcasing asset-based approaches inspired by individual reflection, research, and experience, this volume offers a fresh and timely perspective on grief and trauma within higher education and illustrates how these approaches can serve as opportunities for hope and allyship.

Featuring a broad range of contributions from scholars and professionals involved in educational research and academia, *Humanizing Grief in Higher Education* explores the varied ways in which students, scholars, and educators experience and navigate grief and trauma. Set into four distinct parts, chapters deploy personal narratives situated within interdisciplinary and transdisciplinary research frameworks to illustrate how issues such as race, gender, socio-economic class, and politics intersect with experiences of personal and professional grief in the academy. A variety of intersectional fields of study—from positive psychology, counselling, feminist and queer theories, to trauma theory and disability studies—informs an interdisciplinary framework for processing traumatic experiences and finding ways to hope. These narrative explorations are positioned as key to developing a sense of hope amongst the grieving and those supporting them.

This text will benefit researchers, doctoral students, and academics in the fields of higher education, teacher education, trauma studies, and mental health education. Those interested in positive and educational psychology, as well as grief counselling in adults, will also enjoy this volume. Finally, this collection serves as a companion for those who find themselves grappling with losses, broadly defined.

Nicole Sieben is Assistant Professor of Secondary English Education, Coordinator of the Graduate English Education Programs, and Director of the Graduate Education Programs at SUNY College at Old Westbury, USA.

Stephanie Anne Shelton is Assistant Professor of Qualitative Research in the College of Education, and Affiliate Faculty Member in the Department of Gender and Race Studies at The University of Alabama, USA.

Routledge Research in Higher Education

For more information about this series, please visit: www.routledge.com/Routledge-Research-in-Higher-Education/book-series/RRHE

Humanizing Grief in Higher Education

Narratives of Allyship and Hope

Edited by Nicole Sieben and Stephanie Anne Shelton

Routledge
Taylor & Francis Group

NEW YORK AND LONDON

First published 2021
by Routledge
52 Vanderbilt Avenue, New York, NY 10017

and by Routledge
2 Park Square, Milton Park, Abingdon, Oxon, OX14 4RN

Routledge is an imprint of the Taylor & Francis Group, an informa business

Library of Congress Cataloging-in-Publication Data
A catalog record for this title has been requested

Names: Sieben, Nicole, editor. | Shelton, Stephanie Anne, 1978- editor.
Title: Humanizing grief in higher education : narratives of allyship and hope / edited by Nicole Sieben and Stephanie Anne Shelton.
Description: New York, NY : Routledge, 2021. | Series: Routledge research in higher education | Includes bibliographical references and index.
Identifiers: LCCN 2020046662 | ISBN 9780367345488 (hardback) | ISBN 9780429326493 (ebook)
Subjects: LCSH: College students—Psychology. | College teachers—Psychology. | Education, Higher—Psychological aspects. | College teaching—Psychological aspects. | Grief. | Narrative inquiry (Research method)
Classification: LCC LB3609 .H768 2021 | DDC 378.1/98–dc23
LC record available at https://lccn.loc.gov/2020046662

ISBN: 978-0-367-34548-8 (hbk)
ISBN: 978-0-429-32649-3 (ebk)
ISBN: 978-0-367-75079-4 (pbk)

Typeset in Baskerville
by KnowledgeWorks Global Ltd.

This book is dedicated to the eternal memory of our beloved fathers and the inimitable strength of our beautiful mothers.

Table of Contents

List of Figures

Contributors

Cara Anderson is an English teacher at Aspen Ridge Middle School in Ishpeming, Michigan. She has published in the *Language Arts Journal of Michigan* and presented at the annual fall conferences of the Michigan Council of Teachers of English and the Assembly on Literature for Adolescents of *NCTE* (*ALAN*), as well as the Upper Peninsula *Teaching and Learning Conference*. She is a National Writing Project Teacher Consultant (Northern Shores Writing Project) and has taught English to students in grades 7–12 in Michigan and previously taught at an alternative program in Salina, Kansas. I would like to dedicate this chapter to those we have lost and those who helped us through the grieving process.

Alison L. Black is a Senior Lecturer and arts-based/narrative researcher in the School of Education, University of the Sunshine Coast. Her research and scholarly work seeks to foster reflection and connection. Ali is interested in storied and visual approaches for supporting knowledge construction, representation of knowledge, and ongoing meaning making. This chapter with Linda is an expression of gratitude and hope, but also of grief for the loss of loved ones, of species, and the losses yet to come.

Katherine C. Brown is a Mental Health Counselor in Memphis, Tennessee and enjoys helping clients work through loss and grief and toward healing and hope. She completed her graduate work at the University of Memphis, where she deepened her understanding of bereavement within a framework of qualitative research and poststructural theory. This chapter is dedicated in loving memory to her mother, Trudy Brown, Master Gardener, stewardess of nature, lover of lolling about in rivers. Mom, you introduced me to the natural world and showed me how to be gentle. When you died, my heart broke, yet you have also helped me heal. I also dedicate this chapter to those lost loved ones whose specters continue to haunt me, and to all those that hum, buzz, bark, crinkle, and crunch, and still others that do not emit sound yet nevertheless have quite a lot to say.

Christina Christie is a Licensed Clinical Social Worker and Certified Alcohol and Drug Counselor. Her specialty area is children and families, with a strong focus on the neurobiology of relationships. Christina received her Master of Social Work degree from the University of Maine and her B.A. in Psychology from the University of Maine Farmington.

S. Adam Crawley is an Assistant Professor of Literacy Education at Oklahoma State University where he teaches courses about literature and literacy across content areas in K-8 classrooms. A former elementary teacher and on-going advocate for culturally diverse, responsive, and relevant pedagogy, his research explores depictions in LGBTQ-inclusive children's literature along with such texts' use and censorship in public schools. Via presentations and service, he is involved in the National Council of Teachers of English, Literacy Research Association, and American Educational Research Association. His scholarship is published in *Voices from the Middle, The ALAN Review, The Journal of Children's Literature, Bookbird: An International Journal of Children's Literature, Taboo: The Journal of Culture and Education,* and *English Journal.* He is grateful to share his narrative in this book and dedicates the chapter to his past elementary students, those who mentor him, and all educators navigating their LGBTQ identities in the classroom.

Jennifer S. Dail is a Professor of English education in the Department of English at Kennesaw State University in the metro-Atlanta area of Georgia. She also directs the Kennesaw Mountain Writing Project (KMWP), a National Writing Project site serving teachers Pre-K through college in all content areas. Dail served as coeditor of SIGNAL Journal, the International Literacy Association's journal focusing on young adult literature, from 2008 to 2013. She is also an active member of several educational organizations including the National Council of Teachers of English (NCTE) and the National Writing Project (NWP). She serves on the board of the Georgia Council of Teachers of English (GCTE) as the First Vice President and Conference Director. Dail has published multiple articles on young adult literature and technology in The ALAN Review and has written book chapters focusing on this work as well. She also co-edited *Toward a More Visual Literacy: Shifting the Paradigm with Digital Tools and Young Adult Literature* (Rowman and Littlefield, 2018) and *Young Adult Literature and the Digital World: Textual Engagement through Visual Literacy* (Rowman and Littlefield, 2018), both with Shelbie Witte and Steven Bickmore.

Mandie B. Dunn is Assistant Professor of English Education at the University of South Florida. Her research investigates the complexity of teachers' roles as professionals who do relational work and respond to multiple and competing stakeholders. Her chapter is dedicated to the teachers in her dissertation study: Ann, Jerry, Emma, Rachel, Rose, Tara, and Tiffani (names are pseudonyms).

Toby Emert is a Professor in the Department of Theater and Dance at Agnes Scott College, a liberal arts college for women, near Atlanta, Georgia. He is a former middle and high school English and drama teacher and has conducted professional development workshops for teachers across the United States on topics related to digital literacies, arts-based instructional strategies, and creative drama. For the past decade, he has worked closely with the refugee community in Clarkston, Georgia, directing summer programming and developing participatory action research projects. His scholarship focuses on digital storytelling, refugee-background learners, and queer issues in education. He co-edited the collection *"Come Closer": Critical Perspectives on Theatre of the Oppressed* for Peter Lang's Counterpoints series and currently serves as the co-editor of *English Journal*, a publication of the National Council of Teachers of English (NCTE).

Donita Grissom holds a B.S. in Elementary Education and a specialization in Early Childhood; a Master's Degree in Instruction and Curriculum, with an emphasis in teacher training in the field of ESOL; and, a Ph.D. in TESOL. She is a professional educational consultant, coach, and curriculum developer, training teachers in methods of teaching English to speakers of other languages nationally and internationally. Her research interests are hope, social emotional learning, preservice education, and teacher training. Dr. Grissom's teaching experience has been in K-12 classrooms, high school teaching Language Arts through ESOL, and adult ESOL classes. She is a former ESOL Curriculum Specialist for Seminole County Public Schools, one of the highest achieving districts in Florida. Dr. Grissom now teaches graduate and undergraduate English as a Second Language methods and culture courses at the University of Central Florida.

Kate Shands Haq has been a professional educator since 1985. She has taught in urban and rural schools in Western New York, primarily as an elementary classroom teacher and literacy coach in public schools. Currently, Kate teaches English Language Arts and Social Studies to middle school students at The Park School, an independent progressive school in Buffalo, New York. Kate earned her Ph.D. in Curriculum, Instruction and the Learning Sciences with a focus on Literacy at SUNY Buffalo in 2018. Mother of three sons, community activist, and education advocate, Kate's research interests include the intersection of homeless adolescents, literacy, and civic engagement as well as teachers' work, policy, and identity. This chapter is dedicated to the young people who empathetically and wholeheartedly shared their stories, their love, and their energy to make our community better. Your bravery and generosity live on through improved conditions for others. Thank you!

Linda Henderson is a Senior Lecturer and feminist early years researcher in the Faculty of Education, Monash University. She embodies her research and work through practices that honor the land upon which she works. She values and respects her connections with all living things and seeks to generate hope and healing in her work. She treasures friendship and connections. This chapter with Ali is an expression of my deep gratitude of the friendship we have, but also an expression of honoring the grief for the losses that have shaped and formed my heart and my soul.

Danielle Lee is a Visiting Assistant Professor of English at SUNY College at Old Westbury. Danielle teaches writing intensive courses ranging from English composition to Shakespeare and the classics, to Africana and multicultural literatures. Danielle also studied trauma and its representation in literature while earning her doctorate.

Stacia L. Long is a Ph.D. candidate in the Department of Language and Literacy at The University of Georgia. From 2011 to 2015, she was a high school English teacher in Texas before working on her master's degree at The University of Texas at Austin. At UGA, in addition to teaching in the undergraduate English Education program, she served as an editorial board member of the *Journal of Language and Literacy Education* in the roles of Children's and Young Adult Book Review Editor, Principal Editor, and Conference Co-Chair. She chaired the NCTE English Language Arts Teacher Educators-Graduate Strand from 2019 to 2021. Her research interests include narrative inquiry and teacher emotions. Her dissertation focuses on the effects of students' sexual violence on teachers' emotions and relationships, and how student sexual violence is depicted in the media. This chapter is dedicated to her grandparents, who passed away during the production of this chapter.

Elsie Lindy Olan is an Associate Professor and Track Coordinator for Secondary English Language Arts in the School of Teacher Education at the University of Central Florida. She has over 25 years of teaching experience. Her work has been published in *English Education, English Leadership Quarterly, Research in the Teaching of English, Education and Learning Research Journal, Argentinian Journal of Applied Linguistics,* and *Language Arts.* Her current research on teacher education, leadership, and diversity is shared in a co-edited book series, *Transformative Pedagogies for Teacher Education,* from Information Age

Publishing, Inc. Elsie Lindy's work and research has been presented at conferences in Mexico, Spain, United Kingdom, Tokyo, and the United States. Dr. Olan dedicates this chapter to her hope agents, her students, and colleagues. Their words and actions helped me move towards self-realization, sustainable hope, and personal growth, while critically thinking about ways to approach grief and become a better me.

Josefa Pace is in Literacy Studies. Through ethnographic research and discourse and narrative analysis, Josefa examines writing and digital rhetoric on culture, identity, and gender. Josefa received a BFA in Theatre and BA in English with a minor in Italian. She obtained her Masters in English/Creative Writing. She also completed coursework in Women's History and Social Work. She has been teaching on the college level in varied capacities at colleges in New York and California for almost 15 years. She teaches a range of courses in writing studies and composition, literature, literacy, and interdisciplinary classes. She would like to dedicate this chapter to her family, students, and the four women as they are integral to her personal and academic experiences. Most especially, she is inspired by her nephew and niece as they embrace each day anew and with unconditional love and ingenuity.

Kia Jane Richmond is Professor of English at Northern Michigan University in Marquette, Michigan, directs the English Education program and supervises student teachers in Michigan and Wisconsin. Her research focuses on teacher-student relationships, psychology and young adult literature, and English Education pedagogy. Her publications have appeared in *English Education, Journal of Literacy and Language Education, The ALAN Review, Language Arts Journal of Michigan,* and *Composition Studies.* Her latest book, *Mental Illness in Young Adult Literature: Exploring Real Struggles through Fictional Characters,* was published by ABC-CLIO/Libraries Unlimited in 2019. I would like to dedicate this chapter to those we have lost and those who helped us through the grieving process.

Ericka Roland is an Assistant Professor in the Department of Educational Leadership and Policy Studies' Higher Education Administration program at the University of Texas at Arlington. Her research examines critical leadership development in postsecondary educational settings through two interconnected lines of inquiry: 1) the dynamics of dialogical relationships; and 2) the lived leadership experiences of historically minoritized persons. Ericka's research topics include leadership development; dialogical Relationships; popular culture; critical pedagogy; equity in higher education and mentoring. This chapter is dedicated to graduate students who were/are grieving while dissertating.

Katie Rybakova is Assistant Professor of Education at Thomas College and the executive director of the Maine Association for Middle Level Education. She earned her doctorate from Florida State University in Curriculum and Instruction. Her expertise is in young adult literature and digital literacies, but her interests vary depending on her students' needs. This chapter is dedicated to them—the preservice teachers who give her hope in the future of education.

Stephanie Anne Shelton is Assistant Professor of Qualitative Research in the College of Education at The University of Alabama, and affiliate faculty member in the Department of Gender and Race Studies. Research interests include examining intersections of gender identities, gender expressions, sexualities, race, and class in educational contexts. Publications have appeared in *English Education*, the *International Journal of Qualitative Studies in Education*, *Qualitative Inquiry*, *Qualitative Research Journal*, *Sex Education*, and *Teaching and Teacher Education*. Her published books, in addition to this collection, are *Feminism and Intersectionality in Academia: Women's Narratives and Experiences in Higher Education* and *Narratives of Hope and Grief in Higher Education*.

Nicole Sieben is Assistant Professor of Secondary English Education at the State University of New York (SUNY) College at Old Westbury where she is also the Director of Graduate Education Programs and the Coordinator for the Graduate Programs in English Education. A former high school English teacher in New York, Sieben's research focuses on building "writing hope" in secondary and postsecondary education, social justice practices, and professional development in K-12 schools. Sieben is author of the book, *Writing Hope Strategies for Writing Success in Secondary Schools: A Strengths-Based Approach to Teaching Writing* (2018), co-editor of the book, *Narratives of Hope and Grief in Higher Education* (2020), journal co-editor for the special issue of *English Education* "Designing Professional Development for Equity and Social Justice," and column editor (2018–2020) for *English Journal*'s Books-in-Action column. Her work has recently been published in *English Education, Teaching and Teacher Education, English Journal,* and *English Leadership Quarterly*.

Peter Smagorinsky is distinguished Research Professor in the Department of Language and Literacy Education at The University of Georgia, emeritus; and Distinguished Visiting Scholar at the Universidad de Guadalajara, Jalisco, Mexico. From 2012 to 2020, he served as the faculty advisor to the student-edited *Journal of Language and Literacy Education* at UGA. Recent awards include the 2020 Horace Mann League Outstanding Public Educator Award, 2018 International Federation for the Teaching of English Award, and 2018 Distinguished Scholar recognition by the National Conference on Research in Language and Literacy. His research and teaching take a sociocultural approach to issues of literacy education and related social concerns. Recent books include *Learning to Teach English and Language Arts: A Vygotskian Perspective on Beginning Teachers' Pedagogical Concept Development* and *Developing Culturally and Historical Sensitive Teacher Education: Global Lessons from a Literacy Education Program*, the latter co-edited with Guadalajaran colleagues Yolanda Gayol and Patricia Rosas.

Kara M. Taylor is a Clinical Assistant Professor, IUPUI School of Education. She is a public intellectual who centers her work around narrative inquiry, critical reflection, fugitive literate practices, and healing spaces. Dr. Taylor is a former middle-school teacher, and still engages with urban elementary schools in her work as a Curriculum Designer, Instructional Coach, and Educational Consultant. Dr. Taylor regards her research work as her art that fuses her background in creative writing to create narratives that center the silenced voices of marginalized communities.

Nick Thompson is Assistant Professor of English Education in the Department of English at Kennesaw State University. He taught high school English for 10 years in Georgia before pursuing his doctorate at The University of Georgia. His primary research focuses on preservice and in-service teacher learning and professional development, but the tragic loss of one of his students has inspired him to seek understanding of the nature of teachers' bereavement. He has presented on this work at the annual meetings of the National Council of Teachers of English (NCTE), Georgia Council of Teachers of English (GCTE), and the American Education Research Association (AERA).

Margaret Rose Torrell is an Associate Professor of English at the State University of New York: College at Old Westbury where she teaches courses in disability studies, autobiography, women's literature, English literature, and Composition. Her work in disability studies focuses on literary representations of disability, especially the intersections of disability, gender, and trauma. She has also authored book chapters and articles on critical pedagogy and other issues in education.

Katahdin (Kate) Cook Whitt is a STEM Education Specialist at the Maine Mathematics and Science Alliance. Dr. Cook's work focuses on designing, implementing, and researching rigorous and equitable curriculum materials and professional learning experiences for three-dimensional science learning. She is particularly interested in supporting educators in finding ways to engage learners in making sense of local phenomena by exploring key science ideas using the science and engineering practices. Dr. Cook began her career as a high school life sciences teacher at the Dayton Regional STEM School in Ohio. She then served as an Assistant Professor of Education at Thomas College in Maine prior to joining the Maine Mathematics and Science Alliance in 2019. Dr. Cook holds an Ed.D. in Organizational Studies (Learning Organizations) from Wright State University, an M.S. Ed. in Secondary Science Education from Northwestern University, and a B.A. in Neuroscience and Music History/Theory from Oberlin College.

Shelbie Witte is the Chuck and Kim Watson Endowed Chair in Education and Professor in Adolescent Literacy and English Education at Oklahoma State University, where she directs the OSU Writing Project and the Initiative for 21st Century Literacies Research. She serves as editor (with Sara Kajder) of *Voices from the Middle*, NCTE's premiere middle-level journal. Witte has published extensively in the area of 21st Century Literacies, including *Writing Can Change Everything* (National Council of Teachers of English, 2020) and *Literacy Engagement through Peritextual Analysis* (American Library Association and National Council of Teachers of English, 2019) with Don Latham and Melissa Gross.

Leora Wolf-Prusan is an educator, facilitator, and trainer based in Los Angeles, California. A former teacher, teacher coach, district leader coach, and now federal project director on programs related to racial justice, mental health, school wellness and teacher development, her work operates through a framework in which public health, social work, and education intersect. While deeply involved in grief work, Wolf-Prusan is also a full-spectrum doula and passionate about birth justice. She received a BA in international relations and a BA in Spanish with a minor in Social & Ethnic Relations from the University of California, Davis; a teaching credential from Mills College; and an Ed.D. in educational leadership from the University of California, Los Angeles. Leora dedicates this chapter to the teachers who have advocated for their grief to be seen, tended to, and validated; to the students no longer with us; to the scholars in whose soil her scholarship grows; and the many educators who inspire hope and continued commitment to cultivate school communities vibrant with learning, connection, belonging and healing.

Adam Wolfsdorf is an Adjunct Professor at NYU's Steinhardt School of Education. He is also an original founder and the English Department Chair at Bay Ridge Preparatory. Wolfsdorf holds a Ph.D. in English Education from Columbia University, where he served as the Coordinator of the INSTEP Master's program. He has published extensively in *Changing English, The F. Scott Fitzgerald Review, English Education, English Journal,* and *The Columbia Literary Journal.* Dr. Wolfsdorf has book chapters in *From Disagreement to Discourse (IAP)* and *Deep Reading, Vol. 2 (NCTE).* Outside of the English classroom, Wolfsdorf has performed professionally for 25-years. He appeared in the national tours of the Broadway musicals *RENT* (with Neil Patrick Harris) and *Grease.* He fronts the nationally touring rock band, *The Energy (MTV, NBC, ABC,* and *ESPN).* Wolfsdorf received his MA in Psychology and Education from *Columbia University,* and a BA in English from *Harvard.*

Christopher Worthman is a Professor in the College of Education at DePaul University in Chicago. He has taught at the middle school, high school, and collegiate levels and has developed and facilitated community-based critical literacy programs for pregnant teens and teenage mothers. Along with preparing future English teachers, he presently teaches in Cook County Correctional Facilities as part of the Inside-Out Prison Exchange Program®. His research focuses on the in- and out-of-school literacy practices of youth and young adults. He dedicates this chapter to those marching today and always for justice and Black Lives Matter. Their stories and the stories of the people for whom they march give hope to a better future for all.

Foreword

In her 2010 book *Human Development and Political Violence,* Colette Daiute studied young people's efforts to move forward from the genocide, conflict, and violence they had experienced during the breakup of the former Yugoslavia. She questioned the notion that such young people are necessarily handicapped and damaged by their experiences with trauma, grief, and loss. Rather, she assumed that their feelings can be reflected on and reconstructed through a writing workshop she established to help them construct more hopeful and resilient social futures. The workshop provided a therapeutic means of mediating their understanding of the past and projection of a hopeful, agentive future via narratives and other texts. The past was prologue and present; as William Faulkner (1951, p. 73) once said, "The past is never dead. It's not even past." Rather, however, than dwelling on the past, the workshop was designed to create an emotionally healthy vision of future possibilities through which the young adults could conceive of a way forward.

The mythologies of many cultures have included figures that represent looking back and looking forward simultaneously. The Roman god Janus, also the term for a gateway, faces both backward and forward and symbolizes both end and beginning. The Akan tribe in Ghana relies on the image of a mythical bird whose feet face forward and head looks backward, such that the past sets the stage for the future. These ancient beliefs are present in the ideas embodied in this book: loss and grief may serve as the substance on which to build a new future.

This impressive collection, edited by Nicole Sieben and Stephanie Anne Shelton, was inspired by their own grieving after the loss of their fathers. This experience led them to assemble a volume that looks at the experience of loss in academia, particularly profound loss that produces seismic emotions. The contributors provide frameworks and narratives of grief that both reflect on the experience of loss and construct pathways of hope for a social future. This hope is buoyed by allies who support them through their process of rebuilding a sense that life may yet move forward in positive ways. The chapters in this collection, orchestrated with wisdom and sensitivity by the editors, echo Daiute's efforts to help youth from the Western Balkans move forward from the debilitating traumas experienced during catastrophic national and ethnic conflict. Like the youth in Daiute's workshop, the contributors to this volume use narrative means that build on the immense feelings of emptiness, stasis, sadness, disillusionment, and other feelings that follow from a major loss. The past is ever-present in this recovery. Yet it doesn't prevent people from looking forward and incorporating grief into a new outlook, a new phase of reckoning and rebuilding.

The focus of this volume is higher education, although it's impossible to separate it from the K-12 world because most contributors have taught in both arenas, often reflecting on one from the vantage point of the other. Neither schools, nor universities are set up for compassionate care of teachers or students. I attribute this ethos of emotional distance to the powerful influence of the European Enlightenment, which provides the rationalistic basis for much education. In this conception, emotions are frivolous distractions from clear thinking. Undoubtedly, this conception also has roots in historic notions of masculinity, given the hierarchical roles that males have always played in schools. The K-12 teaching force has steadily been occupied by women, with about 75–85% of the national faculty women (and 85% White; see Loewus, 2017) and 85% of school superintendents men (Glass, n.d.). As Gilligan (1982) outlined convincingly, men and women (assuming the gender binary of her day) differ according to their tendencies toward authoritarian, disaffective, hierarchical, categorical thinking (masculine) and relational, caring, nurturing (feminine) dispositions. Who's in charge does seem to matter in which values comprise the deep structure of a school or university. Throw in a neoliberal environment in which everything is reduced to numbers rather than relationships, and you have a perfect storm of conditions that render the emotional life of people in schools somewhere between irrelevant and obstructive.

Meanwhile, the people populating schools live lives heavily affected by affect. And contrary to the belief in cold rationalism driving enlightenment-based educational systems, there is good reason to believe that all of the emphasis on scientific reason misconceptualizes human cognition and social life. If Haidt (2012) is right—and I believe he is (Smagorinsky, 2018)—rationality is an illusion. All thinking, in contrast, is fundamentally emotional. The rational arguments that people present are undergirded by emotion more than reason, with logic applied to emotional decisions after the fact as a way to justify beliefs in scientistic terms that have credibility for their rational appearance, while in fact being motivated by gut feelings.

As the chapters in this volume attest, however, emotions run high in educational settings, and overlooking them produces a hostile environment for those experiencing loss and grief. Undoubtedly, some students have had relatives who have died many times over, remarkably concurrent with due dates and tests. But many, if not most, people endure real traumatic loss while being a student or teacher, and genuinely need time and space to grieve and process their experiences. Schools and universities that reduce everyone to numbers make it harder to give attention to the relationships that matter during times of loss. They also make it harder for relationships to have salience in the daily lives of people in education, at least from the standpoint of administrators.

I have been told by the research dean in my college of education that nobody on a university faculty can ever be great if they don't pull in lots of external grant funds; publications, to this dean, only matter if they generate funds. My value as an instructor is largely determined by enrollments, not teaching quality. My annual reviews and promotion cases have never included attention to relationships, only volume. Aside from having a tepid record with grants, I have done fine with volume-related assessments. But they only measure part of what I do as a teacher.

Nobody has counted the number of students who have found my undergraduate class a safe space for emotional sharing (see Smagorinsky, 2019, and other publications listed at http://www.peters-magorinsky.net/SL/index.html, for details on the course, which serves as the Foundations Requirement for English Education majors). Such a sharing, however, is a common occurrence in my undergraduate course. Students tell me that how I begin the course affects what they feel safe talking about. I start by sharing that I'm on the autism spectrum, accompanied by high chronic anxiety, an obsessive-compulsive personality, a mild case of Tourette syndrome, a fear of flying and public speaking (tempered by drugs), and other vulnerabilities. I share with them an essay (Smagorinsky, 2011) that details losses of my own: my being widowed the night before school started, seven weeks after my marriage at the age of 29; my feelings when learning of mental illness in my family, including my own case of Asperger's syndrome; and other intensely emotional times when my life as a teacher has been affected by traumatic loss and recovery.

By making myself vulnerable, I offer myself as an ally, and the class often takes the opening seriously. The class has been the site of many personal revelations. Several students have come out for the first time to their classmates as gay or lesbian. A couple have talked about a highly personal problem they have had with irritable bowel syndrome, not a typical topic for a university classroom. Many have acknowledged depression, bipolar personalities, high anxiety, and other facets of their personal makeups. It's an opening they don't find often in the classroom, and providing them with a safe space to share is a big part of what makes the course work, at least according to course evaluations. But aside from the numeric rating that the course evaluations provide based on student averages, what happens in the class is ignored when members of my department assess my teaching quality.

Educational settings, I conclude, are not designed to acknowledge the emotional side of life or consider it in a performance evaluation. Meanwhile, people experience loss and trauma all of the time, and need support. This volume by Sieben and Shelton includes attention to both the forms of interpersonal support that might be available through allyship, and means of moving forward from loss through constructive, imaginative visions of a new future. Many universities provide what they call safe spaces (Yee, n.d.). What I wonder is why there needs to be a designated safe space, rather than having the university community as a whole serve as an emotionally supportive space. The idea of a safe space suggests that the rest of the university can be as callous and insensitive as it wants, because there's a place to retreat to when times are emotionally tough, where they can go during a time of grief when the institution sends the message: quit whining and get back to work.

This collection sends a very different message. It assumes that people will experience trauma in their lives, and that it's a collective responsibility to help them through it. Institutional indifference to pain is assumed, leaving allyship to those who care enough to invest time that won't be rewarded when their careers are evaluated, but who see a human responsibility to support people in emotional need. That's the sort of effort that makes institutions places of community, places that people return to because they feel an attachment to them, places that people donate to as alums, places that people recruit new generations to attend based on emotional bonds developed during affective ordeals.

The sort of connection to people and places afforded by such compassion includes both immediate support and the belief in a possible future. Allyship and hope. I know from personal experience that not all efforts at allyship provide affirmation or support; some are downright bizarre, such as the woman who told me that my wife had died on purpose because she'd never been happier and wanted to end on a high note (she died in her sleep of unknown causes). Another person in my English Department insisted to my department chair that I be fired that year because I was clearly struggling with my emotions and not bringing my A-game to class every day. Even well-intentioned support often missed the mark; one friend on the faculty attempted to console me by telling me to take courage and be strong. I felt in contrast that it was a time to be weak.

Allyship and hope, then, are not guaranteed simply by showing up and saying what comes to mind. It's how you show up that matters, and many people have no idea of how to support a person struggling to keep it together. This excellent volume should provide a roadmap for understanding the importance of constructing relationship-driven educational environments that support the inevitable loss and trauma that affect the people in the community, and help build from devastation a new possibility for a positive social future. That's an impressive achievement, one that I hope will contribute to an ethos of care in education and help spawn a new generation of scholarship on loss and grief.

Peter Smagorinsky,
The University of Georgia

References

Daiute, C. (2010). *Human development & political violence.* Cambridge University Press.

Faulkner, W. (1951). *Requiem for a nun.* Random House.

Gilligan, C. (1982). *In a different voice: Psychological theory and women's development.* Harvard University Press.

Glass, T. E. (n. d.). *Where are all the women superintendents?* AASA. Retrieved March 11, 2020 from https://www.aasa.org/SchoolAdministratorArticle. aspx?id=14492terms=women

Haidt, J. (2012). *The righteous mind: Why good people are divided by politics and religion.* Vintage.

Loewus, L. (2017, August 15). The nation's teaching force is still mostly white and female. *Education Week.* Retrieved March 11, 2020 from https://www.edweek. org/ew/articles/2017/08/15/the-nations-teaching-force-is-still-mostly.html

Smagorinsky, P. (2011). Confessions of a mad professor: An autoethnographic consideration of neuroatypicality, extranormativity, and education. *Teachers College Record, 113*, 1701–1732. Available at http://www.petersmagorinsky.net/ About/PDF/TCR/TCR2011.pdf

Smagorinsky, P. (2018). Emotion, reason, and argument: Teaching persuasive writing in tense times. *English Journal, 107*(5), 98–101. Available at http:// www.petersmagorinsky.net/About/PDF/EJ/EJ2018.pdf

Smagorinsky, P. (2019). Inquiry and service-learning in teacher education. In E. A. Kahn, A. Bouque, D. Forde, T. M. McCann, & C. C. Walter (Eds.), *An invitation to inquiry: Possibilities for immersive literacy processes* (pp. 119–136). Rowman & Littlefield.

Yee, M. (n. d.). *Why 'safe spaces' are important for mental health — especially on college campuses.* Healthline. Retrieved March 11, 2020 from https://www.healthline. com/health/mental-health/safe-spaces-college#1

Acknowledgments

We thank our families—both personal and professional—for their companionship in our times of grief, and for the hope that they have helped us to find and celebrate.

We thank Lindy L. Johnson at The College of William & Mary, for being the one who initially introduced us to one another at the first *JoLLE* Conference. That moment sparked a series of collaborations that we continue to be grateful for.

We extend so much gratitude to Peter Smagorinsky at The University of Georgia, who created a beautiful foreword to this work and has constantly encouraged us and supported this project through its many stages. Thank you for caring about and for us as people and scholars.

We are grateful to Carlson Coogler, Shelly Melchior, and Boden Robertson, whose critical behind-the-scenes work helped to make this book possible.

We wholeheartedly thank the authors of this book for their willingness to think through and share these critical academic frameworks of grief and hope, amidst their personal encounters with both, in order to examine the ways that grief and hope shape higher education.

Nicole would first like to acknowledge her co-editor and partner in this work, Stephanie Anne Shelton, without whom none of this would be possible. It has been a hope-filled journey to work with you on this project and build a community of companionship and hope in higher education together along the way. Nicole also thanks her family members who are at the center of her life. You all are my whole heart—my mother, Madelyn; my sister, Joanna and her family; my husband, Dave, and our son, Nicholas; and my deeply missed father, Marc and grandmother, Maria, whose love and light are with me every step of the way. I love you all infinitely. I am everything I am and everything I can and will be because of you and your love. Thank you also to Kristin, Attie, and Uncle Joe for always being a phone call or (short or long) car ride away for all of us. Your love lifts us up. Nicole is grateful to each person who has companioned her in this grief journey along the way: to those who have sat with me in grief for a while, but who are no longer on this journey with me today, I extend my appreciation to you for traveling pathways with me for a time; and to those who are traveling pathways to hope and healing and loving and living in these moments with me right now, including those who have joined me anew on this journey of finding hope, I am grateful for you. Thank you for being a text, a phone/ Zoom call, a prayer, or a car/plane/train ride away. More than I can ever express, your offer of a hug; a kind word; an act of love; a sentiment of empathy; a sharing of a story, a reading, a picture, or a memory has companioned me in my grief in meaningful ways. The depth of your impact cannot be overstated.

Stephanie, first and foremost, is grateful to her co-editor and co-author, Nicole Sieben, for her constant support, love, and generosity over years of friendship. Not a single page of this book would exist without you. I am also grateful to my colleagues (and #qualleagues) at The University of Alabama, particularly the #UAQUAL Crew. Thank you to Peter Smagorinsky, Meghan E. Barnes, Michelle M. Falter, and Margaret Robbins for driving all the way to the boondocks of Warthen, Georgia, to mourn my father's death with me, and for all of my UGA and UA academic families, who have supported me in invaluable ways. Thank you to the extensive GHP family for your incredible support, particularly to Lisa Shull, Ricky Parmer, and Jobie Johnson. Thank you to Margaret Shelton, and to Carrie and Becky Brown, for helping me to recall wonderful memories and to find comfort and joy in those shared moments. Thank you, Jasper, for being the best writing support dog on the planet. And, finally, thank you to Mama, Belle, Tray, Laurie, Colin, Declan, and Genevieve for your impossible support and constant hilarity.

1 Introduction- Intersecting Hope with Actionable Frameworks in the Academy

Allyship in Grief

Nicole Sieben and Stephanie Anne Shelton

We are both educational researchers with our work situated in frameworks that provide hope and allyship through struggle and strength in academic and life circumstances, and we often consider ways in which our work can manifest aloud. This volume is one such approach of doing so. Together with other scholars across a variety of fields in higher education, we present this collection as a companion to those in the academies who are experiencing, or who inevitably will experience, grief, in all of its forms.

Our Positionality in the Work

Nicole's Found Frameworks: Hope and Writing Hope

As a hope researcher, I've learned a lot from *hope theory* in the last few years. In my study of hope—the hope construct grounded in positive psychology originally conceptualized by Snyder (1996)—I have learned that hope is a future-casting concept that combines will/agency (motivation) and ways/pathways (strategies) knowledge in order to help people achieve intentionally set, self-determined goals. The components of will and ways in the hope concept work together in a feedback loop to inform one another as people move toward their goals: strategies inform motivation, and motivation encourages the use of strategies. They work together to keep momentum moving forward.

Over the past ten years, I have studied hope as it pertains to increasing secondary and postsecondary students' chances of academic success and life fulfillment, and I have specifically focused on researching the influence that hope can have in a person's writing development. In 2012, a construct that I called "writing hope" emerged out of my doctoral work. Defined simply, writing hope is the will and the ways to accomplish self-determined, worthwhile writing goals (Sieben, 2013). In conjunction with this "writing hope" theory, I also developed a valid and reliable Writing Hope Scale (Sieben & Rose, 2012) with my then-dissertation chair that measures a person's writing hope levels. Across multiple large-scale studies, writing hope levels have been able to significantly predict writing competency levels and general hope levels in secondary school and college students and in adults across various fields.

This contextualization of hope in education and writing is necessary to describe in the foregrounding of this book because it allows for a historical understanding of how I arrived at hope as an action plan for surviving grief. Before I began researching hope, I understood hope to be used synonymously with wishing, as a whimsical comforting idea that is often associated with blind faith that has more to do with believing and less to do with knowing that having hope can move people through even the toughest of times. Initially, my experiences as a hope researcher were contextualized within my own understanding and privileged existence as a person who had experienced minimal hardship and pain throughout my first 30 years of life. Then, in July 2014, my heart was shattered and my world was upended as my father passed away suddenly without warning and without any hope for reversing the circumstances. In the hours, days, and weeks following my father's death, I became disillusioned with the idea of "hope" as I once knew it. If hope was supposed to ameliorate all hardship and move me in the direction of fulfillment and success, how could it fix my circumstances when it could not reverse my father's death? How was I supposed to rely on hope to move me forward when all I wanted to do was go backwards to a time when my father was still alive?

After weeks and months of reflection, research, reading, and conversations with mentors and coaches, all of which became a large part of my journey in hope once again, I learned that I needed to allow hope to evolve with me and for me. And, one of the most lifesaving things that I have learned along the way is that as we hope, we have to create pathways for ourselves in order to advance toward our goals; no one else can do this for us. Others can provide companionship for us in grief and hope, but the desire to grow needs to come from inside of us (i.e., agency) and not from external forces. Even when hope creators in my life helped me to find ways to hope and identify new goals, I needed to want these outcomes (and have agency to pursue them) in order to find pathways I would actually attempt to follow. And, this did not mean creating one pathway and following it. It meant devising many possible pathways so that if one pathway presented challenges or obstacles (which they often did), I could redirect my course or start anew toward my goals so that eventually I could reach them (or an altered version of them). Having hope in grief, I learned, was often about adjusting my goals so that they were attainable versions of the ones I had originally planned for my survival. For me, one of the issues of experiencing these life-altering losses was the realization that I could not go on as I had once before and continue toward my original goals using my previous pathways; I needed to go on as I had not needed to before and instead work toward significantly shifted life goals given my new circumstances.

Throughout my life, I have set frequent goals for myself: some long-term, some short-term, and some reach goals. This is a routine practice I learned from my father who had a habit of writing a list of daily goals each morning, including on the morning of his unexpected passing. One goal I never thought I'd have in my life, at what I consider to be a young age, is the newly persistent goal of surviving the sudden death of my most beloved father. Once it became something that I had to do, I realized there was going to be a need for many, many pathways toward survival. In this case, there were roadblocks everywhere, so I needed numerous pathways that I could travel concurrently to make progress toward my goal. And, if on some days some pathways were impassible, I traveled different grief pathways that day knowing that I at least had to keep moving. That's what I continue to do: I keep moving and hoping that these pathways lead me to my continuous goal of surviving this devastating loss. Since the loss of my father in 2014, I have also newly faced the loss of my maternal grandmother, a mother-figure in my life who lived with me all of my childhood and into my adult life. This loss in 2019, just months before the birth of my son, Nicholas (whom my grandmother played a role in naming), brought on a new wave of grief that brought with it additional challenges and a need for novel pathways to survival. Already in the midst of this book project, the frameworks within these chapters provided some vital companionship, and conversations with allies like Stephanie provided additional support that was much needed during a time of reinvigorated grief.

Necessarily, I think it is critical to note that I share my grief pathways as an example of a few ways through grief toward hope, but not as a "how to" or a "fix-all." Everyone's survival and struggle with grief is unique, and we all need different sources of allyship through it. For me, writing (and reading) about pathways of grief has provided me with companionship and has helped me to survive, but having hope does not mean I don't still struggle. I will always struggle with these life-changing losses, I imagine, but now I have multiple ways of coping and framing grief that bring me closer to my goal of surviving these intimate tragedies.

To end this section on a personal note, because processing grief—even through academic frameworks and research—is quite personal, I share one additional perspective. My grief, much like my writing process, is messy. Just like my writing process is non-linear, so too is my grieving process: both are recursive processes that ebb and flow depending on specific circumstances of the moment and situation. I often find myself back in moments of heavy grieving, crying without knowing when the tears will stop flowing and wishing without logic that my father and my grandmother could be back here with us. I still ask "Why?" even though there are no satisfying answers that I've found over time, especially with my father's untimely passing, a medical error ending his life. I still wonder "What if?" they were still alive and life could carry on, more or less, as it was. "How would life be different" for my mother, my sister, and me (and the rest of our family)? I still dream about times when grief was not as prevalent in my life, but… traveling several intentional pathways through hope in my grieving has made my grief more manageable for me. Knowing that I can turn to hope, in all its varied forms, to see me through the different ebbs and flows of grief helps me to survive and gives me courage to persist. I hope, in many ways, this book provides that gift of hope and allyship to others too.

Stephanie's Found Framework: Allyship

The intertwined simultaneity of grief and hope is closely enmeshed in my identity as a queer person living in the U.S.'s "Deep South." This region of the United States, also referred to as the "Bible Belt," has long been associated with socio-politically and religiously informed conservative policies that have, over centuries, resisted gender-based equalities and LGBTQ+ rights (Shelton & Lester, 2018). One of few large-scale studies examining LGBTQ+ experiences in this region determined that the anti-LGBTQ+ sentiments found across the United States were "amplified in the South" (GLSEN, 2012). This region is my home. It is where I was born, where I came of age, where I have been educated, and where I have been an educator. The ways that I understand "grief" and "hope" are forever bound to this space and my work in education.

When I was a high school teacher, I worked in a community where it was clear that who I was and how I loved were disallowed. The local newspaper, for example, ran a full-page editorial written by a community leader declaring marriage equality and LGBTQ+ people "against God's will." A local pastor called my school superintendent to complain that I was a negative influence on one of his parishioner's grandchildren, because I taught her American literature and openly acknowledged that I am queer. These moments were sources of deep grief, as I mourned for students who feared coming out to families, for my school as it resisted any explicit policies to support and protect LGBTQ+ students, for myself when I found my professionalism and teaching abilities called into question because of who I am.

Like Nicole, though, I found that grief rarely travels alone. Alongside it much of the time, though harder to find in grief's looming shadow, is hope. Colleagues, who I was sure held anti-LGBTQ+ beliefs, shared stories of gay sons, trans-uncles, and their staunch support for me. Students readily engaged with LGBTQ+ topics, researched and applied queer theories, and celebrated newfound appreciations for diversity in our classroom (Shelton, 2017). These relationships were critical to me finding, applying, and sharing hope in what would have otherwise been dark and troubling times. The term "ally" has long been invoked relative to supporting LGBTQ+ communities, but much of the literature discusses ally work as something anyone with the right training might do (see Shelton, 2018, for discussion). "Ally" regularly failed to encompass for me the deep-seated connections, contexts, and insuppressible humanity of those who offered hope in the face of substantial oppression and grief.

In an effort to redefine ally work to include these elements, I propose a framework of "allyship" instead. This word literally and figuratively expands "ally" to include the degrees to which true support, authentic community, and meaningful acceptance of others necessarily include understanding and interactions that extend beyond a safe space training or cursory claim of support. Allyship is in constant companionship with hope and with others, and makes navigating grief not always easier but always more possible.

I drew on and further stretched this notion of allyship when my father passed away only a few months after Nicole had lost her father in 2014. I was a doctoral student at the time in the throes of dissertation writing and, following the funeral, separated from family as I returned to academe. My grief was more complex than just my father's death. I grieved that, as I am a first-generation college student, he would never know or celebrate my doctoral graduation. I grieved that because I had been away at school, I had not been with him in his last days or hours. I grieved that my mother grieved without my support. I grieved because I was forced to grieve alone, in my small apartment, in the glow of my laptop screen's display of my dissertation draft.

This was certainly a different form of grief than I experienced when a classroom teacher, but it threatened the same isolation and uncertainty. And, as before, allyship offered hope that moved alongside, and sometimes ahead of, this grief. Faculty members, doctoral program friends, and friends from other institutions, including Nicole, immediately reached out to support me. Without the pre-existing relationships that they and I drew on, those moments of support would have likely felt hollow to me, perhaps obligatory for them. However, as they came to my aid, offering help with responsibilities, meals, even laundry, it was the companionship that mattered most.

I do not professionally theorize on hope as Nicole does, but I have lived enough life to understand its elusiveness, its contradictions, and its necessity. Grief always makes itself known. Hope requires intentionality and active seeking—on the part of the one searching for it and the ones working to offer it. Allyship offers a form of hopeful support that pulls deeply from places of care, concern, and human-ness. Allyship does not offer simple answers; instead, it offers a version of hope that is fragile in the face of near-crushing grief and undeniably powerful in its determination of move with and through sorrow. Allyship synthesizes the best of ally work, with its commitment to justice and unshakeable support in challenging contexts, and our most beautiful relationships, with the tears, laughter, and beautiful memories that accompany those connections.

Situating the Work in Higher Education

Hope

In 2016, the *Journal of Pedagogy* charged "educational researchers, teachers, thinkers, and pedagogues… to find and accelerate the hope that is always already present" in our work and in our lives by taking on the task of "creating hope" (Casey, 2016, p. 6). This book, with chapters written by "educational researchers, teachers, thinkers, and pedagogues" in various fields of higher education, answers this call. As Vinz (2013) has said, "hope is an action plan for success," and we wish to recognize that it can be an action plan for survival through grief and loss, too. Hope is not passive—it is not a wish. It is a goal pursued and a (re)imagined passion personified. It can be what sustains us through the darkest of times in our lives, our schools, and our political and personal spaces. At a time when so much is uncertain, hope can companion us through.

As Casey (2016) recognizes, "there is a kind of violence that can be perpetuated by insisting on hope when it is clear that so much of what we have been hoping for has been decried, delegitimized, and[/or] seemingly rejected by so many in our societies" (p. 5). He notes how important it is to grieve "in the wake of the unthinkable and abominable" but also cautions "we cannot allow our grief to constrain us to the point of defeat" (p. 5). With this agentic call in mind, we present this edited collection to offer pathways forward to academics, researchers, teachers, pedagogues, and thinkers who grapple with grief in a variety of forms.

The forthcoming chapters explore a variety of possible pathways through grief, examined by scholars who have found frameworks that provide critical action steps forward and accessible avenues to processing. As editors of this work, we aim to provide two unique frameworks in this introduction through our scholarship on "writing hope" (Sieben, 2016, 2018) and queering the notion of what it means to be an ally (Shelton, 2017, 2018). Together, we look at critical intersections of our work that may provide nuanced understandings of allyship through grief in a way that can sustain collective, borrowed, and/or personal hope.

With Casey's (2016) words echoed, we affirm, "this hope is not naïve" but is the source of our pedagogical and personal "engagements with the world, with texts, and with contexts," (p.6) and we would add, with people who "make hope happen" (Lopez, 2013). Just as grief manifests in our lives in many forms, so too does each pathway forward in grief and hope. It is our hope that this work provides a critical resource of hope to those in the academy (and others) who may feel the effects of an otherwise solitary journey of grief to create an awareness of solidarity and support that some may not realize exists in our academic circles. We wish to acknowledge that while we know for many grieving is a lifelong journey, it does not need to be a journey embarked on alone. Through hope, which is also a "journey with all the obstacles and all the successes and everything in between" (Sieben, 2018, p. xxiv), we can companion one another in this work. This book may provide some of what is needed to move *forward* (not necessarily to move *past*, but to move *forward* or *through*) in our collective and individual grief experiences. Because hope is a forward-thinking concept (Lopez, 2013), we use the notion of hope to foreground this work on moving forward through grief.

(Queering the Notion of) Allyship

Another concept that informs this collection and its individual chapters is the notion of "queering" allyship. Queerness, as a theoretical concept, regularly gets taken up as a means of challenging taken-for-granted norms. That element remains true here. After all, a key aim of this book is to push against grief as existing without hope, while also troubling the notion that hope is easy or constant. However, there is more to queerness as we connect it with allyship. As we noted before, allyship extends ally work to move in concert with relationships and hopefulness. The queer aspect stretches allyship further, to acknowledge the degrees to which hope and support are inevitably, necessarily, and sometimes frustratingly contextual.

When Stephanie experienced anti-LGBTQ+ sentiments as a high school teacher, she was regularly exasperated at the degrees to which ally work seemed divorced of contexts (Shelton, 2019a, 2019b). What she was able to accomplish in a conservative rural community in the Bible Belt would look undeniably different than what, for example, Nicole might attempt in a different place, space, and time. What either of us dared to challenge in our seventh year of teaching were substantively different than our first year. Time changed. What we do now as university professors is substantially different from what either of us was willing or able to even try just a few years ago. Time and space change. These shifts matter. Who we are in a given moment, or in a particular place, matters.

Thus, queering allyship necessarily positions the concept as slippery, as flexible, as visceral. All of the messiness of being people who confront and stumble through grief while flailing about for hope requires this additional layer of understanding how allyship looks and works. Or, sometimes, how it does not look or work. Queering allyship means rejecting any universal truth about how grief, hope, or relationships should or might happen, not just across people but also across individual moments or places. As we each grieved our father's death, there were moments when we were overwhelmed with tears, when our chests were wracked with sobs and our eyes swollen with crying. In the next instance, we were joyfully laughing as we recalled funny stories of our fathers (both of our fathers were quick-witted comedians). The sadness and happiness were not in conflict; those contradictions were all necessary parts of navigating hope and grief together. And, effective allyship offers elasticity to honor those sudden and seemingly paradoxical shifts. Because making hope actionable and making grief manageable require pushing against long-held norms and embracing the jumbled messiness of hurt and hope co-existing.

The Chapters

In these pages, authors share frameworks and narratives of pathways that illustrate progress and struggle with grief in the hopes that some of these strategies may provide action steps for readers to find and re-define hope in their own academic and personal lives. Divided into four parts, this collection situates this humanization of grief work into the following:

Part I: Allyship through Writing and Literature
Part II: Communities of Hope and Healing
Part III: Grieving for/with Students and Teachers
Part IV: Finding Hope through Activism

Through a guided exploration of various academic frameworks and strategies, readers can move toward a re-definition of allyship and hope that encourages a self-definition of survival. This emphasis on self-definition puts less pressure on the grieving to achieve the societally imposed goal of "happiness now" that often is heard in the discourse of those trying to comfort the grieving. Though kind intentions are surely present, the expectation for a grieving heart to work toward the goal of "happiness" often seems an impossible feat to achieve. Instead, a self-definition of hope and survival can serve to create a more authentic space for continuous healing, which we have found to be necessary in this journey of grief that was thrust upon us and not chosen.

Additionally, the chapters—written by a range of scholars in the field—provide frameworks that will offer readers important ways forward in the wake of unimaginable loss (defined in a variety of ways such as loss of a person in death, loss of circumstances, loss of status, identity, friendships, finances, political hope). In Part I: Allyship through Writing and Literature, Torrell's chapter "Changing Cultural Constructions of Grief through the Shared Story: Lessons from Disability Studies" begins this section by connecting a disabilities studies framework with narrative writing and grief frameworks. It examines how we might consider reframing conversations about grief in a way that repositions it as a normative part of life, a condition not to be fixed. In the next chapter, "Agency in Writing: Managing Narratives of Trauma in Student Writing," Lee discusses the ways in which discussions about trauma can be framed by literature that can ally students through grief work. Then Wolfsdorf recounts his experiences as an English teacher grappling with discussions on death in *Hamlet* in the chapter "'Conceit Upon her Father': An Unintentional Confrontation with Grief and Hope in the English Classroom." Following this, Witte and Dail examine in "'The Grief that Fills One's Heart': Pairing Loss Narratives and Graphic Young Adult Literature" how reading young adult literature and writing narrative can open up spaces for critical dialogue to unfold in teacher education and English language arts education. To close this section, Henderson and Black's chapter "Opening to the Hauntings of Grief and Mourning: Writing Our Way towards Hope" reveals how writing in all of its forms with a supportive ally allows hope to blossom.

In Part II: Communities of Hope and Healing, the chapter authors use a variety of hope frameworks to navigate ways of healing in the face of unimaginable grief and loss. The first three chapters in this section engage Snyder's (1996) hope theory framework to navigate various expressions of grief to find hope and healing in their respective communities. First, in "Opportunities Lost and Found: A Gay Educator's Grief and Process of Hope," Crawley examines how hope frameworks and specific, intentional pathways helped him to navigate his grief over lost opportunities (for himself and his students) that he experienced as an elementary school teacher who found ways of healing during his doctoral research and university teaching. Next in "Finding Hope Through Hope Agents and Narratives in Times of Mourning," the authors, Olan and Grissom, share their intimate experiences with personal loss and grief that became intertwined with milestone moments in their academic careers that left them struggling to find hope and peace amidst the sadness. Through conversations with colleagues and students, both found hope in the messiness of grief. In "Collaborative Empathy as a Pathway to Hope: Grief and Teacher Education," Richmond and Anderson detail the ways in with their shared empathy as student and teacher educator helped each to navigate unexpected grief in their lives and to find hope in the process. Worthman's chapter, "'Why I Hate the Wind': Magical Realism and Re-Presenting Trauma," uses a magical realism framework to explore his childhood trauma over the loss of his mother and beautifully navigates ways to hope through storytelling and narration. Finally, Brown's chapter "It *Is* Contagious, Honey" closes this section with a stunning recreation of conversations she had with her late mother about gardening, her mother's chronic illness, and the close, intellectual and intimate relationship they shared.

Part III: Grieving with/for Students, the largest section in this collection, includes chapters written by scholars who have lost students and/or family members in the midst of trying to maintain teaching responsibilities and found little time to mourn, grieve, and process their losses. In the first chapter of this section, Dunn explains how the emotional labor teachers put into their work often goes unnoticed or taken for granted. Through her work detailed in "Hiding behind Closed Classroom Doors and Opening up Space for Sharing Grief," we come to understand the ways in which teachers' emotional needs should be considered when they are experiencing grief in their own lives and in their classrooms. This chapter sets the context for the other chapters that follow. The next three chapters take up Snyder's (1996) hope theory in the pursuit of healing grief. In "Designing 'Patterns' after Hurricane Sandy Uproots Structures," Pace examines how super-complexity theory can ally us in our grief during traumatic events that claim our spaces and our sense of comfort. In this work, Pace shows how allyship from professors can provide reliable support systems when all other structures have been uprooted. Next, Long discusses the impacts of secondary trauma that teachers experience in "Grieving when Students Make the News: Two Teachers' Reflections" through hope, critical witnessing, and allyship frameworks. The chapter examines the consequences on schools, teachers, and their identities as members of a school community in the wake of media coverage that pathologized the school based on the conduct of a few. In Thompson's "When a Teacher Lost a Student: A Narrative Pathway through Grief," hope theory, socioculturalism, and narrative play a role in a teacher's quest for making meaning of and healing from the trauma of witnessing a student's death in the classroom. Then "Grief as the Pathway to Hope in the Teaching Profession" by Wolf-Prusan explores the relationship between hope, grief, and how the student-teacher relationship impacts the teacher's self and contribution to collective identity and purpose. In the final chapter of this section, "How Experiences with Student Grief Inform Our Practice: Teaching Teachers to Navigate Healing Processes," Rybakova, Whitt, and Christie show the ways in which teachers can navigate student trauma and grief in the classroom through a "Counselor's Corner" feature that illuminates the healing process through understandings of interpersonal neurobiology and the brain's trait of neuroplasticity.

The final section of the book, Part IV: Finding Hope through Activism, includes chapters that examine grieving through pathways of activism, which inspire hope and healing. In "My Father's Keeper: Pathway to Grief-Inspired Activism," Roland shares the personal, traumatic loss of her father and the ways in which she navigated the injustice of and the media's racist representation of his death. Roland profoundly illuminates the omnipresence of oppression in the lives, deaths and grief of Black people, and how such oppression led to her grief-inspired activism as a pathway to hope. Next, Taylor's "When the Music Changes, So Does the Dance: Critical Racial Events as Told Through a Narrative Inquiry Beat" draws on narrative inquiry to examine how self-reflection on critical incidents regarding racialized events influence one's work in education and how written and spoken reflections can illuminate issues of race, class, and/or gender. In "Homeless Adolescents, Grief, and Advocacy for Others: Hope for the Future," Haq uses positioning theory and narrative inquiry to focus on the ways that youth position themselves as agentive in helping peers navigate their complex living situations. Through allyship and advocacy, hope is found. Finally, in "Visualizing Hope: Digital Storytelling with Refugee-background Children," Emert details a university-school partnership that provides mentoring and curricular support to Refugee-background children. The project of focus, a digital storytelling project, invites Refugee-background children to narrate important moments of their lives using digital tools, and this project not only supports skill development, but also hope growth.

Each chapter uniquely positions hope and allyship within and across various disciplines and frameworks to bring companionship in the grief we face or inevitably will face in the academy. Though each chapter is uniquely situated, all chapters conceptualized in this work answer Freire's (2006) invitation to create an "armed love" and actionable hope that is so desperately needed in our educational, political, social, and personal communities.

Conclusion

As humans *being* with our grief and activating our hope, we find it important to acknowledge that everyone's journey through and to hope is different. As allies in this work, both to one another and others, we affirm that we are here in this together. We each still struggle with grief, and we probably always will. But through this work, we have found hope-filled pathways that companion us through.

As readers embark on this journey with us, we would like to invite those interested to frame their reading with two potentially persistent questions: (1) *How will I know when I've found hope in my grief? (What does this hope look like?)* and (2) *What are my pathways of hoping and grieving that will help me survive? (What allyship do I need to move me forward and through my grief?)* These questions are for each person to decide individually. For each of us, working on this book with a co-editor who has long been an ally and friend in this grief journey is a start—it is one pathway of the many we travel in this journey of grief, in this quest for hope. It is our collective hope for readers of this book that this work will help others explore these questions too. This book will take readers through the frameworks that academics across a variety of fields have considered as allies to their grieving hearts, and their chapters will detail strategies they have employed over the years in their own grief journeys. Together, we offer this allyship in the quest for hope alongside the grief, all the while acknowledging that all of this is messy and complex, but so is being human. What can make these journeys hopeful are the connections and commitments we make to one another (and ourselves) across the academy and beyond.

References

Casey, Z. A. (2016). Sustaining and (re)creating hope. *Journal of Pedagogy, 7*(2), 5–8.

Freire, P. (2006). *Teachers as cultural workers: Letters to those who dare teach.* Westview Press.

GLSEN. (2012, December 11). Strengths & silences: The experiences of lesbian, gay, bisexual and transgender students in rural and small town schools. https://www.glsen.org/research/strengths-and-silences-lgbtq-students-rural-and-small-towns

Lopez, S. J. (2013). *Making hope happen: Create the future you want for yourself and others.* Simon & Schuster, Inc.

Shelton, S. A. (2017). "White people are gay, but so are some of my kids": Examining the intersections of race, sexuality, and gender. *Bank Street Journal: Occasional Paper Series, Queering Education, 2017*(37), 109–129.

Shelton, S. A. (2018). Queering intersectional literacies to redefine female sexualities: A case study. *Literacy Research: Theory, Method, and Practice, 67*(1), 1–16.

Shelton, S. A. (2019a). Examining sociocultural factors' effects on LGBTQ teacher ally work. *English Education, 51*(3), 292–315.

Shelton, S. A. (2019b). "When I do 'bad stuff,' I make the most difference": Exploring doubt, demoralization, and contradictions in LGBTQIA+ ally work. *International Journal of Qualitative Studies in Education, 32*(6), 591–605.

Shelton, S. A., & Lester, A. O. (2018). Finding possibilities in the impossible: A celebratory narrative of trans youth experiences in the Southeastern USA. *Sex Education, 18*(4), 391–405.

Sieben, N. (2013). *Writing hope, self-regulation, and self-efficacy as predictors of writing ability in first-year college students* (Publication No. 3594312) [Doctoral dissertation, Hofstra University]. ProQuest Dissertations Publishing.

Sieben, N. (2016). Teaching writing hope for a just writing society. *The English Record, 67*(1), 99–121.

Sieben, N. (2018). *Writing hope strategies for writing success in secondary schools: A strengths-based approach to teaching writing.* Brill | Sense Publishers.

Sieben, N., & Rose, S. (2012, August). *Self-regulation, self-efficacy, and hope as predictors of writing ability [Paper].* American Psychological Association, Orlando, FL.

Snyder, C. R. (1996). To hope, to lose, and hope again. *Journal of Personal and Interpersonal Loss, 1*(1), 1–16.

Vinz, R. (2013). *Hope is a thing with feathers: Finding flight … futures [Keynote].* Conference on English Education (CEE), Summer Conference, Fort Collins, CO.

Part I
Allyship through Writing and Literature

2 Changing Cultural Constructions of Grief through the Shared Story
Lessons from Disability Studies

Margaret Rose Torrell

This chapter applies a disability studies framework to the grief narrative, focusing on the sociocultural and political dimension of the shared grief story. The main premise is that just as the disability life story can promote sociocultural change in mainstream conceptions about disability, the shared grief story can make interventions in cultural beliefs about grief and the grieving. In grief studies, the grief narrative has been used as a therapeutic measure to help the bereaved make meaning out of loss (Neimeyer, 1999), but the social construction of grief has been found to have a significant impact on those efforts (Neimeyer et al., 2014). In the field of literary scholarship, studies of the representation of grief have also identified the social construction of grief as problematic, leading to feelings of social marginalization (Gilbert, 2006; Prodromou, 2015). However, while it has been accepted that grieving is made more complicated by negative social constructions, grief studies theorists working in various disciplines have only begun to articulate the potential for grief narratives to intervene in those social constructions.

In applying a disability studies framework to grief studies, this chapter explores how the grief narrative can promote a cultural change in thinking about grief itself. The first section identifies the benefits of an allyship between disability and grief studies and explores an approach to grief that shifts focus away from healing the griever to diminishing the power of the cultural, social, and political forces that construct and police grief. The second section applies disability life writing theory to the grief narrative, addressing the specific role the narrative can play in offering alternatives to social constructions. In particular, I identify four emancipatory strategies used in disability life writing that, when applied to the shared grief story, have potential to promote a reconceptualization of the grief experience: a focus on the human, the acknowledgement of pain, the assertion of community, and the recognition of a diversity of grief experiences. The final section uses lessons from disability studies to make recommendations for pathways forward in the project to redefine how we conceive of and experience grief.

Disability Studies and Grief Studies as Allies

In contemporary culture, both disability and grief are negatively constructed in similar ways to help reassure those in mainstream culture that such fates won't befall them. Thus, while disability and grief are not the same, they trigger similar anxieties in mainstream culture: fears of being out of control; fears of loss, pain, and change; fears about becoming a burden, unproductive, dependent, and pitiful, for example. Disability studies theorist Siebers (2011) explains, "For better or worse, disability often comes to stand for the precariousness of the human condition, for the fact that individual human beings are susceptible to change, decline over time, and die" (p. 5). Grief represents similar messages about the transience of life and the fundamental lack of control we have over our futures and ourselves. The very presence of the grieving person reminds us that we could lose someone close to us or our own lives at any moment, or we could lose it—feel loss so deeply that we are not able to control our emotions.

As a result, both disability and grief have been conceptualized by mainstream culture using a *deficit model* that delineates between *normals* and those whose presence upsets what is deemed to be "normal." The deficit model for understanding disability assumes that able-bodiedness is the norm and views disabled identity as devalued and "wrong." As a result, disability appears to be an individual problem or a personal tragedy that requires cure, rehabilitation, or other intervention to make the person as "normal" as possible (Brueggemann, 2013; Oliver, 2009). The goal is to fix the individual so that they can fit into a very narrow definition of the "normal"—read valuable—human life. Failing that, the practice is to isolate those lives that don't fit. For example, disabled people can be kept from public view in environments that are built for able-bodies and can be socially separated by such psychologically distancing maneuvers as viewing disabled lives as pitiful, tragic, or inspirational. These social constructions of disability have been identified as a main source of trouble for disabled lives and a main impediment to equality (Brueggemann, 2013; Fries, 2003; Linton, 2006).

The social construction of grief is also dependent upon a deficit model. Neimeyer et al. (2014) argue that grief is situated within a cultural framework that polices its expression: "individuals are subjected to and sometimes subjugated by a dominant narrative of grief, which constructs their identity as bereaved people, and which regulates their proper performance of their role of mourners" (p. 493). The social rules governing the expression of grief place limits on it and work toward isolating it from public view—for example, grieving is currently conceived of as something done in private and is rarely witnessed in public (Neimeyer et al., 2014). Additionally, grievers whose experiences fall outside of the socially sanctioned responses to grief "are labelled abberant ... In contemporary psychotherapeutic culture, aberrant grief is pathological" (Neimeyer et al., 2014), in need of cure.

Similarly, Gilbert (2006) finds that there is a "mystifying oppression" of grief in contemporary western culture that she describes as "a pervasive social imperative to silence, isolate, or forbid mourning" (p. xx). Grievers become a social contaminant, "something people would indeed like to isolate" and, in addition to the pain of loss, feel a sense of "wrongness" or "embarrassment" as the bereaved (p. xx). Prodromou (2015) finds that the grief experience is scripted in one of two main ways—as something one has healed from or as something one will never heal from, leaving no place for experiences that fall in between. Moreover, mainstream expectations about the loss of a loved one don't allow for differences in how grief might be experienced from a socially marginalized perspective, in more emotionally frayed relationships where estrangement and abuse may have occurred, or in cases where violence or negligence may have caused the loved one's death. While a significant loss is itself painful, the rules that govern how one can express and feel that loss cause additional isolation, pain, and confusion.

A frequent response to such negative social construction in disability studies has been to put pressure on the social construction itself and the sociocultural and political structures that create it. Disability studies therefore rejects, challenges, and provides alternates to the deficit model. As Siebers (2011) explains:

> Disability studies does not treat disease or disability, hoping to cure or avoid them; it studies the social meanings, symbols, and stigmas attached to disability identity and asks how they relate to enforced systems of exclusion and oppression, attacking the widespread belief that having an able body and mind determines whether one is a quality human being. (pp. 3–4)

In disability studies, a focus is not on "fixing" disabled bodies so that they fit the able-bodied norm; instead, it is the ableist and exclusionary beliefs and practices of the culture that need "fixing"—study, rehabilitation, and repair. Further, the recognition that mainstream definitions of disability are fictions created by ableist anxiety facilitates reclaiming disability identity so that disability is redefined by disabled people in their own ways and on their own terms (Brueggemann, 2013; Siebers, 2011).

In a similar way, grief studies might also claim that it is not the griever who must be stifled or hidden away, but instead the loss- and emotion-avoidant culture that needs reform to allow a place for a range of human emotions and experiences. The acknowledgment that mainstream conceptions of grief are severely limited can promote the telling and circulation of alternate and more authentic stories about the grief experience, ultimately contributing to a change in the cultural understandings of grief.

Changing Representation through the Life Story

The life narrative can play a particularly important role in identifying and challenging stigmatizing representations of disability and grief. However, social constructions can put pressure on how authentically such a life can be described. Narratives about disability, like narratives about grief, are subject to formulaic plots that reassure mainstream culture of their separation from such experiences. Disability studies and life-writing theorist Couser (2012) finds that a disability memoir is more likely to be published and well-received if it conforms to a number of preferred *rhetorics*, or narrative patterns, that uphold social constructions of disability. These include "a story of triumph over adversity" in which the life-writer overcomes the challenges of the disability (p. 33); "the rhetoric of horror" which paints disability "as a dreadful condition, to be shunned or avoided" (p. 34); "the rhetoric of spiritual compensation" in which the writer understands disability as a spiritual gift (p. 36); and "the rhetoric of nostalgia" in which the autobiographer mourns for a body that once wasn't disabled (p. 38). Each of these patterns uses a deficit approach to disability, reinforcing the notion that disability is a private matter to be cured, compensated for, or dreaded; the need for social and political action to bring about changes that lead to greater equality is missing.

The grief narrative is subject to similar pressures from social expectations. In psychology, Neimeyer et al. (2014) assert "the public voicing and performance of grief and its associated rituals are functionally scripted in a way that supports broader social systems and those who wield power within them" (p. 496). In her literary study of grief memoirs, Prodromou (2015) finds "the standard model of grief with its cookie-cutter style of recovery" problematic because it reinforces a fictional binary in which one is either completely over grief or one experiences unending grief with no room for a more complicated, in-between experience of grief (p. 4). Gilbert (2006) in her cultural and literary examination of grief finds that mourners are pressured to muffle their grief, creating additional barriers to telling their stories, especially on their own terms.

However, at the same time that there is pressure to conform the life story to mainstream expectations, it is the life story—out of all of the literary genres—that may have the greatest capacity to make interventions in the ways marginalized identities are represented. As Couser (2012) has theorized: "autobiography has considerable potential to counter stigmatizing or patronizing portrayals of disability because it is a medium in which disabled people may have a high degree of control over their own images" (p. 31). The autobiography, then, becomes a space where a person can construct their own life on their own terms in ways that can counteract the harmful constructions of mainstream culture. In contrast to the aforementioned narrative patterns that uphold the status quo, Couser identifies an autobiographical pattern he terms "emancipation," which works toward freeing disability from negative mainstream perceptions and represents "disability not as a flaw...but as the prejudicial construct of normative culture," placing the disability experience "within the context of an ongoing personal and collective struggle for recognition of the value and rights of people with disabilities" (p. 47). Such autobiographies push back against pressure to portray disability as deviant and a private misfortune to assert more realistic and positive messages about disabled lives and call attention to the need for cultural and political change.

Four emancipatory life-writing strategies used in disability autobiographies have particular application to grief studies. First, there is an assertion that disability identity is simply part of what it means to be human. This resituates disability from being considered "abnormal" and frightening to being conceptualized as part of life (Brueggemann, 2013). Likewise, the fear surrounding grief and loss might be offset by the assertion that they are part of what it means to be human and are actually more ordinary than they appear to be in a culture that is trained to look away from them. Prodromou (2015) notes that there are many literary works that deal with death and grief; however, because there is a social contract prohibiting the open discussion of such topics, they are simply invisible to readers, further accentuating the isolation associated with grief. Life stories which help to situate grief within a spectrum of human experiences will help to render grief experiences more visible and ordinary, offsetting cultural anxieties about loss.

Second, there is a call to discuss bodily contingencies such as pain that cannot be ameliorated by change in socio-political treatment of disability. While such examinations refer mainly to physical pain, grief studies may substitute the pain of loss. Discussions of pain often take a constructionist approach, noting that there is a tendency to devalue lives that experience pain, and call for alternative ways to conceptualize lives in pain (Brueggemann, 2013; Mintz, 2015; Siebers, 2011). Overall, there is an assertion that the experience of pain is not antithetical to a good life, but instead is part of a spectrum of experience. For example, Mintz (2015) identifies writers who "craft pain in ways that resist its supposed horror, encouraging their readers to react differently to pain experiences that might otherwise feel overwhelmingly lonely, frightening, even hostile. They write a pain that affirms rather than annihilates selfhood" (p. 6). In a similar way, grief studies may seek out alternate representations of grief that situate the anguish and other painful qualities of grief as part of, not a barrier to, a good life.

Third, there is a focus on understanding disabled people as part of a thriving community and culture (Brueggemann, 2013). This representation counters the isolation created by mainstream notions of disability, builds positive associations, and helps to marshal political advocacy. Likewise, the development of a group identity for grievers is tantamount to changing cultural constructions of grief. Stories that situate a griever within supportive communities of grievers work against the construct of grief as an isolated, personal matter and represent the bereaved as a cultural group whose experiences are valid and visible.

Fourth, disability autobiography frequently celebrates diversity in terms of types of disability, ways of experiencing disability, and intersections with other cultural identities. Similarly, grief studies can expand the narrow cultural representations of grief by welcoming a diversity of grief stories that are complicated by such factors as estrangement and abuse or death by violence or negligence. In addition, grief studies can welcome a diversity of grievers to tell their stories, resulting in a greater understanding of how grief intersects with race, gender, sexuality, class, and other alignments.

Such reconceptualizations—the focus on the human, the acknowledgement of pain, the assertion of community, the recognition of diversity—are particularly useful in targeting some of the most damaging social constructions connected to disability. For example, disability autobiographies by Mairs (1996), Clare (1999), Fries (2003), and Linton (2006) assert a strong and vibrant disability culture that participates in such activities as art, dance, celebrations, political activism, advanced education, and travel and which enjoys community, family, friendship, romance, love, and sex. There are also frank discussions of living with such bodily realities as pain and immobility; these occur alongside an assertion that such lives have intrinsic value, and the narratives point to the social construction of disability as one of, if not the most, problematic part of living with a disability. Each autobiographer is careful not to universalize by speaking for others and suggests there is a diversity of experiences of disability and myriad intersections with other cultural identities such as race, gender, sexuality, and class. Each in their own way uses the life story to represent disabled lives as complex, rich, valuable human lives and advocate for socio-political change.

In disability studies, then, the presence of many stories nurtures a sense of a thriving disability community and works to offset the prevalence of mainstream narratives that favor a deficit model of disability. Similarly, a diversity of grief stories might be infused into the culture to promote a change in the cultural constructions and experiences of grief. The emancipatory potential of the grief narrative has already begun to be recognized. Neimeyer et al. (2014) find that the bereaved person can "actively resist" social scripts for the proper expression of grief in the grief narrative (p. 496). Gilbert (2006) argues that the very impulse to write about grief is a reaction against the social compulsion to silence grief. Prodromou (2015) seeks out what she calls memoirs of "textured recovery" that work against the healed-from-grief/never-healed-from-grief binary, situate grief as a "universal experience," and conceptualize grievers as a "community of mourners" (pp. 4–6, 12). Such life stories have potential to destigmatize the experience of grief.

Pathways Forward

Both Neimeyer et al. (2014) and Prodromou (2015) recognize that studies of the social construction of grief are still in their infancy—there is more work to be done. Toward that end, insights from disability studies suggest that the following pathways might be productive in changing the culture of grief. First, we can turn a spotlight on the cultural representations of grief, making them more visible and identifying the need for advocacy to change insidious negative representations of grief. For example, we might mindfully ask of a literary work, movie, or any cultural production: What is the message about grief being communicated? How does it uphold or provide an alternative to negative constructions of grief?

Second, we can join with other fields to fight against devaluing social constructions. In addition to disability studies, trauma studies and pain studies can be productive allies to grief studies because they all articulate ways to challenge social fears of pain, loss, and mortality. It's important to note that mainstream conceptions of disability and grief may present some obstacles to allyhood between disability studies, grief studies, and other fields. For example, the ableist misperception that disabled people routinely experience grief over the loss of their ability could be perpetuated in such a partnership and would be undesirable from a disability studies standpoint; similarly, the experience of grief may be identified as a disability and further aligned with the deficit model, not an ideal outcome for grief studies. Many of these obstacles, however, originate from mainstream misperceptions about disability and grief, pain and loss, and indicate the crucial need to work together to dismantle them.

Third, perhaps most urgently, we can call for the circulation of narratives, written and spoken in public and in private spaces, that reflect many facets and experiences of grief. This pathway will have a generative effect: as more varied models for grieving become culturally available, as death is spoken about more freely, grievers will be more empowered to fight against oppressive conceptions of grief and to tell their own stories about loss on their own terms. The proliferation of grief stories will decenter mainstream definitions of grief, contributing to cultural change.

In conclusion, just as the shared disability story changes our understanding of disability, personal narratives of grief can alter beliefs about grief. The shared grief story can identify and challenge stereotypes and systems of oppression connected to grief. It can suggest that grief—with all of its pain and unpredictability—is part of a changed but good life. Providing alternate patterns to counter fairly narrow mainstream expectations, it can suggest that grief is experienced in a diversity of ways. It can also promote a sense of community among grieving people. Situated in a disability studies framework, the shared grief story is a social justice action that allows those with intimate experiences of grief to provide an authentic spectrum of what it is like to live with grief. Making available a variety of grief stories transmits more holistic understandings of grief and promotes a sense of shared experiences, of community, of strength.

References

Brueggemann, B. J. (2013). Disability studies/Disability culture. In M. L. Wehmeyer (Ed.), *The Oxford handbook of positive psychology and disability* (pp. 279–299). Oxford University Press.

Clare, E. (1999). *Exile and pride: Disability, queerness, and liberation.* South End Press.

Couser, G. T. (2012). *Signifying bodies: Disability in contemporary life writing.* University of Michigan Press.

Fries, K. (2003). *Body remember: A memoir.* University of Wisconsin Press.

Gilbert, G. M. (2006). *Death's door: Modern dying and the ways we grieve.* W. W. Norton.

Linton, S. (2006). *My body politic: A memoir.* University of Michigan Press.

Mairs, N. (1996). *Waist-high in the world: A life among the nondisabled.* Beacon Press.

Mintz, S. B. (2015). *Hurt and Pain: Literature and the suffering body.* Bloomsbury Academic.

Neimeyer, R. A. (1999). Narrative strategies in grief therapy. *Journal of Constructivist Psychology, 12*(1), 65–85. doi: 10.1080/107205399266226.

Neimeyer, R. A., Klass, D., & Dennis, M. R. (2014). A social constructionist account of grief: Loss and the narration of meaning. *Death Studies, 38*(8), 485–498. doi: 10.1080/07481187.2014.913454.

Oliver, M. (2009). The social model in context. In T. Titchkosky and R. Michalko (Eds.), *Rethinking normalcy: A disability studies reader* (pp. 19–30). Canadian Scholars' Press.

Prodromou, A. K. (2015). *Navigating loss in women's contemporary memoir.* Palgrave MacMillan.

Siebers, T. (2011). *Disability theory.* University of Michigan Press.

3 Agency in Writing

Managing Narratives of Trauma in Student Writing

Danielle Lee

Writing, in and of itself, is a very personal journey that most do not know how to embark on. Students assume that writing, particularly writing done by published authors, flows from mind to pen in a fell swoop of ideas, grammatical magnificence, and perfect sentence structure. However, the reality for most students entails staring anxiously into their laptop screen trying to figure out how to begin their writing assignment. The task is particularly daunting when the assignment calls for the student to share an impactful moment from their lives and write about it in vivid detail. As teachers, we try to create assignments that challenge students to think and express themselves in ways either unfamiliar or frightening. We also complicate this process by asking students to engage and analyze their physical and emotional responses to literature, coining the exercise "analysis."

The English classroom demands students critically engage with a text to reveal truths, constructions, presentations, and to a fair degree, misrepresentations of culture, society, race, and gender, to name a few. One overarching goal is to train students to perform critical interpretations of the human condition as depicted from a variety of perspectives within their sociohistorical contexts. More importantly, exposure to sociocultural, socioeconomic, and sociohistorical narratives help students recognize themselves within these frameworks so they can reach an understanding of the world around them and themselves within it. One of the most important tools used to get students situated in this way of thinking is to have them critically respond not only to the mechanics of the texts, but also to how they are personally impacted by these representations. However, the inclusion of a personal response to a text can be problematic when students are responding to depictions of traumatic events on micro- and macro-levels like sexual assault, racism, death, natural disasters, and terrorism. This is especially true if the texts reflect a personal traumatic experience the student is struggling with and needs professional intervention.

For instance, in *Blu's Hanging*, Yamanaka (1997) portrays Hawaiian racial and cultural politics between Japanese and Kanaka Maoli people.

At the center of the novel is the tragic Ogata family who is dealing with a myriad of difficult issues like drug addiction, abandonment, and sexual identity. The protagonist, Blu, is an 11-year-old boy who subsequently commits suicide because of being raped by his uncle. While the cultural politics in the novel offer material for rich class discussions from both literary and historical perspectives, sexual identity and the assault on a child are topics that demand care when exploring these very difficult topics.

The complication is no different with a text like DeLillo's (2007) *Falling Man,* which is the fictional story of 9/11 survivor Keith Neudecker who recalls his experience that day in vivid detail. Part of the draw to DeLillo's book is the authenticity of the experience he depicts, but more so because the title references the iconic picture of a man falling headfirst from the towers. The photo taken by Associated Press photo-journalist Richard Drew (2001) became a worldwide iconic image representing the tragedy of that fateful day and a compelling narrative of the falling man's—loosely identified as Jonathan Briley—last minutes of his life. September 11th narratives such as DeLillo's, demand educators be particularly mindful that many college students reading this text were small children who may have lost parents and other family members on that day. However, literary representations of violence and trauma date back to antiquity. Sophocles's *Antigone* (441/2004) is rife with violence and death. Shakespeare's ten tragedies, including *Othello* (1603/1975), *Hamlet* (1603/1994), *Macbeth* (1623/2005), and *Julius Caesar* (1623/2004), tackled the themes of rape, suicide, murder, and war. *Titus Andronicus* (1594) is particularly violent in the depiction of Lavinia's rape and the mutilation of her hands and tongue. Tamora, Queen of the Goths, consumes her sons in a meat pie. *Romeo and Juliet* (1595/2004) ends in a double teen suicide. The titular character of Aphra Behn's *Ooronoko* (1688/2000) murdered his pregnant wife and disemboweled himself. There is not a single literary period that does not have a canonical text without some kind of trauma experienced by the protagonist. While texts from the earlier periods may be relatable to some extent, later 20th and 21st century texts both inside and outside of the canon may more realistically reflect the lives of the students in our classrooms right now. A safe choice for English classroom educators concerned about teaching sensitive material that may trigger a student dealing with trauma would be to search for books that explore the topic in broad and general terms. However, that would mean not teaching important texts like the autobiography *Narrative of the Life of Frederick Douglass* (1845/2016), Virginia Woolf's *Mrs. Dalloway* (1925/1981), Margaret Atwood's *The Handmaid's Tale* (1985), or Toni Morrison's *Paradise* (1998), just to name some. To avoid these kinds of canonical works would also mean participating in the marginalization and isolation of texts dangerously and/or irresponsibly deemed "risky."

Even though trauma on global, national, and personal levels these days is openly shared via every outlet of social media available, teachers are compelled to be mindful of how the open discussion of certain events may affect a student when there are at least twenty other people in the classroom weighing in on what may be a classmate's personal experience. Therefore, empathy on the part of the teacher is more than just being respectful to a possible experience, but it is also critical to the instructor's interactions with all students, as we cannot valorize traumatic experience over any other. As a writing teacher, however, I argue that part of the most effective results of empathetic teaching happens in the one-on-one discussion between student and professor in personal writing as in a narrative writing assignment.

Developing Student Agency

The exchange between teacher and student during this process can be a positive transformational experience that Read and Read (1998) describe as the shifting of "focus from a dyadic, hierarchical teacher-student relationship to a collective relationship where students become agents, subjects in the process of producing knowledge" (p. 113). More importantly, this shift also allows space for the development of hope where none may have been previously present, which has exponential benefits to the student and their development as a writer moving forward. Sieben (2018), drawing from Freire (2004) and Giroux (2003), explains there is a "need for hope within the context of critical pedagogy, calling for teachers to engage students in a conscious process of understanding that allows students to make meaning from their own lived experiences and emerge from struggle if necessary" (p. 3). Therefore, instruction in the acquisition of analytical skills is necessary for that meaning to develop. Narrative writing assignments help students understand what it means to create meaning as they understand it. For some students, there is little else about their personal lives that makes sense until they have the structure and language to do so. A narrative writing assignment exposes the student writing they have a personal vested interest in. This does not mean that exposing their personal lives is critical or necessary to be a good student writer. However, I do believe the expression of how the student defines, recalls, and reiterates a traumatic experience gives that student a sense of agency that none of us who have experienced trauma may feel. Anderson and MacCurdy (2000) would agree, stating:

> By writing about traumatic experiences, we discover and rediscover them, move them out of the ephemeral flow and space of talk onto the more permanent surface of the page, where they can be considered, reconsidered, left, and taken up again. Through the dual

possibilities of permanence and revision, the chief healing effect of writing is thus to recover and to exert a measure of control over that which we can never control—the past. (p. 7)

The control Anderson and MacCurdy are talking about also extends to how the student's story is told, and hence why the development of voice is critical to academic writing. Voice, as social and political construct, is largely intersectional. Gender, race, ethnicity and culture play a significant role in the development of voice and language as these all affect the expression of experience and identity. When a student is asked to analyze voice as part of the narrative structure of a text, race and gender are often used as clues to help students understand and relate to a character's experience. As Morgan (1998) states:

Our students write about violence and substance abuse and broken families because they're writing about what they have lived and witnessed firsthand, what they care most deeply about. Their crises, past or present, mirror the condition of our society, reflect what has become more and more ordinary. (p. 324)

Our role as the writing teacher is not to break down the student's experience but to help them academically frame the writing of the experience. Our job is to facilitate the mechanics of academic writing, regardless of the topic. This also includes helping students identify and develop their voice, recognize their voice has authority, as well as understanding writing for a specific audience. In the process of writing about their experiences, there is an opportunity for the student to discover and possibly redefine the concept of hope. The process of drafting, revising, and editing such an assignment may seem like a formula for the re-traumatizing of the student for some critics who discourage these kinds of writing on the basis of teachers not playing psychologist, but I argue each segment of the writing process helps develop hope because the student can revisit the assignment and grow an academic distance that allows them to see the assignment through the lens of the writing process, thereby providing more agency to the student as they decide what parts of their story need revision. Once a student believes they have found their voice, they now have more power over how they feel about both the traumatic memory and their writing.

In my third year of teaching English Composition and assigning a narrative paper, one of my students talked about how she met her current boyfriend. At first, I believed it to be a typical high school love story. Boy meets girl, they fall in love, and live happily ever after. The story was really about her first interaction with him at their high school's theater where she was suffering a major panic attack. He was the first person she spoke to about her anxiety and her use of cutting as a way to relieve the enormous emotional pressure she carried with her. This student wrote in vivid detail about her experience and how her boyfriend simply listening to her while sitting on the floor of a dark theater was a life-changing moment. The telling of this story, in her opinion, helped her see just how much this interaction had meant to her. She claimed to have felt empowered and additionally grateful for this memory, as it was a gauge for how far she had come since starting college.

MacCurdy (2007) defends student writing about traumatic experiences stating the act of writing "allow[s] us to put to words to our difficult moments... it is not only cathartic, but it also creates understanding" (p. 2) and, in turn, hope. My approach to this student's story was not to comment on the topic of her narrative, but on how she told the story. My process for grading her paper was to focus on language, description, sentence structure, and voice as to not cross any ethical lines because of my understanding of what my role is. I did not feel it necessary to ask for more clarification or offer her any advice for how to handle her anxiety or cutting. Thankfully, she had already stated by the end of the narrative that she had sought help for both at the encouragement of her boyfriend and was on a healthy path, albeit with a couple of setbacks along the way. Had she not, I would have been bound by law to ask if she needed any assistance the campus or any off-campus services could offer.

Our Role as Writing Teachers

Over the years, the word I have repeatedly heard from students about their choice to write about trauma is "trust." They trust me with these very personal narratives because they believe they will not be judged and can speak freely. In the second chapter of Berman's book *Empathic Teaching: Education for Life* (2004), an examination of empathy and its value to both the student and teacher is drawn from his analysis of how psychoanalyst Heinz Kohut and psychologist Carl Rogers approach psychotherapy and education. Both Rogers and Kohut (as cited in Berman, 2004) believe empathy is a positive and critical tool that enhances life and the understanding of experience. According to Rogers (1980), a person-centered approach to teaching with empathy is at the root of a positive interaction between student and teacher. Rogers connects this positive interaction to the student's perception of the teacher by articulating that "when the facilitator is a real person, being what he or she is, entering into relationships with the learners without presenting a front or façade, the facilitator is more likely to be effective" (p. 271). For Rogers, the act of being heard bears a level of validation that is critical to the relationship between student and teacher. For both Rogers and Kohut, there is a positive connection between psychotherapy and education with empathy as a driving force for student success.

There is a fair amount of criticism about teachers embarking on writing assignments that may lead to students reliving and therefore re-traumatizing themselves by re-visiting the event. Rightly so, the fear is that writing teachers are acting as pseudo-psychologists. However, writing about an experience is a way for students to make sense of the event and how they have, and perhaps still are, processing it. Writing also provides a space for students to be open about their feelings without being interrupted or told they are wrong. When I give my students a narrative assignment asking them to describe an impactful moment of their lives, it is up to the student to choose which moment they want to share. In the seven years I have been teaching and using this assignment in my composition and literature courses, if it is called for, I make it very clear that the impactful moment is of their choice. The need for the student to share a traumatic memory comes from them. I do not question why they chose that moment, but I have come to understand the decision to do so comes from two places: the need to share it and their trust in me as their instructor.

Informed Empathy

While I believe empathy is a critical component of my pedagogy, I also believe that empathy is a useful tool for self-care when engaging with student narratives that are similar to that of a teacher's own personal experience with trauma. Prior to teaching, I worked in magazine print production for a large trade-publishing house in lower Manhattan. Like so many others, I was a witness to the horrors of 9/11. My company lost eleven employees that day with two of them being on the plane from Boston. Like so many others bearing witness that day, I was later diagnosed with post-traumatic stress disorder, severe anxiety, and depression. The effect on my life was such that I left Manhattan and never returned except for the occasional sightseeing trip or to visit family. When I read student narratives or texts about that day, I am transported back to that anxiety and can remember quite vividly where I was, what I said, and how I felt. I would be remiss if I said my personal trauma had no impact on who I am as a teacher. Thankfully, I have long since overcome my original diagnosis of anxiety and depression. Having done the work to overcome these obstacles, I believe my sense of empathy for others and their pain is conveyed through my teaching in intangible ways. Sometimes I wonder if pain recognizes pain. I very rarely share my story about 9/11 with students unless I find it absolutely necessary to humanize that day in a way that makes it more accessible to the discussion at hand. I do not share this to say I am more empathic or empathetic than anyone else. I share it to say that we as instructors can relate to our students on humanistic levels that do not betray any sense of hierarchical authority or distance. Empathy is a tool that helps us recognize each other's humanity at all levels of grief, trauma, and pain. It is at the root of feeling compassion for others. It is one of the many and most important ways people make sense of themselves, and those around them. Student writing about personal experiences serves as a making-sense tool for both the student and instructor. When it comes to assigning literature with disturbing content, we must be clear about student learning objectives and goals. Tragedy is an unavoidable experience and many of our students have seen much of it in their young lives. To not teach narratives dealing with trauma and tragedy is to negate the voices of the very students we interact with, and it further perpetuates the silences we want our students to break. Voice and hearing are not mutually exclusive; they are critical to validating an experience.

References

Anderson, C. M., & MacCurdy, M. M. (Eds.) (2000). *Writing and healing toward an informed practice.* National Council of Teachers of English.

Atwood, M. (1998). *The Handmaid's tale.* Anchor Books, a division of Penguin Random House LLC.

Behn, A. (2000). *Oroonoko* (C. Gallagher & S. Stern, Eds.). Bedford/St. Martin's Press. (Original work published 1688).

Berman, J. (2004). *Empathic teaching: Education for life.* University of Massachusetts Press.

DeLillo, D. (2007). *Falling man.* MacMillan.

Douglass, F. (2016). *Narrative of the life of Frederick Douglass* (P. Smith, Ed.). Dover Thrift Editions. (Original work published 1845).

Drew, R. (2001). *The falling man* [Photograph]. The Associated Press. http://100photos.time.com/photos/richard-drew-falling-man

Freire, P. (2004). Pedagogy of hope. Continuum.

Giroux, H. (2003). Utopian thinking under the sign of neoliberalism: Towards a critical pedagogy of educated hope. *Democracy and Nature, 9*(1), 91–105.

MacCurdy, M. M. (2007). *The mind's eye: Image and memory in writing about trauma.* University of Massachusetts Press.

Morgan, D. (1998). Ethical issues raised by students' personal writing. *College English, 60*(3), 318–325. https://predator.oldwestbury.edu:2095/stable/378560

Morrison, T. (1998). Paradise. A.A. Knopf.

Read, D., & Read, D. (1998). Special issue: Exploring borderlands: Postcolonial and composition studies. Writing trauma, history, story: The class(room) as borderland. JAC: *A Journal of Composition Theory, 18*(1), 105–121. Retrieved from http://www.jstor.org/stable/20866174

Rogers, C. (1980). *A way of being.* Houghton Mifflin.

Shakespeare, W. (1994). *Hamlet* (G. R. Hibbard, Ed.). Oxford University Press. (Original work published 1603).

Shakespeare, W. (1995). *Titus Andronicus* (J. Bate, Ed.). Routledge. (Original work published in 1594).

Shakespeare, W. (2004). *Julius Caesar* (B. A. Mowat & P. Werstine, Eds). Washington Square Press. (Original work published in 1623).

Shakespeare, W. (2004). *Romeo and Juliet* (B. A. Mowat & P. Werstine, Eds.). Washington Square Press. (Original work published in 1595).

Shakespeare, W. (2005). *Macbeth* (R. Gibson, Ed.). Cambridge University Press. (Original work published 1623).

Shakespeare, W. (2005). *Titus Adronicus* (B. A Mowat & P. Werstine, Eds.). Washington Square Press. (Original work published in 1594).

Shakespeare, W. (2014). *Othello* (3rd revised ed.). (R. Gibson, J. Cole, V. Wienand, & R. Andrews, Eds.). Cambridge University Process. (Original work published 1603).

Sieben, N. (2018). *Writing hope strategies for writing success in secondary schools: A strengths-based approach to teaching writing.* Brill | Sense.

Sophocles (2004). *The Oedipus plays of Sophocles: Oedipus the king, Oedipus at Colonos, Antigone.* (P. Roche, Trans.). Plume. (Original work published ca. 441 BCE).

Woolf, V. (1981). *Mrs. Dalloway.* Harcourt. (Original work published in 1925).

Yamanaka, L. A. (1997). *Blu's hanging.* Harper Perennial.

4 "Conceit Upon her Father"

An Unintentional Confrontation with Bibliotherapy

Adam Wolfsdorf

Literature: Hope Theory, Bibliotherapy, and Allyship

For those navigating grief, literature can function as an ally. For while grief tends to inculcate feelings of loneliness, isolation, and despair, literary engagement can forge connections for the reader (Rosenblatt, 1938), augment self-awareness, and facilitate the journey back to hope and recovery (Crothers, 1916). As F. Scott Fitzgerald wrote to Sheila Graham in 1938, "That is part of the beauty of all literature. You discover that your longings are universal longings, that you're not lonely and isolated from anyone. You belong" (Fitzgerald as cited in Graham & Frank, 1989, p. 196). This sense of belonging, a metaphysical companionship we might refer to as allyship, binds the reader to the literary experience. For the act of reading literature, by its very nature, vivifies our senses, expands our consciousness, and satisfies our will to "see with other imaginations, to feel with other hearts, as well as with our own" (Lewis as cited in Bruns, 2011, p. 15). It is this sense of expansion and belonging that can help to mitigate the devastation of grief and pave a path towards recovery.

Literature's capacity as a vehicle for hope has a lasting tradition. *Bibliotherapy* (Crothers, 1916) is rooted in the belief that literature can facilitate psychological healing. *Hope theory* (Allen, 2008; Appleton, 2001) anchors itself in the principle that how we think and feel has a positive or negative impact on our capacity for hope. When we grieve, hope can feel unattainable (van der Kolk, 2014). But literature, because it has the power to shift mental states and reshape cognitions (Bruns, 2011; Greene, 1988), may provide relief from suffering and rekindle faith (Appleton, 2001). In this sense, grief and literature can work antithetically. For while grief tends to shut down and temporarily cripple hope, engagement with literature may boost emotions, galvanize restorative pathways, and create alternative ways of seeing.

Utilizing bibliotherapy and hope theory, this chapter will explore possibilities in the English classroom for utilizing literature as a mechanism for enhancing hope and helping survivors to cope with personal narratives of despair. Grief is a complicated emotion, one that often feels suffocating and intractable. Survivors of grief often struggle to imagine recovery, and typically feel arrested in the trauma of loss (van der Kolk, 2014). But art, because it can facilitate identification and shift perspective, can be healing. By using a case study involving a high school senior in an honors-level Shakespeare class, this chapter will make the case that literature can therapeutically facilitate emotional healing, by helping survivors ally with fictional characters who suffer from analogous traumas. By more closely examining the connection between hope theory and bibliotherapy, this chapter will make a case for the potentially transformative psychological benefits of literature, and elucidate the rich therapeutic capacities within "words, words, words" (Shakespeare, 1603/1994 2.2.191).

Bibliotherapy: Books as Accessories to Healing

The term bibliotherapy was first coined in 1916 by the Unitarian minister and essayist, Samuel McChord Crothers: "He reviewed the prescriptive use of books in helping patients understand their problems, a technique he titled bibliotherapy" (Heath, Sheen, Leavy, Young, & Money, 2005, p. 563). In his *Atlantic* article, "The Pleasures of an Absentee Landlord", Crothers (1916) wrote:

> Biblio-therapy is such a new science…. Here is a stock of literary depressants …. There are other books that are confused with true stimulants but which are really quite different both in their composition and effects—they are the counter-irritants. (p. 295)

Crothers' early conceptualization of the healing powers of literary works pondered whether literature could be used therapeutically to facilitate transformative emotional effects for readers in psychological distress.

Unlike more conventional psychological treatments, such as psychoanalysis, cognitive behavioral therapy, or psychotropic pharmaceuticals—which are more comprehensive and holistic approaches—bibliotherapy was originally intended as an indirect method administered in conjunction with other approaches. According to Heath et al. (2005):

> Stories are helpful in offering potential insight into personal problems (Forgan, 2002; Pardek, 1996) and in creating a safe distance, bringing a child or adolescent indirectly to the edge of sensitive issues, possibly too threatening and painful to face directly (Corr, 2003–2004). (p. 564)

A key issue at play is the concept of psychological distance—both the psychological distance that the individual has in relation to her own traumatic experience, and also the way that literature, since it tells stories about people other than the reader, can help survivors to safely approach, process, and potentially rework transferential feelings associated with their own traumatic memories. In the bibliotherapeutic process, the book is utilized as a conduit, allowing the survivor to unconsciously and then perhaps consciously navigate her own suffering (Heath et al., 2005).

As Scheff (1979) argues in *Catharsis in Healing, Ritual, and Drama*, the relative efficacy of bibliotherapy may depend on the individual's psychological readiness for confronting the transferential feelings associated with the trauma. Since trauma survivors exist on a continuum (van der Kolk, 2014), it may be the case that a survivor at one phase of recovery may not be capable of aesthetic textual engagement, but may significantly benefit from such engagement at a later phase in her healing (Scheff, 1979). As with most therapeutic processes, timing and personal readiness are fundamentally crucial.

The remainder of this chapter will focus on one such circumstance involving a 17-year-old high school senior enrolled in an honors-level Shakespeare course. *Hamlet* was the text we were reading. Unbeknownst to me at the time, the student was caught in the throes of a personal traumatic experience. I wish I could say it was all intentional, but what happened over the course of that 10-week unit accidentally facilitated her grieving process. It was bibliotherapy all right, except neither she nor I knew it.

A Case Study: *Hamlet*, Yana, and Unintentional Bibliotherapy

"Go, bid the soldiers shoot," (Shakespeare, 1603/1994 5.2.448). The words moved out from my lips, lifting into the air and reverberating along the walls of the classroom. Eighteen adolescent Shakespeare students soaked in the words of a play that moves from the ambiguity of an opening question, "Who's there?" (1.1.1), to the finality of Fortinbras's closing imperative. For ten weeks, we'd examined every line, symbol, and soliloquy of Royal Denmark, discoursing extensively over Shakespeare's death of fathers, and the potent complexity of "words, words, words" (2.2.191).

Mostly satisfied, I'd left the classroom late that early winter afternoon, but not before Yana (pseudonym) stopped me: "Would you be willing to read my college essay? I'd love to hear your thoughts before I submit it." Yana was a top student, destined for big things. I told her, "I'd be happy to", and meant it. Later that evening, I took out Yana's essay. I was convinced it would require, at most, some subtle tweaks. I began reading: In the summer of 2015, we lost our father suddenly. He'd been in the Ukraine for six years, since we'd immigrated to the States. Every summer my mother, sister, little brother, and I waited for the day that he would join us. Now that day will never come.

Had I been holding a glass, it would have fallen from my hand and shattered. For the past ten weeks, I had strutted and fretted my hour on the stage, taken on the grief and anguish of *Hamlet* with visceral intensity. I'd encouraged them do the same—casting Ophelias to experience the lunacy of a grief-stricken mind, and Laerteses to embody the rage of forlorn children. It was all death of fathers, from Hamlet Sr. to Polonius and Fortinbras Sr.; a succession of paternal loss and trauma. And there Yana had sat, recently fatherless herself, subject to my rapturous intoxication with tragedy. "Why, what an ass am I!" (Shakespeare, 1603/1994, 2.2.558). What had I done?!

The following morning, I approached Yana with my tail between my legs. I asked her if she'd be willing to grant me an interview. I was writing my dissertation at the time, researching the relative efficacy of trigger warnings in the English classroom. Initially caught off guard by my request, Yana invariably agreed. It was our second year working together, and we had established a strong bond.

In the months that followed, Yana and I engaged in several interviews, focusing on what experiencing *Hamlet* had been like for her in the wake of her father's death. We talked about what it had meant for her to dive into a literary work that touched so close to her personal tragedy (Britzman & Pitt, 2004). There was so much more to understand; so many words needed to unpack the complexity of what it means when fictional grief and personal trauma collide.

The Yana Interviews

One of the things I was genuinely concerned about when I sat down to interview Yana, was that I had unwittingly retraumatized her. Given the play's obvious circumstantial overlap with her life, I wondered whether the psychologically prescient (Scheff, 1979) material, paired with my dramatic teaching style, had violated her emotional life-space. She seemed to convey otherwise:

> You can't avoid things in your life regardless of how much you want to. So it's better to deal with them rather than just pretend that they're not happening...So when it's in a controlled environment like that and, in addition to that, you're feeling like this character is going through... and maybe you opened your mind to "someone else is going through that, someone else is experiencing this," and I think it was more helpful than harmful.

Yana seemed to believe that our *Hamlet* work facilitated her grieving process. In his loss and pain, Hamlet may have been a suitable literary figure capable of mirroring and embodying some of Yana's despair. She continued:

> I thought it was therapeutic. It was always an escape to see into [Hamlet's] mind, but at the same time kind of open my mind.... Just thinking about situations that I might not normally want to think about but nonetheless are sometimes necessary to think about.

This point felt important to me. Depending on an individual's psychological readiness relative to their traumatic experience, she may not be willing or capable of directly processing the hurt (van der Kolk, 2014; Wolfsdorf, 2017, 2018). Yet literature's modality as fiction may provide safety and allyship for students, an indirect opportunity for them to digest emotional conflicts in their own lives. For teachers capable of promoting student-centered, brave spaces (Arao & Clemens, 2013) where risk taking and vulnerability are encouraged, the literature classroom can encourage students to wrestle with grief without feeling pressured to divulge or disclose personal information:

> I think that if there's any situation where you should be open to relating to something or even being open to thinking about something that you might not necessarily wanna think about, it's best to do it in a situation like that, where you could live your life through maybe a character.

Feeling safe is an essential feature for trauma survivors (Stolorow, 2007; van der Kolk, 2014). And literature may be safer than we imagine, in large part because it is the author, rather than the reader, who leads with vulnerability, disclosing the grief and suffering through the characters she pens. Similar to how Winnicott envisioned the role of toys for developing children, the text may serve symbolically as a transitional object for the grief-stricken mind, allowing survivors to transact in a psychologically healing manner (Bruns, 2011). For Yana, Hamlet's struggle facilitated her grieving process, helped her to process the trauma, and seemed to aid in her recovery. This is an essential feature of Appleton's (2001) hope theory: the belief that art can be used to facilitate recovery and the reconstitution of positive expectations for life and the future. In Yana's case, *Hamlet* was the right bibliotherapeutic text, a component of her pathway back to faith, resilience, and hope.

The Play's the Thing

During one of Hamlet's low moments early in the play, Rosencrantz and Guildenstern attempt to cheer up their college buddy by announcing that the players are coming to Elsinore. The very instant he hears about the actors' arrival, Hamlet abandons his despair and shifts into unbridled enthusiasm:

> He that plays the king shall be welcome; his majesty shall have tribute of me.... and the lady shall say her mind freely, or the blank verse shall halt for't. (Shakespeare, 1603/1994, 2.2.309–10)

As the actors file in to Elsinore, Hamlet greets them heartily, conveying an enthusiasm absent in previous scenes: "You are welcome, masters; welcome, all. I am glad to see thee well. Welcome, good friends" (Shakespeare, 1603/1994, 2.2.402). Nostalgic, Hamlet urges that they recite a speech from Ovid's *Aeneid*: the scene recounting Priam's slaughter.

Up until this point in the play, the Prince has been reeling from the loss of his father. Donning an "inky cloak" and sighing "windy suspiration of forced breath" (Shakespeare, 1603/1994, 1.2.79), Hamlet has been coping with trauma, while actively planting the seeds to avenge his father's "foul and most unnatural murder" (1.5.25). But with the Players' entrance, art facilitates Hamlet's connection to his suffering. Though he will use the actors later to "catch the conscience of the King" (2.2.581), he first uses them to help identify his own grieving process.

Like the distraught reader who chooses a book because it mirrors her own suffering, Hamlet requests a monologue touching upon his own traumas. "Anon he finds him/Striking too short at Greeks" (Shakespeare, 1603/1994, 2.2.446). The Player King recites the tale of Priam's slaughter, a scene which captures Hamlet's own inner struggles. In a world where Hamlet has felt shut out and disregarded by the denial of his grief, the players' theatricalization offers Hamlet a window into the authenticity of his own experiences, mirrors his anguish, and in the process affirms his suffering. In Shakespeare's play, Hamlet does, invariably, come to a place of relative acceptance: If it be now, 'tis not to come. If it be not to come, it will be now. If it be not now, yet it will come. The readiness is all. Since no man of aught he leaves knows, what is't to leave betimes? Let be. (Shakespeare, 1603/1994, 5.2.192-198)

In *Hamlet* (1.2), he is fixated on the difference between perception and reality: "seems madam, nay it is" (1.2.76); by *Hamlet* (3.1), he's wrestling with the decision to live or die: "to be or not to be" (3.1.56); by *Hamlet* (5.1), he's learned to "let be" (5.1.198). Since each of these lines deliberately navigates some form of the infinitive "to be", i.e. seeming to be, being or not being, and letting be, and since the first occurrence takes place near the top of the play, the second in the middle of the play, and the third close to the end, we might conclude that *Hamlet*, as an artwork, is a play about being. Life, too, is a play about being; about how, at times, we must navigate the "slings and arrows of outrageous fortune" in order to "take arms against a sea of troubles" (3.1.59). And though we may not end them, we may learn to acquire the types of insights and emotional fortitude necessary to stomach the difficult journey from the "poison of deep grief" (4.5.80) to the first true glimmerings of hope: "My father—methinks I see my father" (1.2.183). And literature, if it's taught thoughtfully, can help.

References

Allen, J. G. (2008). *Coping with trauma: Hope through understanding.* American Psychiatric Publishing.

Appleton, V. (2001). Avenues of hope: Art therapy and the resolution of trauma. *Art Therapy, 18*(1), 6–13.

Arao, B., & Clemens, K. (2013). From safe spaces to brave spaces: A new way to frame dialogue around diversity and social justice from the art of effective facilitation. In L. M. Landreman (Ed.), *The art of effective facilitation: Reflections from social justice educators* (pp. 135–150). Stylus Publishing.

Britzman, D. P., & Pitt, A. J. (2004). Pedagogy and clinical knowledge: Some psychoanalytic observations on losing and refinding significance. *Journal of Advanced Composition, 24*(2), 353–374. http://www.jstor.org/stable/20866629

Bruns, C. V. (2011). *Why literature? The value of literary reading and what it means for teaching.* Continuum.

Crothers, S. (1916). *Pleasures of an absentee landlord: And other essays.* Houghton Mifflin.

Graham, S., & Frank, G. (1989). *Beloved infidel.* Quality Paperback Book Club.

Greene, M. (1988). *The dialect of freedom.* Teachers College Press.

Heath, M. A., Sheen, D., Leavy, D., Young, E. L., & Money, K. (2005). Bibliotherapy: A resource to facilitate emotional healing and growth. *School Psychology International, 26*(5), 563–580.

Rosenblatt, L. M. (1938). *Literature as exploration.* D. Appleton Century.

Scheff, T. J. (1979). *Catharsis in healing, ritual, and drama.* University of California Press.

Shakespeare, W. (1994). *Hamlet* (R. Andrews & R. Gibson, Eds.). Cambridge University Press. (Original work published in 1603).

Stolorow, R. D. (2007). *Trauma and human existence: Autobiographical, psychoanalytic, and philosophical reflections.* Taylor and Francis.

van der Kolk, B. A. (2014). *The body keeps the score: Brain, mind, and body in the healing of trauma.* Viking.

Wolfsdorf, A. (2017). Reflecting on functioning in trigger happy. *America. Changing English, 24*(3), 299–318.

Wolfsdorf, A. (2018). When it comes to high school English, let's put away the triggers. *English Journal, 108*(1), 39–44.

5 "The Grief that Fills One's Heart"

Pairing Loss Narratives and Graphic Young Adult Literature

Shelbie Witte and Jennifer S. Dail

Loss and its accompanying grief come in many forms, which we, like our students, have both experienced in many ways. It is impossible to consider taking up conversations of loss and grief with our students without considering our own instances. We have both lived through the significant loss of family, friends, pets, relationships and experiences. Each loss has impacted us differently, but ultimately, each has inherently changed us. As other chapters in this collection demonstrate, grief results from many types of events, and we often do not even recognize it in its early stages when the loss is not an obviously significant one, such as death. In this chapter, we explore our work in pairing graphic young adult literature with the writing of loss narratives with preservice and in-service teachers.

Reading and Discussing *Drowned City*

We grounded our work in the young adult graphic novel *Drowned City: Hurricane Katrina and New Orleans*, written and illustrated by Don Brown (2015). This dramatic novel served as a common loss experience for all participants and illustrates the multiple dimensions of grief and loss experienced by the citizens of New Orleans in August of 2005, immediately following the landfall of Hurricane Katrina. The 15 preservice participants in this study were located in a face-to-face Teaching of Young Adult Literature course at Oklahoma State University, while the 10 in-service participants in this study were in an online graduate English education course through Kennesaw State University. Both groups of participants read and discussed *Drowned City* in preparation for the larger focus assignment of writing their own loss narratives.

We shared some reflection strategies with our participants, including mindfulness activities and ways to center our thinking on the self and drawing upon our senses during these times of loss. Frankly, we knew revisiting these times of loss could be emotional experiences, and we wanted to provide the classes with opportunities to reflect in healthy ways as well as provide opportunities to re-center into the present once these memories came to the surface.

In discussing and writing their narratives, the two groups of participants did not collaborate. Rather, we wanted to identify and name the themes from class discussions and writing across the two groups as opposed to co-creating work across universities. Additionally, collaboration felt as if it would disrupt the safety of the individual classroom spaces given the risks we were asking students to take.

The participants in both groups were quick to make connections between reading *Drowned City* and the loss narratives they would write. During our prewriting conversations, both groups recognized the topic of loss as important because students in secondary classrooms face loss themselves. Before reading *Drowned City*, most of the participants gravitated toward more personal examples such as a loss of a parent. But following the reading of *Drowned City*, they were able to acknowledge the trauma associated with natural disasters and recognize examples of the grief and loss in their own lives because of natural disasters. For example, many of our teachers in Shelbie's class have the recent lived experiences of tornadoes and floods and remember clearly the news of schools or school districts, businesses, and families who suffered life and property losses because of these natural disasters.

Regardless of the type of loss, participants saw value in this sort of work in overall classroom dynamics. For example, they viewed discussing loss with their own students as a means of developing more personal relationships with and among them. They noted that students show interest in connecting with others' experiences. The participants also acknowledged that loss is a difficult topic to write about but is one that invites personal, authentic writing. To that end, they noted that adults often deal with pain and loss through writing and felt that students deserved that opportunity as well. Because of the authentic nature of the writing, participants felt that it had a great potential for classroom impact, which must always be balanced with the greater risk of difficult conversations that it creates in classrooms for both teachers and students. And because of that increased risk, it is necessary to lay the groundwork for this type of writing in classrooms. Writing that is personal can also be uncomfortable and can open vulnerable spaces.

As participants continued in their discussions of *Drowned City*, they concluded that looking at the complexity of loss could bring hope to students. We used this opportunity to discuss definitions of hope and used as a framework Nekolaichuk et al.'s (1999) three dimensions of hope experiences—personal spirit, risk, and authentic caring— with a basic understanding of hope as a way of finding meaning in life, taking risks in spite of uncertainty, and experiencing credible and caring relationships. Participants also broadened their view of what constitutes loss. One noted, "Writing about loss gives memory to something that happened and can offer a way to reclaim the narrative" while citing the example of addiction as a form of loss.

The participants in this study also made broader connections to the loss in *Drowned City* and loss among students in their classrooms. An overarching theme was the recognition that people lost everything in Hurricane Katrina and that their identities and personal connections were wrapped up in that. In Jennifer's class, this was really unpacked for others by two teachers with personal connections to New Orleans and Katrina. Participants felt that reading a text such as this builds empathy in students and asks them to reflect more critically on their own experiences. They also felt it makes students less desensitized about an event from which they are personally removed. They felt that texts such as this humanize people. One participant noted that here "we view an event through a narrative" and experience it where our previous knowledge was "fed to us" through news outlets. This is important when we consider that over half the participants were in middle school when Katrina occurred and only have peripheral memories of the event. They also commented specifically about the graphic narrative mode of the text noting that it "helps us understand things from a different perspective." The images enhanced their experiences with the narrative.

Writing Loss Narratives

Participants were told that as a follow-up to their discussions of loss prevalent in *Drowned City*, they would be asked to describe a time in which they experienced grief as a result of a loss. They were encouraged to choose a dimension of loss to explore with which they felt comfortable because they would be sharing it within their classroom communities. They were also invited to express the narrative of their loss through a variety of modes (e.g., storytelling, graphic illustrations, poems, songs, art, or even dance). And, as is always the case with our work as instructors, we wrote alongside to experience the assignment and navigate the successes and challenges of this assignment with them.

We also proposed a variety of examples of loss participants might consider ranging from the loss of a pet, to loss of a loved one, to moving, to natural disaster, to pregnancy or to some aspect of their health. We wanted to invite participants to explore what felt safe to them. Finally, they took their narratives through the writing process, including participating in writing workshops with classmates to refine their pieces.

The Student Products

It came as no surprise that the writing of the loss narratives was more difficult for some than others. Several of our participants were experiencing recent losses, with the events current and at the forefront of

Figure 5.1 James' Visual Representation of Loss Following the Death of his Grandfather, IRB Permitted Data

their minds. Their grief was still fresh, and as we wrote together in the face-to-face class, grief was clearly present in the room and on the faces of the participants as they reflected and shared their writing with one another. James (all names are pseudonyms) shared a visual representation of the loss he felt losing his grandfather to a heart attack only weeks before the activity.

Many of the loss narratives were reflective pieces, having the gift of time to offer another perspective. Rose articulated the importance of this time and distance:

> If you would have asked me a year ago to do this, I would not have been able to. I tend to keep my emotions inside, hidden away from others, but this assignment allowed me to step outside of my comfort zone and truly let out some of my deepest thoughts that I have never shared.

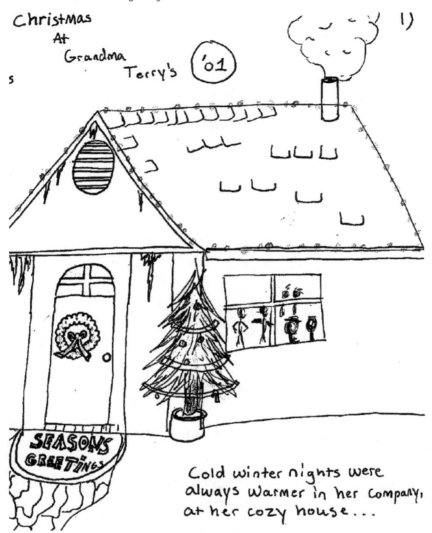

Figure 5.2 Matthew's Sense of Christmas before his Grandmother's Death, IRB Permitted Data

Matthew documented what Christmas was like while his grandmother was alive versus how Christmas was experienced after the loss of the family figurehead. The visual representation of the loss of joy was evident as he described the ways in which branches of families often go their separate ways after losing the head of the family.

And while time often heals the wounds of loss, the distance from the event offers perspective. Luke was and is quite angry as depicted in his editor's

Figure 5.3 Matthew's Sense of Christmas after his Grandmother's Death, IRB Permitted Data

note. As a child of divorce, Luke had grown to understand how the choices his parents had made in their divorce continued to impact him as an adult.

As instructors for the course, we were also drawn to the choices of genres our participants chose to use in their loss narratives. From prose narratives, to digital stories, to songs, we did not have any preconceived notions of what we may receive, and we were pleasantly surprised at the range of genres depicted in our sample. While one may assume emotional writing might evoke more traditionally expressive genres such as

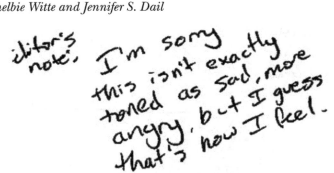

Figure 5.4 Luke's Editor's Note, IRB Permitted Data (Witte, S. (2018). What Have We Lost? Using Young Adult Literature Narratives to Examine Grief Journeys. ED-18-145, Oklahoma State University).

poetry, we were excited to see the range of narratives, including graphic and digital approaches that were used. We believe that allowing genre choice was critical in the opportunity for our students to express their losses and grief in authentic responses.

Transferring the Experience to Teaching

An additional component of this assignment asked students to consider how the writing of loss narratives applied to their teaching through a brief reflective analysis (Appendix A).

Most of our participants expressed a clear understanding of the value of writing loss narratives and reading young adult literature about loss. The activities resonated with Holly, a teacher candidate, who remarked:

> I have students who sit in my classroom each year that have parents, siblings, relatives, and friends who have passed away and other students who have lost pets, homes, and other meaningful items in unimaginable ways. Students, who from the outside look completely fine, but who are battling their own demons on the inside.

While a few preservice teachers expressed concerns about how to approach discussions of grief, death, and hope with students and their parents, more seemed concerned about how to develop a rationale for their administrators. Ultimately, teachers are not licensed therapists; therefore, we also discussed the importance of involving those that can guide us in this work. It can be worthwhile to involve a counseling expert in the classroom work around writing loss narratives.

Conclusion

We often assume that grief looks a certain way—sadness, tears, and depression—but as these narratives reminded us, grief takes many forms, including anger. We also understand that as educators, we have a responsibility to not only allow students the opportunity to examine and express their losses, but also have opportunities to share in empathetic conversations, feeling into the lives of others (Mirra, 2018, p. 4). As Lily explains:

> I never really thought about how to connect the loss and grief experienced in the reading to my students' own lives and personal experiences. I feel like maybe I was afraid for students to open up old wounds or share about experiences that weren't entirely healed. Maybe I was afraid that my superiors would be skeptical of having these kinds of conversations in class. However, after completing this assignment I have learned that writing about loss is a form of healing.

The shared experiences of loss provide an opportunity for all students to realize each has far more in common with their peers than they might recognize. It is the people and things we lose that brings us closer to understanding each other and ourselves. And ultimately, these shared experiences and understandings bring us back to hope. It is hope that propels us forward from our grief and the shared experiences of grief that bring empathy to our interactions with others who are struggling. Through both the self-reflection and self-awareness that result from this work, as well as the allyship that connects all who experience grief, hope floats. And, it is the hope that moves us forward.

References

Brown, D. (2015). *Drowned city: Hurricane Katrina & New Orleans*. Houghton Mifflin Harcourt.

Mirra, N. (2018). *Educating for empathy: Literacy learning and civic engagement*. Teachers College Press.

Nekolaichuk, C. L., Jevne, R. F., & Maguire, T. O. (1999). Structuring the meaning of hope in health and illness. *Social Science & Medicine, 48*(5), 591–605. doi: 10.1016/s0277-9536(98)00348-7.

Appendix A

Loss Narrative Assignment

Project: Loss Narrative
Due: October 22
65 points

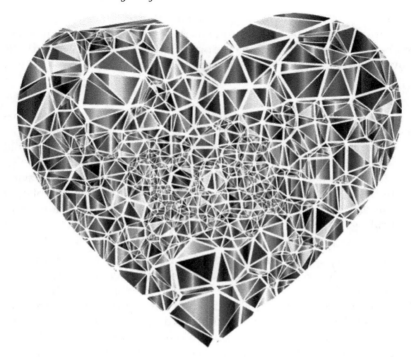

This assignment meets the following course objectives:

1 Develop a principled approach to teaching English language arts that supports the development of adolescents' literacy practices.

Important Dates
October 1 (module 6): Read *Drowned City*
Week of October 2–8 (module 7): Thinking about *Drowned City* (Learning Activity #14)
Week of October 2–8 (module 7): Submit a DRAFT of Loss Narrative
Week of October 9–15 (module 8): Peer Review of Loss Narratives (Learning Activity #18)
Sunday, October 22 (module 9): Submit final version of project

---

Step 1:

What Am I Writing About?

After discussing the multiple dimensions of loss prevalent in *Drowned City: Hurricane Katrina and New Orleans*, we will take an introspective lens to responding to this text. You will be asked to describe a time in which you experienced grief as the result of a loss. There are many levels and dimensions of loss to explore, so choose one that you feel comfortable writing about and sharing with the classroom community. You will have the opportunity to express the narrative of your loss through a variety of modes (e.g., storytelling, graphic illustrations, poems, songs, art, or even dance).

Narratives are stories. They may be written, they may be fictional, but they may also be deeply ingrained stories that tell who we are and how we relate to each other and to place and time. We might think of these as our autobiographical narratives. When we experience loss, our identity is challenged and may even shift, depending upon the nature of that loss. When we experience loss, grief is also the natural emotion accompanying it. Grief theorists believe that the "sharing of autobiographical memory narratives of loss … is a major way to maintain and/or reconfigure a healthy sense of identity after a loss" (Baddeley & Singer, 2009).

I am asking that you consider a time when you experienced grief as a result of loss. The loss can take any form. The following are possible examples of loss; however, you are not limited to these in any way:

- Loss of a pet
- Death of a family member
- Death of a friend
- Moving to a new community
- Loss of a home or personal object to a natural disaster such as fire, hurricane, or tornado
- Loss of a pregnancy
- Loss of some aspect of your health

As you can see, there are many levels and dimensions of loss to explore, so choose one that you feel comfortable writing about and sharing with the classroom community.

Step 2:

How Should My Final Product Look?

You can express the narrative of your loss through a variety of modes. These might include but are not limited to:

- Storytelling (oral or written)
- Graphic illustrations
- Poems
- Songs
- Art
- Dance

Note: if you choose a performative element (oral storytelling, singing a song, performing a dance), you will need to record it on video and share it with the class.

Step 3:

How Does This Apply to My Teaching?

The final component of this assignment is a reflective analysis where you unpack your thinking and make connections to your classroom practice. This is a brief (2–3 pages) paper. Your analysis should be written as a cohesive paper rather than in question/answer format in response to the prompts. In your analysis, you should address the following prompts:

- What were you trying to accomplish in your loss narrative that may not have been clear to the reader?
- What was difficult about writing this type of narrative? Dig deeper than the obvious, "It is hard to write about loss" component here.
- How might you incorporate a similar assignment or allow space for these sorts of discussions around literature and real-world events in your classroom? Why would you want to do that? What rationale you might offer a skeptical administrator or parent.

Evaluation Criteria:

I want you to have space to take some risks here and dig deeply with some authentic writing and to really consider the space you might make for that in your own classrooms. To that end, the evaluation for this project will be different from that of other projects; it will be holistic. You are striving to fulfill the following criteria and leave an overall positive impression on the reader with regards to your work quality and effort.

Your final product should:

- Have an original voice and fully represent you
- Be presented in an appropriate mode for the topic and for what you are trying to accomplish as a writer
- Be authentic by way of offering and inviting some emotion
- Be polished and well edited
- Address all of the prompts in the reflective analysis

Reference

Baddeley, J., & Singer, J. A. (2009). A loss in the family: Silence, memory, and narrative identity after bereavement. *Memory, 18*(2), 198–707. doi: 10.1080/09658210903143858.

6 Opening to the Hauntings of Grief and Mourning

Writing our Way toward Hope

Linda Henderson and Alison L. Black

Journeying toward the Gateway to Hope

We are two women academics and friends. We have encountered the loss of relationships of various kinds. We have experienced the loss of loved ones through death, illness, and separation; disconnection with our bodies and ourselves; the absence of health, home and place. In our work/lives, we have felt the academy's cruelty, the (dis)counting of our time, knowledge and contribution. We have carried stress and mourned the loss of dreams.

But, we are learning "grief is but a gate, and our tears a kind of key opening a place of wonder that's been locked away" (Abram, 2010, p. 309). We are learning the power of friendship through writing, the value of relational and storied processes, of artful and contemplative methodologies.

Through our writing together, we are learning our sorrow songs matter. The sharing of song lines is a "source of contact and rapport with the surrounding terrain" (Abram, 2010, p. 306). Our writing is bringing air and alchemy—allowing hope and healing in—supporting the seeding of new beginnings and possibilities across our work/lives.

We are recognizing the hope we seek is desperately needed not only by us—but by many in our educational, social, and personal communities. We draw on bell hooks (2003), who as a black feminist writer/researcher writes:

> hope stretches the limits of what is possible. It is linked with that basic trust in life without which we could not get from one day to the next...To live by hope is to believe that it is worth taking the next step: that our actions, our families, and cultures and society have meaning, are worth living and dying for. (pp. xiv-xv)

Thinking about our work/lives in the academy, our writing together is opening spaces for critical engagement with what is troubling us, for responding to the care-less structures in the neoliberal university—structures that misguidedly count only certain ways of knowing (Bloom, 1998). As is seen in the pages of this collection, others are troubling alongside us, witnessing and writing through their own hauntings of grief and loss (Anders & Lester, 2019). We are encountering one another, recognizing one another. People grieving. People hoping. People healing.

Collectively, there is a growing recognition that tears must be cried, that tears are a necessary elixir for hope and healing. And so, with this chapter we are choosing to make visible, and public, something of our intimate navigation of personal, environmental and institutional grief. It is our "methodology of the heart" (Pelias, 2010, p. 1), our believing that "grief is but a gate" to (re)storying and restoration (Abram, 2010, p. 309).

Hopeful Methodologies

We know the power of story, of the arts, and how these invoke in us and others personal and social responses—transformation even—bringing "past and the future into the present" and supporting a "pedagogy of hope" (Denzin, 2017, p. 9). Contemplative practices create spaces for thinking deeply about the personal and professional, and give us courage to step into the unfamiliar, to "let go of ourselves" and "relax into something different" (Walsh, 2018, p. 3). We seek, like Allegranti and Wyatt (2014), to "open a space with and for others", to show what can happen "as the pen shifts in our hand, as we dance and move, with and between gestures, with and between each other; as we perform ourselves and our losses into being" (p. 536).

These hopeful pedagogies help us "catch glimpses", "moments" of life beyond our institutional grief—to engage in a kind of "attunement with the world and with other people" (Walsh, 2018, p. 2). Our contemplative storying "speaks to the future" and asserts we *"can* be free from essentializing, naturalizing, constraining, and oppressive identifications" (Bloom, 1998, p. 11).

What follows in our chapter is a palimpsest—a scattering of storylines, poetry, imagery, art-making; fragments and traces of sorrow songs and hopeful glimpses. Rather than contextualizing these pieces and explaining the fullness of what they represent, we ask readers to allow these artful fragments to settle into whatever form feels meaningful and resonant. We invite reader participation in this scholarship of connection and vulnerability, in these "layers and cycles of witnessing" (Allegranti & Wyatt, 2014, p. 536), and these sites of feeling, possibility and healing (See also Black, 2018a, 2018b; Henderson & Black, 2018). Attune, and move with and between the fragments of our lines and lives, our gestures, hauntings, hopes and dreams (Denzin, 2017; Walsh 2018).

Sorrow Songs and Song Lines

...The verdict is guilty... ...sex crimes... ...my father... ... prison...

...and there it is, your final breath mum... ...I spiral into despair...

...the house we left still hasn't sold... ...six years of limbo...

...Your dad has passed away overseas...
...the will is being contested... ...no inheritance for you...

...disillusionment with the academy... ...probation again...
...career slippage... ...overwork, never-ending demands...

...I had a brother, but he died from AIDs...
...I hold the scarf he once wore... ...my parents didn't accept him...

...I drove her to the airport... ...a momentary flash... ...she is gone... ...I dreamt she came home...

...blood tests haven't improved... ...blood pressure way up...

Falling into grief
Tripping, stumbling
Against the pain, the sharpness of grief's edges
Rubbing and scratching against the heart, the soul
Tearing and ripping open that which used to appear
Intact
Whole
Falling
Breaking
Into a thousand pieces
A million tiny shards
Wrenching loss
Eyes swollen
A river of tears falling upon the earth

***

The swirling darkness of grief. Trauma. Black shadows of death, despair and dis-ease. Loss upon loss upon loss upon loss...

Is there something more? More than this darkness? More than the loss you/I feel within your/my body, within your/my family, within your/my life, within your/my academic work, within the natural world around us all?

How do we move beyond the heartache?

Somehow, we step into the circle. Two academics, women, friends.

Figure 6.1 Holding Hands and Hearts

Holding each other in folds of friendship. Ripples of tentative sharing, a revealing of lives. Becoming visible. Vulnerable.

Holding space. Holding suffering. Holding hands. Holding hearts.

***

Be yourself. Love yourself. Leave yourself. Risk the risk. Follow it. The terror of it. Face it head-on, heart on. Lose it. Let go. Lose everything. Loose everything. Everything loose. Losing self. Self-losing. Lose. Lies. Real eyes. Realize. Relies. What lies ahead? Allies. Eyes. I's. Let go. Let go. Let go.

Writhing. Writing. Righting.

Writhing with ideas, emotions, fears. Daring to dare.

Writing yourself/myself on the page.

Righting yourself/myself and finding balance. Your/My right to be free. Whole. More yourself/myself.

Let go. Let go. Let go. Take off the armour.

Unwrap the layers of self-protection. The fear. The pain.

Let the layers fall away.

Lean into this grief. Right in. Write in.

Let loose. Loosen it. Lose it.

Writhe. Write. Right. Just as you are.

You are allowed to be you. I am allowed to be me.

Nothing is lost. You are not lost. I am not lost.

We are here, together.

Risking the risk. Loosening.

Allowing grief to break [us?] open

***

There is a tenderness in y/our company. Somehow, together it is easier to touch the wounds and the scars. To imagine healing. To let go. To exhale. To inhale. To breathe deeply. To lean towards the sun. To feel its warmth.

What is now becoming through our songs of tears and tears?

Our sorrow songs and song lines call across the water, across the land, across time. An ancient alchemy.

Song lines of love and loss beckon healing and renewal. Transformation. Like wildflowers breaking through the ground, birdsong warbling in our ears. Our hearts are softening, attuning to intimacy and relationship.

Here is such a song that has emerged for us. Listen closely to its rhythm, inhale its fragrance:

> *Stand tall and proud*
>
> *You are strong*
>
> *Brave*
>
> *Warrior*
>
> *Woman*
>
> *Claim your space*

Refuse to be small

Or Invisible

You are worthy

Worthier than you know

Bring forth your light

Heart, speak your wisdom

Sing your ancient knowledge

Your ancient longings

Bring forth that which can only be touched

In silence and stillness

Breathing in,

Breathing out.

***

We are two academics, women, friends.

Holding each other in folds of friendship.

Slowly, compassionately, care-fully.

Connecting our heartlines and song lines.
Writing our bodies, our hearts, ourselves, our sorrow songs.
Writing our spirits and dreams.
Coming alive again through our meaning-making.
Seeing hope in the face of the other.

Companioned on the Journey: The Gifts of "Being With", of "Wit(h)nessing"

Grief has opened the pathways for our coming together, for our becoming friends and co-creators. We live in different states of Australia. We have met in person only twice. Yet, we have become sisters—sisters who know what it is to be estranged and violated, sisters who hold space for the other to be as they are.

We seem to take turn-about in leading the other gently toward the ways and forms grief has manifested/manifests in our work/lives.

Her gentle sweet embrace,

Caressing the air between us.

That which remains between two

Unspoken. A whisper or murmur—invoking,

Language, subjectivity, words,

Bodily figurations of breath.

In our writing together, we have risked the intimate unveiling of dark stories and hauntings. We have put our stories on the page, in emails, messages and shared folders. We have disclosed secrets and scandal. We have sent each other honest ramblings, heartfelt offerings, stories of the lives we have lived and are living, of our walks on the earth and by the sea. We've shared photos, videos, artwork, poetry, snippets of songs and singing, memories and moments. A collection of connections.

The universe really is doing something; talking to us as we read-write-share-despair-sigh-cry-laugh together. In these cycles of writing and sharing, we have come to realize we are no longer frightened of grief (Abram, 2010). In "dropping deep into the sorrow", we are "find[ing] therein a necessary elixir to the numbness" (Abram, 2010, p. 309). We have "encountered one another" and "allowed our tears to fall easily to the ground" (Abram, 2010, p. 309).

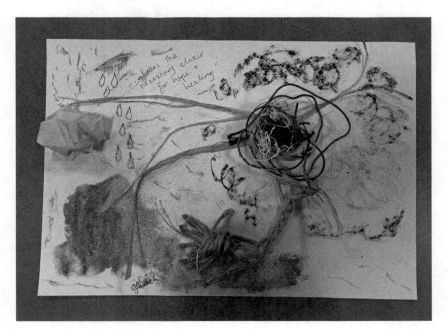

Figure 6.2 No Longer Frightened of Grief

Source: Collage, Linda Henderson, "Tears, the necessary elixir"

Neimeyer (1999) suggests that "meaning reconstruction" in response to loss is the central process in grieving (p. 67). Reconstruction has been our organic process. Our relational meaning-making has been central to our connection, facilitating our shared and individual "grief work" (Neimeyer, 1999). Our writing together maps our climb down into the depths of experience and our journey toward self-respect, self-care, and friendship. It maps the journeys we take and re-take as we grapple with setbacks and the daily matter of living a life.

We have, through our vulnerable shedding of skins and protective facades, come to understand sorrow is an entrance to healing. We liken this to Estes's (1995) call for woman to "do the work of turning toward home" (p. 288). Like some ancient ritual, we write to feel the pulse of new beginnings as we turn toward home and sing out loud

Figure 6.3 Mapping Journeys and Ancestors

Source: Painting, Ali Black, "They walk beside me"

our sorrow songs. We have, through our writing/art-making, actively connected with the voices of generations and ancestors. Exploring spiritual/ontological/philosophical and embodied ways of knowing has supported our listening to the stories of our hearts. It has supported more spacious ways of being, sensing, thinking and responding (Walsh, 2018).

Through the singing of our sorrow songs, we are teaching our heads and necks and hearts to engage in a looking inward, outward and upward. And in this looking, we are moving toward dignity and hope, our worth and the sun.

Together we are writing with, and through, the darkness, the haunting, the turmoil and the loss—the loss we feel within our bodies, our academic work, within society and the more-than-human world, the loss of loved ones and the loss of hope (Walsh, 2018).

Of course, our writing of loss is not easy. The act of it can aggravate the wounding, sometimes opening afresh life's scar tissue, dropping us again into our almost unbearable sorrows (Henderson & Black, 2018). But, we are no longer alone. We are moving deeply into relationship. With our pedagogies of hope and our methodologies of the heart, our contemplative writing activates connection, compassion, care—a witness/with-ness consciousness (Walsh & Bai, 2014). We are "wit(h) nessing" across time and space, connecting to each other and to our stories by "fully being with and beside the other in remembrance and experience" (Snowber & Bickel, 2014, p. 76). We are holding space, holding our stories, holding our meaning-making, holding each other in friendship.

> We are found in each other's stories, and our stories utter one another—my story utters your story, your story utters my story. Art gives us the ability to go into the threshold of our own sorrow; it is the entrance point to our sorrow, and the entrance point to our own joy. (Snowber & Bickel, 2014, p. 76)

Being "with"—with each other, our art-making and our storied fragments—brings us and has brought us to entrance points, to gateways: to sorrow, hope and joy. Before, alone, we saw only sorrow and despair. Now, with our shared songs and song lines we are opening toward other experiences, other possibilities. There is a growing sense of space. Space to breathe. Space to see. Space to listen. Space to be present.

Our narratives and storied artefacts move us tenderly and alchemically toward a deeper intimacy with ourselves, each other and the earth. Writing and representing our tears, we remember, receive and feel our way toward healing. Our alchemic writing and representations offer ways of moving through our grieving, ways of (re)constructing, (re) imagining and sustaining hope even in the face of the losses we have known and will continue to know (Bloom, 1998). It offers pathways and maps for seeing the journeys we have made, how we have responded and grown. It makes real our lives, our histories (Bloom, 1998). We can see who we are:

Strong

Brave

Warrior

Women

Grounding our writing in our experiences of sorrow, stories we have privately given to each other "under a promise" to protect (Denzin, 2017, p. 15), we commit to sharing more widely our relationship with sorrow, and our relationship of being-with. We share our meaning-making in order to "speak to the human dignity, the suffering, the hopes, the dreams, the lives gained, and the lives lost" (Denzin, 2017, p. 15). We share to give testimony to the human ability "to endure, to prevail, and to triumph over the structural forces that threaten at any moment to annihilate all of us" (Denzin, 2017, p. 15). Each person's sorrow story can offer hope as we move toward deeper, creative and vulnerable collaborations, and find ways to speak ourselves into existence, "resist[ing] stereotypes...objectification," and validating y/our experiences as "rich sources of feminist insight" and knowledge (Bloom, 1998, p. 147). These ways of writing, making, knowing and being have power to break open and name spaces of oppression and patriarchy in the academy. And, the beauty is—it occurs under the sign of hope (Bloom, 1998).

We know our writing together, our renewed awareness, our sharing more widely, is troubling how we view our academic work—work that is "often draped in loss" (Anders & Lester, 2019, p. 926). It is troubling what it is we think/know we have to do—now and in the future. Our desire to "open up to the other side" (Henderson & Black, 2018, p. 4), to locate and reveal ourselves and our losses and commitments has had unanticipated effects. It is connecting us to something larger, to something else—to defiance, community, the relational, advocacy, resistance and "calls for what could be otherwise" (Anders & Lester, 2019, p. 930). Our writing has become a resource for reimagining—and not just ourselves, but the academy too. And so, we conclude where we began:

> Grief is but a gate, and our tears a kind of key opening a place of wonder that's been locked away. Suddenly we notice the sustaining resonance between the drumming heart within our chest and the pulse rising from under the ground. (Abram, 2010, p. 309)

References

Abram, D. (2010). *Becoming animal: An earthly cosmology.* Vintage Books.

Allegranti, B., & Wyatt, J. (2014). Witnessing loss: A feminist material-discursive account. *Qualitative Inquiry, 20*(4), 533–543.

Anders, A., & Lester, J. (2019). Examining loss: Postcritical ethnography and the pursuit of what could be otherwise. *Qualitative Inquiry, 25*(9–10), 925–935. https://doi.org/10.1177/1077800418784327

Black, A. L. (2018a). Digesting a life: Embodying transformation through creative writing. *New Writing: The International Journal for the Practice and Theory of Creative Writing, 16*(1), 50–58.

Black, A. L. (2018b). Time to remember: A portrait of my mother, *TEXT Journal*, Special Issue No 50, October.

Bloom, L. R. (1998). *Under the sign of hope: Feminist methodology and narrative interpretation.* State University of New York Press.

Denzin, N. (2017). Critical qualitative inquiry. *Qualitative Inquiry, 23*(1), 8–16.

Estes, C. P. (1995). *Woman who run with the wolves: Myths and stories of the wild woman archetype.* Ballantine Books.

Henderson, L., & Black, A. (2018). Splitting the world open: Writing stories of mourning and loss. *Qualitative Inquiry, 24*(4), 260–269.

hooks, b. (2003). *Teaching community: A pedagogy of hope.* Routledge.

Neimeyer, R. A. (1999). Narrative strategies in grief therapy. *Journal of Constructivist Psychology, 12*(1), 65–85.

Pelias, R. (2010). *Methodology of the heart: Evoking academic and daily life.* Alta Mira Press.

Snowber, C., & Bickel, B. (2014). Companions with mystery: Arts, spirit, and the ecstatic. In C. Leggo, S. Walsh, & B. Bickel (Eds.), *Arts-based and contemplative practices in research and teaching: Honoring presence* (pp. 67–87). Routledge.

Walsh, S. (2018). *Contemplative and artful openings: Researching women and teaching.* Routledge.

Walsh, S., & Bai, H. (2014). Writing witness consciousness. In C. Leggo, S. Walsh, & B. Bickel (Eds.), *Arts-based and contemplative practices in research and teaching: Honoring presence* (pp. 24–44). Routledge.

Part II
Communities of Hope and Healing

7 Opportunities Lost and Found

A Gay Educator's Grief and Process of Hope

S. Adam Crawley

Before entering academia, I taught 12 years in elementary public schools. During those years, I remained closeted as a gay man who refrained from using LGBTQ+-inclusive teaching practices, lied when students inquired about my personal relationships and sexual orientation, and—beyond writing discipline referrals or mildly redirecting—failed to respond to bullying about students' gender performances or perceived sexual orientations. My (in)actions stemmed from fear due to actual and perceived vulnerabilities. Therefore, I did not use, and thus lost, opportunities to provide windows and mirrors (Bishop, 1990) via personal example or texts, facilitate critical conversations, and counteract injustice.

In my classrooms, I taught youth diverse in race, ethnicity, social class, dis/ability, and religion among other ways of being. My students also lived in homes with diverse family structures. Though many lived with a mother and father, others resided with a single parent or grandparent(s), and some had same-sex parents. Further, though I was unaware of my students' own non-heterosexual orientations or non-cisgender identities when teaching them, I had students who non-normatively performed gender. I have since learned some of my past students—now young adults—identify as gay, lesbian, bisexual, transgender, and/or queer. Research indicates I undoubtedly taught other youth who identified then or later as LGBTQ+, question(ed) their identities, and/or had LGBTQ+ family members (GLSEN & Harris Interactive, 2012; Lopez, 2013; The Williams Institute, 2016).

Now, I reflect on my past students, how I served them, and how I might have served them better. With my passion for inclusive teaching, especially related to sexuality and gender, I grieve so many lost opportunities. For my past students, I consider how peers during my youth verbally and physically harassed me and realize many contemporary youth unfortunately share similar experiences (Kosciw, Greytak, Zongrone, Clark, & Truong, 2018). I also grieve not being my authentic self with colleagues and students, thus depriving myself personally along with depriving my students of teaching practices that affirm people who are gender and/or sexually diverse. My grief catalyzes and propels my scholarship about LGBTQ+-inclusive teaching.

Theoretical Framework

Queer theory and hope theory—complementing frameworks—inform my experiences and this narrative. Within queer theory, I find Muñoz's (2009) concept of queer utopia particularly salient to this reflection. Queer utopia looks to the future and how it might, or can, be different from the present. Muñoz described queer utopia as a time of collective belonging, a time without nervousness and fear, a time of *hope* in which queer individuals can live openly without succumbing to normalcy: "Utopia lets us imagine a space outside of heteronormativity...and offers a critique of the present, of what is, by casting a picture of what *can and perhaps will be*" (p. 35, emphasis in original). When describing utopia, Muñoz distinguished between possibility and potentiality: possibilities might happen, whereas potentialities are eminent, present but not yet fully realized, and thus on the horizon. Further, Muñoz asserted that people—and specifically queer people—"must insist on a queer futurity because the present is so poisonous and insolvent" (p. 30). The recognition of the present as a site of grief and thus a desire for a different, better future connects to hope theory's future-casting focus (Snyder, 2002).

Although people may not overcome grief, they might work through or ease it via hope: "[Hope] can help our students [and ourselves] to imagine scenarios in which they could feel happy or fulfilled, when perhaps they are not" (Sieben, 2018, p. 21). In other words, much like Muñoz's (2009) queer utopia, hope theory entails envisioning more positive and promising futures. However, hope theory adds to the concept of queer utopia by suggesting specific steps to address grief and move through or forward.

I understand the steps for working through grief—and even toward a queer utopia—as directly related to Snyder's (2002) three-part hope framework: goals, pathways, and agency. In short, goals are the visions of what to attain; pathways are the strategies to undertake toward the goal, and agency entails the motivation and ability to use the pathways to achieve the goal (Snyder, 2000). Further, Snyder (2002) conceptualized high-hope and low-hope, with high-hope involving obtainable goals achievable with known, specific pathways. In some instances, high-hope people may even adapt their goals and strategies to make "the seemingly unreachable...become reachable" (Snyder, 2002, p. 251). In this way, high-hope parallels potentiality as described by Muñoz (2009) as more definite and tangible than a possibility which may be associated with low-hope. This is not to say, however, that people with low-hope cannot develop high-hope. Low-hope individuals may still be so immersed in grief or their current situation that they have not yet determined—or are not yet ready to pursue—pathways for moving through and forward despite knowing their goal. Over time, these individuals may conceptualize increasingly concrete pathways and enact agency toward the goal, thus developing high-hope (Kibby, 2015; McDermott & Snyder, 1999).

I was a person with low-hope during much of my elementary classroom career. I felt alone and that I had to hide central components of my identity from colleagues and students, thus failing to serve students needing windows and mirrors of non-heterosexual orientations. I was uncertain my goal of becoming my more authentic self in the classroom was even a possibility. However, as I began graduate school, my hope increased. In the following sections, I share how goals, pathways, and agency help me move through and forward though continuing to remember and grieve my past.

Goals: Considering Who I Wanted to Be(come)

As described above with queer utopia, one way to navigate grief is to envision a more bearable or fulfilling future. In other words, to imagine what a life beyond the present grief might look like. Such a projection is similar to a goal. Sieben (2018) asked, "In times when you may find yourself in grief, what goals will you set for yourself? How will you work towards achieving these goals" (p. 24)? These are important questions, and the first question takes strong consideration before the reflective and difficult work needed to address the second.

In the elementary classroom, my goal was to become my more authentic self, a man open with his students and colleagues about being gay. Little did I realize at the time that this goal would later lead to other goals I would set for myself, such as how to teach for equity, be increasingly inclusive, and engage others in such work. At the time, I was simply hopeful for my own queer utopia within the microcosm of my classroom and school. However, while I regretted my closeted situation, I hadn't yet begun to grieve—both for myself and for my students—because I didn't realize another existence was possible or understand fully the damage I was causing. My grief began to surface as I entered graduate school. Through various experiences, I reflected on how my professional and personal experiences inform(ed) one another. I also learned pathways I wish I had known throughout my childhood, adolescence, and current adulthood. I began to realize and grieve the many lost opportunities in my elementary classroom. However, several pathways helped me move through and forward while continuing to reflect on and be catalyzed by my past.

Pathways: Learning from Complementary Strategies

Returning to Sieben's (2018) questions—"what goals will you set for yourself? How will you work towards achieving these goals?" (p. 24), the second question suggests the next step following goal creation. It's necessary to consider how to achieve those goals. Hope scholars use the term pathways for the strategies and steps developed for reaching goals. Snyder (2002) wrote, "Hope is defined as the perceived capability to derive pathways to desired goals" (p. 249). In other words, hope involves not only articulating a goal but also determining strategies for working toward it. Knowing specific strategies helps the goal become more tangible and thus increases hope.

During graduate school, my grief about lost opportunities heightened concurrently with learning pathways for a different futurity. In particular, two pathways—reading widely and developing networks—helped me to realize I was not alone in being a non-heterosexual educator with vulnerabilities. The pathways also showed the possibility of being a more authentic self and teaching inclusively. These pathways were by no means linear but rather recursive, and they are on-going for me.

Reading Widely

As a literacy educator, I value texts. Reading a variety of texts, often repeatedly and across time, has been an integral pathway toward my goal. I find three types of texts particularly informative: children's and young adult (YA) literature, empirical research, and policies and legislation.

Children's and YA Literature. Nearly a decade into my elementary teaching career, I first saw books that were mirrors (Bishop, 1990) for me. In the first semester of my master's program, I took a culturally diverse children's literature course during which we read *And Tango Makes Three* (Richardson & Parnell, 2005) and *The Misfits* (Howe, 2001). Each book depicts same-sex relationships and/or attractions. Reading these books and discussing them in the graduate course was a pivotal moment for me, in that I not only saw representations of others like me but I also saw resources positioned for use with youth and conversed with colleagues about teaching practices and my own gay identity. These experiences—the books and conversations—provided me hope. The books and conversations catalyzed my interest to learn what other LGBTQ+-inclusive children's literature existed. Since that course, I read widely children's and YA literature to discover more texts I could share with students as well as diversify my own understandings of LGBTQ+ people's experiences and the representations currently (un)available via texts.

Empirical Research. While reading LGBTQ+-inclusive children's and YA literature provided mirrors and windows for me and served as one pathway, that alone was not enough. I still grieved not knowing if or how to include such texts in my own classroom. Fortunately, I began reading—first through graduate coursework and then independently—studies conducted by and with educators in elementary classrooms. From Schall and Kauffmann's (2003) one day in a fourth/fifth grade multiage class, to Ryan and Hermann-Wilmarth's (2018) on-going work with teachers across various schools and grades, I have seen how non-heterosexual educators can exist and thrive, as well as how educators—regardless of sexual orientation—can inclusively teach. Such educators and their work have become models and mentors for me through their writing.

Policies and Legislation. Relative to if and how non-heterosexual educators can openly exist and how inclusive teaching can occur, my hope has further developed through learning policies and legislation. While policies and legislation exist that explicitly or implicitly prohibit being out or teaching inclusively, I am bolstered by contrary local and national statements. For example, school districts increasingly list sexual orientation, gender identity, and gender expression in their non-discrimination statements for youth, families, and employees. Related, GLSEN (the Gay, Lesbian, and Straight Education Network) (n.d.) provides online information about state-level policies and legislation (https://www.glsen.org/article/state-maps). Even in local contexts where policies or legislation may thwart inclusive teaching, documents such as the National Council of Teachers of English's Position Statements on the Right to Read (2018b) (http://www2.ncte.org/statement/righttoreadguideline) and Gender and Language (2018a) (https://ncte.org/statement/genderfairuseoflang) are incredibly useful, supportive of my efforts, and instill hope in me for my own place and possibilities within the field of education.

Developing Networks

During the past few years, I have not only continued to read widely but also met educators (K-12 and higher education) and others (e.g., children's and YA authors) who identify as LGBTQ+ and/or are committed to inclusive work. Thus, I have developed a network of others, an essential pathway for my hope that helps me think toward the future while remaining reflective about my lost opportunities. Such a network has been an incredible support to me, and support from others can be a critical component of hope (Sieben, 2018; Sieben & Hultberg, 2015). Like reading various texts, developing a network reminds me I am not alone in my identity or efforts. Developing a network, along with the pathway of reading widely, has helped me move toward the third element of hope: agency.

Agency: Being Motivated and Able

Having a goal and developing pathways are important steps in working through or overcoming grief, but hope also involves agency. Agency entails the motivation and ability to use pathways to achieve the goal (Snyder, 2000), and both components are integral.

Relative to motivation, Snyder (2002) stated high-hope individuals "embrace such self-talk agency phrases as, 'I can do this,' and 'I am not going to be stopped'" (p. 251). Mantras like these echo in my mind, and the motivation is propelled by multiple factors: attending to my grief about lost opportunities for myself and the students I served, knowing the continued injustices in schools and society writ large, and learning of other educators' work toward inclusive and increasingly queer learning spaces (e.g., Ryan & Hermann-Wilmarth, 2018; Schall & Kauffmann, 2003). These micro and macro aspects, some negative and some positive—coupled with remembering my primary goal of being my authentic self and teaching inclusively—provide me motivation that contributes to agency.

Not only am I motivated; I also now have greater ability than I once did or felt possible. Because of the pathways—reading widely and developing networks—I have a fuller understanding that I can be out professionally and how to more inclusively work. I am also acutely aware and attentive to how my current position in academia affords me abilities to be agentive in ways I didn't feel possible when in the elementary classroom. Further, my being privilege adjacent (Jiménez, 2019)—benefitting from being white, cisgender, and a man—makes my ability to be out and teach inclusively more possible than it may be for others. I recognize that for many educators, especially at the elementary level, such ability—despite their motivation—might be or seem less available. Autonomy, directly related to agency, is crucial to consider. Others' actual or perceived lack of autonomy is an aspect I now grieve and thus propels my creation of new goals to work toward via my current and developing pathways.

Conclusion

Despite my goals, pathways, and agency, I still grieve my twelve years of being closeted in the elementary classroom and how I could have better served students. I cannot change my past, but I can change the present and future for myself and hopefully others. I also would be remiss to not share that I still sometimes find myself in instances where I revert to my past (in)actions. For example, when I enter an elementary school or other context in which I'm not familiar, I sometimes refrain from sharing about myself if I'm uncertain about how others might respond or how I might be vulnerable. I'm not proud of this. My past experiences, fears, and vulnerabilities remain deeply ingrained in me, and so I continue to work toward my goals.

As a teacher-educator and researcher inquiring into, advocating for, and implementing LGBTQ+-inclusive practices at the elementary level, I believe transparency about my past experiences and practices is important. Research about LGBTQ+-inclusive teaching at the elementary level continues to grow. In some scholarship, the researchers share how their LGBTQ+ identities influence their work and/or name their former roles as elementary educators. Such disclosure perhaps lends credibility to the researchers' assertions and suggestions. However, scholars rarely— if ever—address their own past experiences. For example: Were they out as a teacher? Did they use inclusive practices in their classrooms? If so, how? If not, why? How did those (lost) opportunities lead to the researcher's current interests and practices, and how do they reconcile their past and present? The lack of such sharing and reflection is not limited to LGBTQ+ related research. Scholars often profess how teaching practices might increasingly attend to particular areas or identities (e.g., technology, race, religion, dis/ability, gender) while lacking transparency about their own past practices, including missteps or (in)action. The narrative I share in this chapter, alongside the contributions of others describing their grief and hope in this book, adds to extant scholarship highlighting how past experiences inform moving through and forward to the future.

References

Bishop, R. S. (1990). Mirrors, windows, and sliding glass doors. *Perspectives, 6*(3), ix–xi. https://scenicregional.org/wp-content/uploads/2017/08/Mirrors-Windows-and-Sliding-Glass-Doors.pdf

GLSEN. (n.d.). *Policy maps.* https://www.glsen.org/article/state-maps

GLSEN and Harris Interactive. (2012). *Playgrounds and prejudice: Elementary school climate in the United States, A survey of teachers and students.* GLSEN. https://www.glsen.org/sites/default/files/2020-04/Playgrounds_Prejudice.pdf

Howe, J. (2001). *The misfits.* Aladdin.

Jiménez, L. (2019, July 2). Bi any other name... *Book toss.* https://booktoss.blog/2019/07/03/bi-any-other-name/

Kibby, M. (2015). Applying 'hope theory' to first year learning: A practice report. *The International Journal of the First Year in Higher Education, 6*(1), 147–153. doi: https://doi.org/10.5204/intjfyhe.v6i1.248.

Kosciw, J. G., Greytak, E. A., Zongrone, A. D., Clark, C. M., & Truong, N. L. (2018). *The 2017 national school climate survey: The experiences of lesbian, gay, bisexual, transgender, and queer youth in our nation's schools.* GLSEN. https://www.glsen.org/sites/default/files/2019-10/GLSEN-2017-National-School-Climate-Survey-NSCS-Full-Report.pdf

Lopez, M. H. (2013, June 13). *Personal milestones in the coming out experience.* Pew Research Center. http://www.pewsocialtrends.org/2013/06/13/the-coming-out-experience-age-when-you-first-thought-knew-told/

McDermott, D., & Snyder, C. R. (1999). *Making hope happen.* New Harbinger Publications.

Muñoz, J. E. (2009). *Cruising utopia: The then and there of queer futurity.* New York University Press.

NCTE. (2018a, October 25). *Statement on gender and language.* https://ncte.org/statement/genderfairuseoflang/

NCTE. (2018b, October 25). *The student's right to read.* https://ncte.org/statement/righttoreadguideline/

Richardson, J., & Parnell, P. (2005). *And Tango makes three.* (H. Cole, Illus.). Simon & Schuster.

Ryan, C. L., & Hermann-Wilmarth, J. M. (2018). *Reading the rainbow: LGBTQ-inclusive literacy instruction in the elementary classroom.* Teachers College Press.

Schall, J., & Kauffmann, G. (2003). Exploring literature with gay and lesbian characters in the elementary school. *Journal of Children's Literature, 29*(1), 36–45.

Sieben, N. (2018). Advocating for the affective: Writing hope into school spaces. *Language Arts Journal of Michigan, 33*(2), 20–27. doi: https://doi.org/10.9707/2168-149X.2177.

Sieben, N., & Hultberg, G. (2015). Collaboration fosters hope. *English Leadership Quarterly,* 37(4), 7–11. https://secure.ncte.org/library/NCTEFiles/Resources/Journals/ELQ/ELQ0374apr2015.pdf

Snyder, C. R. (Ed.) (2000). *Handbook of hope: Theory, measures, and applications.* Academic Press.

Snyder, C. R. (2002). Hope theory: Rainbows in the mind. *Psychological Inquiry,* 13(4), 249–275. http://doi.org/10.1207/S15327965PLI1304_01

The Williams Institute. (2016, March). *LGBT people in Georgia.* https://williams institute.law.ucla.edu/wp-content/uploads/Georgia-fact-sheet.pdf

8   Finding Hope through Hope Agents and Narratives in Times of Mourning

Elsie Lindy Olan and Donita Grissom

Hope is a construct that involves thinking about goals, how to achieve goals, and staying motivated during a goal attainment process (Snyder et al., 1991). In this chapter, we teacher educator researchers share our narratives of mourning the death of loved ones. By utilizing Snyder's hope theory (Snyder et al., 1991), we analyze our narratives of grief through three components of hope: goals, pathway thinking, and agency thinking. It is in this exploration, through dialogic interactions and constructivist approaches that we explain narratives of grief such as the loss of spouse and parent and how these transformed to narratives of hope. The use of "descriptive narratives of school experiences can initiate the kinds of conversations and research that is imperative for teacher development and implicit in the everyday trials and tribulations present in educational institutions" (Olan, 2015, p. 1957). Also, we describe how we dealt with loss, pain, choice, and growth while spreading hope through the act of teaching and working at our educational institutions.

We use Paulo Freire's (1997/2005) notion of armed love and "actionable hope" to foreground our work as we interact and work with teacher candidates, teachers, and teacher advocates. In this interaction and dialogue, we recount how we borrowed the hope of others who became our "hope agents" (Lopez, 2013). Through multiple insights, encouragements, written reflections and reflexive dialogues, attainable goals and actions (hope strategies), we guide and facilitate discussions where teachers move towards self-realization, sustainable hope, and personal growth while thinking about critical ways to approach grief in their lives, classrooms, and communities.

Hope in Action

When hope is in action, people set more goals, both realistic and specific (Snyder, Lehman, Kluck, & Monsson, 2006). Hopeful people perceive they have the ability to develop multiple strategies/pathways to meet their goals or solve their problems (Snyder et al., 1991). Finally, the hopeful person utilizes motivational/agency thinking by perceiving that they can and they will achieve their goals or solve their problems (Snyder et al., 1991). They have an "I will" message motivating them, which helps them navigate through their goals and problems (Snyder et al., 1991). Incredibly, hope can be taught, learned, borrowed, loaned, increased, and is not dependent on income, education, age, gender, race, or childhood background. In fact, it is not even dependent on situational disappointments and traumas (Snyder et al., 1991). Hopeful people have a stronger ability to re-goal, to find alternate pathways to meet goals and solve problems, to garner support, experience less anxiety and distress, and focus on success (Lopez, 2013). Further, they view obstacles as challenges to overcome, experience increased resiliency, and are more energetic and full of life (Snyder et al., 2006). A person who utilizes the three-pronged power of hope can overcome the effects of illness, trauma, and grief and loss of a loved one (Snyder, 2000). People who perceive life with higher hope are armed with a protective factor against depression and anxiety (Kwon, 2000). They possess greater life satisfaction, and higher problem-solving and adaptive skills, and a psychological buffer for challenging situations. High hope can mitigate the effects of acute negative life events (Valle, Huebner, & Suldo, 2006). In contrast, people with lower hope get stuck and are discouraged. Most importantly, they tend to not ask for support and do not acknowledge hope could be one of the most powerful tools for creating the change they desire (Snyder et al., 1991) (For further explanation of high-hope and low-hope characteristics, see Chapter 7, Crawley).

The following narratives will describe how hope empowered two teacher educator researchers in one of the most hopeless moments of their lives.

Narratives

Donita's Encounter with Hope

What a difference a handshake makes! I completed a four-year doctoral graduate degree journey because my late husband persuaded me to promise with a handshake that I would if I received a scholarship.

A dear colleague and friend invited me to apply to a Ph.D. TESOL track program she developed at her university, which included a scholarship. "Seriously, God! Seriously, honey!" Yet, I felt the hand of destiny navigating my life and purpose; however, I just didn't know the specific goal.

Sitting in my office counting the costs of committing to the grueling process of a Ph.D. program, I questioned if this was the direction my life should take. At that very moment, a jet flew over my house. I remembered that jets transporting Haitian survivors—of an earthquake that had left too many dead and injured—were landing in the airport near my home. I was struck by the deepest sorrow and sobbed with heartache.

I cried out to God, "Please help these people who are shattered; please don't let this trauma destroy their emotional development and self-esteem." The specific goal was still unclear, but the urgency to move forward was evident.

After starting my Ph.D. program, I had an online course and therefore did not personally meet my professor. While on campus in the Education Complex, I noticed my current professor's nameplate on her office door. I scheduled a meeting, and when we met, she began our discussion with, "So why are you getting your Ph.D. and what are your research interests?" I looked deep in her eyes and honestly answered, "I don't know!" I felt compelled to tell her my story about the plane of Haitian people. She began to cry and explained, "I am from Haiti. An hour ago I received a grant for computers for Haiti to start an English Language Program. I would love for you to be the Curriculum Developer." I felt destiny lining up!

I worked on several educational projects for Haitians. In fact, I went to Haiti with my professor to assess the continuing educational needs to help Haitians rebuild their lives and rebound from their tragedy. My second trip to Haiti was with my husband, a contractor. One Sunday when we were scheduled to go back to the United States, he decided to stay to continue rebuilding an area in the mountains of Haiti. Sadly, I left my husband standing at the airport. On Thursday, the exact anniversary of the earthquake in Haiti, while conducting and teaching men how to do a planned demolition of one of the buildings they were going to rebuild, bricks fell on his head. They managed to get him back to his lodging. That night he called me around 8:30 and spoke with our grandbaby; however, he didn't tell me about the accident. He said we would talk tomorrow. Tomorrow never came. I got the terrifying phone call no one ever wants to get. They told me my husband was gone. I said, "Gone where?" The bottom line was he did not wake up that morning. He had died in his sleep, apparently from the blow to his head the previous day.

"What! How can this be! My husband and I had a handshake! What am I supposed to do now?" The next month was a blur and I had to take time off from my graduate studies. I seriously only remember bits and pieces, until one day I realized it was time to go back to school. I needed to finish because I still had a goal, although the path felt so uncertain. I called my professor/friend and said, "I am ready to come back. Please help me get through this the best I can." This conversation became the first of many where my professor/friend became my hope agent (Lopez, 2013) in my most critical time of need. In fact, when encountered with any negative life experience, if a person chooses to allow a hope agent in their personal space, their brains are primed to follow them (Lopez, 2013). Hence, I followed my professor/hope agent.

Our conversations back and forth helped me navigate through this most distressing time in my life and kept me on track to earn my Ph.D.

She helped me adjust my goals for graduating, even if it meant me giving up a perfectionist mentality. All in all, turning to her as my hope agent helped me maneuver through this tragedy through the remainder of the Ph.D. program, and helped me with my agency in completing the program.

One day, the professor asked me to meet her for coffee. She asked what I was considering for my dissertation. Oh, that dreaded question. So, I began to explain to her the whole story about Haiti. I really didn't know what to do. However, I told her that I couldn't give up the Haitian population. I told her that I had always been passionate about my English language students who came to our schools with trauma. I always thought there was so much more we should do for them, yet I didn't know what or how. She turned to me and said, "You are too far removed from the traumatic experience of the earthquake to measure trauma; however, you can measure *hope*." Although I couldn't verbalize exactly what that meant, I felt it. This professor became another one of my hope agents by helping me consider this goal for my dissertation, now with greater precision.

I had finished my dissertation focusing on *hope*, specifically the implementation of Snyder's Adult Hope Scale survey (Snyder et al., 1991) to measure illiterate Haitians' hope; however, my inquiry and interest in hope had just begun. I am still learning after earning my Ph.D. and have many goals. My goals are to share hope, speak and write about hope, and be a hope agent for as many people as I can along the way. And, in doing so, my hopelessness from the loss of my loved one has been supplemented by a newfound love for life.

Elsie's Encounter with Hope

As I walked the corridors of my new institution, I felt overpowered with grief and uncertainty. The death of my dad had created this dense cloud that suffocated me, leaving me lightheaded and in a daze. The bitter taste in my mouth was a constant reminder of my feelings of guilt, because I was not near him to see the signs, fix him, or help him regain his strength. I was guilty. I had left my parents to pursue my doctoral studies. I had promised to come back and invite them to live with me, but that was a promise I would never keep. I felt guilty and lost.

During Daddy's wake, I felt my phone vibrate and I noticed the 407 area code the number of the institution I had applied to a visiting position. I shyly excused myself and stepped out to answer the call. I heard the School Director's cheerful voice as he congratulated me. After he repeated his congratulatory statement, I finally muttered "Thank you." He questioned my lack of excitement, and I shared I was in my father's wake. He understood and hung up. I had been offered a visiting line in

Orlando—a three-hour flight away from my parents' home in Puerto Rico. This opportunity was great! How then could I share with my mother and siblings the happiness of being offered my dream job during my dad's wake?

I pondered how my dad's death was making me question my end goal of getting a job to offer my family new opportunities and mobility. Now, I was not only facing uncertainties and impossibilities but I was also second-guessing myself, the decisions I was making, and my goals. I was losing hope, and the feeling of guilt and hopelessness was engulfing my being.

In this juxtaposition of emotions, I thought about how my narrative of loss would influence my teaching. How could I share with my students, preservice teachers, my grief? How could my students help me heal? Would our stories connect or create tension? As Snyder (2000) explains, "a loss of a loved one often shuts down both pathway and agency thinking as more time lapses from the loss, the realization that the loss incurred includes also a loss of pathways to activities once enjoyed with the deceased person" (p. 133). That is where I was. I felt lost and embarrassed. I wanted to hide how excited I was about my new professional endeavors. I reminisced about how happy others felt when they described their goals. For me, surviving the day without crying or feeling remorse was a good day.

As I walked into my educational methods course, I introduced the course syllabus and objectives. I followed by asking the one question I myself could not answer, "What are your goals for this semester? For your daily life?" A student shared her goals, then sheepishly looked at me while inquiring about my goals for the semester. I froze in my tracks. I had to think about a distant or near future. In considering the future, I had to reminisce on the past. A past that festered like an infected wound. I shared with my students about my loss and explained that I did not have a response for the question just asked. I thought about Freire's ideas on transformative educators and the responsibility I have to examine my own actions, interactions and pedagogy. I recalled how Freire (1970) repeatedly describes the essential responsibility that transformative educators have to start "where the people are." He writes:

> You never get there by starting from there, you get there by starting from some here. This means, ultimately, that the educator must not be ignorant of, underestimate, or reject any of the "knowledge of living experience" with which educands come to school. (1970, p. 58)

I needed to meet my students in my painful present with the understanding that my past experiences were definitely informing how I was living my present. My students would share their own struggles, help me articulate my feelings and experiences, and push me to think about how our discussions better informed our pedagogy. I learned how to embrace the discomfort that I felt when disclosing my feeling and experiences with my students.

As I walked out of the classroom, I realized my students were my hope agents; they were going to help me not only establish new goals that could possibly bring new meaning into my life but also help me identify and recognize new pathways and agency thoughts where I could embrace feeling vulnerable and hopeless in times of suffering. My students taught me that I needed to not only ask them to share, but I needed to do that myself. It was in this nonthreatening space, where written and oral narratives were crafted and shared. My students helped me hone into authentic teaching and goal setting for them and myself.

Conclusion

In our penned interaction and dialogue, we have co-constructed meaning of our grief through our navigations of loss, pain, and choices and through others who became our hope agents (Lopez, 2013). Furthermore, through multiple insights, encouragements, written reflections and reflexive dialogues, attainable goals and actions (hope strategies), we share with our students and colleagues how guided and facilitated discussions helped preservice teachers in our classes. We all moved towards self-realization, sustainable hope, and personal growth, while thinking about critical ways to approach grief in our lives, classrooms, and communities.

Hope theory tells us that people can borrow hope (Lopez, 2013). We connect this hopeful thinking and knowledge gleaned from our journeys in finding hope, or hope finding us, to Freire's (2005) notion of armed love (p. 74). This concept turned our experiences and lessons learned into actionable hope as we have interacted and worked with teacher candidates, teachers, and teacher advocates. As Webb (2013) states, "The cognitive dimension of hope in turn grounds and inspires concerted goal-directed action, i.e. the behavioural dimension of hope." (p. 410). We now feel compelled to educate people about hope and how they can become hope agents in others' lives; and in the arena of education, think about how many students' lives teachers can reach, if they know how. This is the amazing power and gift of hope; it keeps on giving. And, academia has become our platform for informing future teachers about hope.

Change in our personal situations is available. Even if we think we have no recourse, truly we do. One does not have to live with heartache forever. Fear, doubt, worry, failure, panic, anxiety, and depression do not have to continue to be constant companions, even through grief and loss. Our perceptions of hopelessness can be transformed into perceptions and actions of hope. Just knowing that where we are now is not where we have to stay, increases our hope. Thus, we become hope agents for many and mentor others to become hope agents.

References

Freire, P. (1970). *Pedagogy of the oppressed.* Continuum.

Freire, P. (2005). *Teachers as cultural workers: Letters to those who dare teach.* (D. Macedo, D. Koike, & A. Oliveira, Trans.). Westview Press. (Original work published 1997).

Kwon, P. (2000). Hope and dysphoria: The moderating role of defense mechanisms. *Journal of Personality, 68*(2), 199–223.

Lopez, S. J. (2013). *Making hope happen: Create the future you want for yourself and others.* Simon and Schuster.

Olan, E. L. (2015). Narratives that inform pre-service secondary English teachers' writing instruction and pedagogy. *Literacy Information and Computer Education Journal, 6*(3), 1956–1963.

Snyder, C. R. (2000). The hope mandala: Coping with the loss of a loved one. In J. Gillham (Ed.), *The science of optimism and hope: Research essays in honor of Martin E. P. Seligman* (pp. 129–142). Templeton Foundation Press.

Snyder, C. R., Harris, C., Anderson, J. R., Holleran, S. A., Irving, L. M., Sigmon, S. T. ... Harney, P. (1991). The will and the ways: Development and validation of an individual-differences measure of hope. *Journal of Personality and Social Psychology, 60*(4), 570.

Snyder, C. R., Lehman, K. A., Kluck, B., & Monsson, Y. (2006). Hope for rehabilitation and vice versa. *Rehabilitation Psychology, 51*(2), 89.

Valle, M. F., Huebner, E., & Suldo, S. M. (2006). An analysis of hope as a psychological strength. *Journal of School Psychology, 44*(5), 393–406. doi: 10.1016/j.jsp.2006.03.005

Webb, D. (2013). Pedagogies of hope. *Studies in Philosophy and Education, 32*(4), 397–414.

9 Collaborative Empathy as a Pathway to Hope

Grief and Teacher Education

Kia Jane Richmond and Cara Anderson

This chapter focuses on collaborative empathy in a relationship between a preservice teacher (Cara) and a teacher educator (Kia), who each experienced the loss of a loved one before working together in an English Education program. Sharing our stories and engaging in empathetic dialogue helped minimize the power differentials between us while helping us through the grieving process. In this chapter, we describe how conversations grounded in empathy provided pathways toward hope and healing.

Theoretical Framework

We identify constructivism as our guiding framework. A constructivist methodology stresses the researcher's role as "an active participant who interacts with the field being explored" (Edmonds & Kennedy, 2013, p. 116). By sharing how the grieving process affected us, we recognize that "knowledge emerging from data is not only 'discovered' but also created" (Edmonds & Kennedy, 2013, p. 116). By using constructivism, we acknowledge the dialogic nature of analyzing data, identifying themes, and writing about our findings.

We also adopted a humanistic psychological lens and identified empathy as a key construct. Carl Rogers (1961) described empathy as one of three significant components in a successful client-therapist relationship: "To sense the client's private world as if it were your own, but without ever losing the 'as if' quality—this is empathy" (p. 284). Empathy involves dialogic interaction—responding to others without depending on one's own emotions (Richmond, 1999, p. 38). Warren (2018) called empathy "the piece of the student-teacher interaction puzzle that connects what a teacher knows or thinks about students and families to what he or she actually *does* when negotiating appropriate responses to students' needs" (Warren, 2018, p. 171).

Method

Participants

We identify as White women. We actively participated in the design and interpretive stages of the study. I (Kia) base my pedagogy on Rogers's (1961) principles of communication in helping relationships:

congruence, unconditional positive regard, and empathetic under-standing. Embracing Rogers's ideas, I focus on empathy in my teacher education courses.

I (Cara) came to Northern Michigan University (NMU) as a post-baccalaureate student majoring in Secondary Education English and History. I earned my bachelor's degree in Theatre Arts and Literature from Eastern Michigan University, subsequently deciding to seek teacher certi-fication at the NMU. By the fall of 2013, I enrolled in EN 309, Teaching of Writing, and EN 350, Methods and Materials of Teaching Secondary English, excited and enthusiastic about student teaching the following term.

Research Site

At the NMU, we spent over 120 hours together in two classes as Cara pre-pared to student teach. In winter 2014, I (Kia) served as Cara's university supervisor, observing her in an English classroom at a local alternative high school and meeting with her during a three-hour monthly sem-inar. After Cara's graduation, we communicated in writing, via email and social media messages; by phone when Cara moved to Kansas to teach high school English; and in person when she returned to teach English at Aspen Ridge Middle School.

Data Collection and Interpretation

For this study, we collected and analyzed narrative pieces from Cara's English Education assignments, written notes from our dialogic inter-actions during a five-year period, and our individual reflections. We also employed a narrative methodology, which Clandinin and Connelly (1989) have called "the description and restorying of the narrative structure of varieties of educational experience" (p. 4). As Clandinin and Connelly (1989) have stated, "In narrative inquiry the individual is shaped by the situation and shapes the situation in the living out of the story and in the storying of the experience" (p. 17). Thus, our choice of methodology emphasized our narrative experiences.

Using an adaptation of grounded theory to facilitate our data analysis, we read the narrative pieces and notes, considering themes that we iden-tified in the process (Charmaz, 2014, p. 32). Once we established themes through collaborative inductive coding, which we charted into five orig-inal findings, we restoried the narratives to highlight ways that empathy occurred during our relationship and the grieving process, focusing on three questions that arose while interpreting data and rereading research on empathy (Rogers, 1975) and hope in teacher education (Sieben, 2018):

- How does the teacher-student relationship develop and evolve based on the experiences of a university teacher educator and a preservice teacher?

- What did we learn from sharing our stories during the grieving process?
- What role does empathy play in the development of the teacher-student relationship?

For example, after examining Cara's freewrites from EN 350, we identified a comment about how grief made Cara feel: "When my mother died abruptly in September 2013, my reality shifted." We then noticed several other statements focused on emotions or changes in self-worth due to grief, e.g., guilt, worthlessness, loss of control, etc. We theorized that these statements were related and categorized them accordingly, then identified the results as findings (a), (b), and (c). In presenting our three findings, we chose to focus on themes rather than chronology to help readers understand our processes of grieving and how collaborative empathy helped create a pathway toward hope.

Findings

We identified three themes about grief, empathy, and the teacher-student relationship of participants. The first finding (a) was that grief causes shifts in reality, feelings of guilt and worthlessness, loss of control over one's situation, feelings of sadness, feeling stuck or at a standstill. Grief can be overwhelming, like a struggle, or feel like an emotional overload.

Grief results in shifts in reality and feelings of guilt, sadness, or being stuck. In my reflective writing, I (Cara) noted:

> When my mother died abruptly in September 2013, my reality shifted. It was the first time in my life where I had been forced to experience the loss of someone close to me. It was incredibly unexpected, and one of the most painful moments of my life thus far.

I found myself "stuck between wanting life to move on and wanting life to stay at a standstill." Feeling trapped in grief, I threw myself into my studies as a coping strategy. This experience with grief was simultaneous with beginning my methods courses with Kia.

When I (Kia) first met Cara, I was grieving the sudden death of my best friend just a year earlier. In my freewrite during EN 350, I described feeling catapulted into a depressive episode that lasted several years: "While I worked regularly with a wonderful therapist and regularly took a prescribed antidepressant, I struggled with symptoms of depression such as anhedonia (lack of interest in pleasurable activities), insomnia, and feelings of guilt and worthlessness."

We began our relationship facing grief as individuals. As Kessler (2004) noted, "Everyone grieves in their own time and sequence of feelings …. Allowing ourselves and others to feel our grief is an act of courage that can transform wounds into gateways to love" (p. 8). As we discovered later, we could move out of these overwhelming emotions through the sharing of our individual stories of loss. During a recent reflection on my mother's passing, I (Cara) described the lack of control I felt and the pathway of hope that Kia provided me:

> The night after my mother's death, I thought to myself, *What am I going to do about school?* I didn't know my professors that well yet, I hoped that they would allow me a day to cope. I specifically remember calling Kia, even though I didn't know her very well at the time. Her reassurance and support automatically allowed me to breathe a little easier. In a way, having the opportunity to express out loud what had happened made my mother's death more tangible, which was painful, but my grief was what connected Kia and I. Her empathy let me know that at least *one* aspect of my life would remain stable. I remember feeling that I had someone that I could go to if that stability felt threatened. That was important to me, especially at a time when my life felt chaotic, a time when I lacked control.

I found that Kia's empathetic support created a sense of stability necessary for me to persevere through the semester and reach my goals.

Our second finding (b) was that grief leads to feelings of isolation; however, sharing the grieving process while employing empathy can help relieve those feelings. Despite being together each week, we both felt isolated in our grief. I (Cara) noticed Kia's listening to the story of my mother's passing and feeling compelled to share her story as our relationship developed. In my reflection, I discussed this process:

> It wasn't long after our conversations that she [Kia] told me about the death of her best friend, also unexpected and uniquely tragic. We talked about good memories, their deaths, our losses. I am almost certain we cried. Most importantly, we grieved, together. Our losses isolated us and we each had our own escapes to distract ourselves from our painful realities. However, the healing really began through our conversations and our shared grief. The isolation became less dark, less all encompassing. Our shared empathy for each other's experiences allow each other to cope, to heal.

My response echoes the idea that empathy can alleviate feelings of isolation during the grieving process and can create allyship in the process. Kia's sharing of her best friend's death was not intended to serve as a *me, too* move. Instead, her motivation was grounded in empathy through self-disclosure. As Kia disclosed her own grief, she hoped I would become more comfortable, fostering a sense of trust within our relationship. This process helped us gain mutual trust, which ultimately began the healing process for each of us.

The act of empathizing while talking about the grieving process can lead to hope and healing through the sharing of emotions, coping skills, memories, and fears. Like Sieben (2018), we define hope "as the will (motivation) and the ways (strategies) to accomplish future goals" (p. 20). Sharing our stories was not intended to change the narratives; instead, we focused on commonalities, which provided hope. It had to do with listening from an *as if* perspective and not from an *I know, too* perspective. As Rogers (1961) argued, we cannot lose the *as if* quality because "this is empathy, and this seems essential to therapy" (p. 284). Empathizing is not trying to one up the other person or fill in the gaps with one's own story. Rather, empathizing is accepting feelings and making space for the grieving person to express emotions without judgment, interruption, or offering a remedy. Additionally, the collaboration is not just about grieving but also moving forward in hope as individuals and as a team. In our relationship, within the educational setting and beyond, we created an active partnership, shared our experiences, and developed and sustained respect for one another. By employing empathy through a collaborative means, feelings of isolation associated with our individual grief subsided.

Our third finding (c) was that the classroom could provide a safe space for students to confront grief, escape, and/or heal. Through our research, we have adapted a term from psychotherapy to describe the empathetic process we have shared: *collaborative empathy*. Hammond and Nichols (2008) described this concept as one that establishes a "collective relationship" that doesn't demand a comprehensive change but means "working a little harder to understand people before challenging them to change …. It requires sustained respect for clients and working in active partnership" (p. 123). Kia's employment of collaborative empathy helped transform the classroom into a safe space for me (Cara), providing a place to confront my grief through writing. In one reflection, I noted:

> I began to write about my mother in class. Kia's class became a safe place where I could choose to escape from my grief or to choose to confront it. This choice was always mine, I never felt forced or pushed, I felt like it was something I could do if I needed to.

Writing became an outlet to both confront and escape feelings of grief.

Our relationship remained a safe space. While Kia offered extra guidance for all her students, she was also available at an emotional level for me as noted in my journal: "There were many nights after class where I would stay, lingering in the background until all the eager, soon-to-be teachers would inquire about their lesson plans or student teacher placements. I stayed for a different reason—for Kia's empathy."

At the end of the semester, I (Cara) felt as though I was beginning the healing process. In my EN 309 portfolio reflection, I wrote to Kia:

> As you already know, this semester has been one of the most stressful semesters I have had so far in my college career. With the death of my mother, I felt as though I unintentionally started off the semester with a rough start. Through the haze of the grief, I pushed through all my classes as best as I could and overall I felt as though I gave it my all. Looking back, I am slightly surprised at how much I was able to learn and accomplish and I am proud that I was able to do so much during such a rough time in my life.

Overall, my motivation to write and reflect was encouraged by Kia's safe environment. I felt comfortable confronting my own grief because Kia had first established trust through collaborative empathy. Ultimately, I began to find hope, moving toward my goal of healing from the grief through reflection and conversation.

Discussion

The themes we identified through this study illustrate the benefits of collaborative empathy in teaching relationships. These findings add to the aforementioned literature on building empathetic teacher-student relationships. Next, we address three questions we posed during data interpretation.

How Does the Teacher-Student Relationship Develop and Evolve Based on the Experiences of a University Teacher Educator and a Preservice Teacher?

Jennings and Greenberg (2009) argued that socially and emotionally competent teachers, in part, create "supportive and encouraging relationships with their students," which we identified as including collaborative empathy (p. 492). Additionally, teachers who had social and emotional competence responded successfully to students' needs, used their emotions and conversations to encourage the learning process, and managed students' classroom behavior (Jennings & Greenberg, 2009, p. 493). I (Kia) noticed that Cara developed in each of these ways during student teaching. At midterm, Cara recorded that she knew "a little about each student, including their academic strengths and struggles" and had learned about "each student's educational success and well-being." Eight weeks later, she wrote, "My classroom environment is a place that is a safe place for students to grow, learn and express their individuality."

Cara's acknowledgment of the benefits of constructing a safe classroom space demonstrated her growth as a teacher with social and emotional competence. She showed self-awareness, social awareness, and emotional management of relationships. Teaching full-time now, Cara recognizes her own emotions and students' emotions. She is aware of how her emotions might affect others and builds "strong and supportive relationships through mutual understanding and cooperation" (Jennings & Greenberg, 2009, p. 495). She also effectively manages her own emotions and relationships with others.

Training teachers to be socially and emotionally competent requires a commitment to their affective and cognitive growth. What Cara described in her own classroom dovetailed with what I (Kia) hoped would happen: that Cara would develop confidence and skills while having her own emotional needs met in a safe learning environment. What I didn't anticipate was having my own emotional needs met while helping Cara through her grieving and development as a teacher. As I watched Cara grow in confidence, I also reflected on my own confidence as a teacher educator.

What Did We Learn from Sharing Our Stories during the Grieving Process?

Students' experiences of grief can be barriers to academic growth. They might not be able to concentrate; likewise, their emotional stability in the classroom could be compromised. In some cases, grieving students might shut down emotionally, which can affect content learning as well. No difference exists when the teacher is the one who is grieving.

In reflecting on themes emerging from data analysis, we realized that though our experiences with grief were painful and isolating, they provided us with a path to healing through collaborative empathy. Each of us found ways to deal with our losses: through writing, conversation, and acceptance of each other where we were. We also discovered growth in our relationship. What started as a typical teacher-student relationship has developed into a friendship and a professional relationship that is still nurtured today.

What Role Does Empathy Play in the Development of the Teacher-Student Relationship?

Research on empathy in teacher education has been well documented (Bouton, 2016; Jaber et al., 2018; Warren, 2018). Bouton (2016) posited multiple reasons for incorporating empathy in teacher education, including preparing preservice teachers to work with a growing diverse student population and promoting social skills and moral development. Additionally, "epistemic empathy," which is "the act of understanding and appreciating someone's cognitive and emotional experience," is vital to "responsive teaching" (Jaber et al., 2018, p. 14). Jaber et al. (2018) demonstrated how engaging in epistemic empathy helped teachers "support learners' agency and sense-making" (p. 22). In our relationship, being sensitive to one another's emotions and experiences motivated us to dialogue regularly, which created an environment in which empathy was sustained.

Warren (2018) focused on the benefits of empathy as a "mechanism for knowing young people, their families, and communities more robustly" (p. 170). Moreover, he identified "perspective taking" as the "anchoring dimension" of "empathy in social interaction" (p. 171). Our data analysis illuminated multiple instances of perspective taking. I (Kia) considered how losing a family member might affect Cara's motivation and performance. In turn, Cara contemplated how she might respond to a future student who experienced such a loss. These perspective-taking actions were grounded in an empathetic stance: without considering the other person's point of view, we could become trapped in our own perspectives, which would limit our ability to engage in collaborative empathy.

By tapping into an empathetic stance, teachers can enhance relationships with students by considering multiple perspectives. Consequently, because being empathetic requires us to be authentic and reach beyond individual positioning, those who engage in collaborative empathy can benefit emotionally and academically.

Conclusion

We began this study to examine collaborative empathy as a pathway to hope in the classroom and beyond. Using a constructivist framework and a humanistic psychological lens, we collected and analyzed narrative data and identified three themes about the teacher-student relationship while exploring our experiences with grief.

This study helped us reflect on our relationship and contemplate others we have had as teachers. Based on what I learned through my relationship with Cara, I (Kia) have used collaborative empathy with other students who have experienced loss, encouraging students to write reflectively and communicate via email, social media, and phone.

Likewise, I (Cara) have drawn on collaborative empathy in relationships with students. I realize how grief has shaped my life and teaching. I often think of my mother and sometimes still grieve. However, I recognize that I am not alone: even though my grief is my own, empathy provides a pathway of hope. My relationship with Kia has evolved, and I now find myself as the teacher of many students, some of whom, unfortunately, have experienced grief. I can empathize and help students through their grieving, which has helped me provide hope.

We invite educators to reflect on their own and students' experiences with grief to construct more rewarding relationships and become more socially and emotionally competent. By being self-aware, managing emotions, and employing collaborative empathy to understand others' emotions, educators can become more active agents of hope while helping students move through the grieving process.

References

Bouton, B. (2016). Empathy research and teacher preparation: Benefits and obstacles. *SRATE Journal,* 45(2), 16–25. http://www.srate.org/journal_archive.html

Charmaz, K. (2014). *Constructing grounded theory* (2nd ed.) Sage.

Clandinin, D. J., & Connelly, F. M. (1989). *Narrative and story in practice and research.* http://eric.ed.gov/?id=ED309681

Edmonds, W. A., & Kennedy, T. D. (2013). *An applied reference guide to research designs: Quantitative, qualitative, and mixed methods.* Sage.

Hammond, R. T., & Nichols, M. P. (2008). How collaborative is structural family therapy? *The Family Journal, 16*(2), 118–124. doi: https://doi.org/10.1177/1066480707313773.

Jaber, L. Z., Southerland, S., & Dake, F. (2018). Cultivating epistemic empathy in preservice teacher education. *Teaching and Teacher Education, 72,* 13–23. https://doi.org/10.1016/j.tate.2018.02.009

Jennings, P. A., & Greenberg, M. T. (2009). The prosocial classroom: Teacher social and emotional competence in relation to student and classroom outcomes. *Review of Educational Research, 79*(1), 491–525. doi: https://doi.org/10.3102/0034654308325693

Kessler, R. (2004). Grief as a gateway to love in teaching. In D. Liston and J. Garrison (Eds.), *Teaching, loving, and learning* (pp. 137–152). RoutledgeFalmer.

Richmond, K. J. (1999). The ethics of empathy: Making connections in the writing classroom. *Journal of the Assembly for Expanded Perspectives on Learning, 5*(1), 37–46. https://trace.tennessee.edu/jaepl/vol5/iss1/6

Rogers, C. (1961). *On becoming a person: A therapist's view of psychotherapy.* Houghton Mifflin.

Rogers, C. R. (1975). Empathetic: An unappreciated way of being. *The Counseling Psychologist, 5*(2), 2–10. doi: https://doi.org/10.1177/001100007500500202

Sieben, N. (2018). *Writing hope strategies for writing success in secondary schools: A strengths-based approach to teaching writing.* Brill | Sense.

Warren, C. A. (2018). Empathy, teacher dispositions, and preparation for culturally responsive pedagogy. *Journal of Teacher Education, 69*(2), 169–183. doi: https://doi.org/10.1177/0022487117712487

10 "Why I Hate the Wind"

Magical Realism and Re-Presenting Trauma

Christopher Worthman

I Hate the Wind, Part 1

***I Hate the Wind. I Hate It with a Passion,
and It Has Been That Way Forever.***

As an 11-year-old, I would ride my bike along country roads, as torrents
of wind swept across fallow fields. I struggled to stay upright and keep
my tear-stung eyes open. How often this happened, I don't know. Once,
a thousand times, it does not matter. I remember it.

I remember, too, setting aside my bike to run. The cold, heat, rain,
snow had no effect. I was unbeatable. The wind, however, set me on my
heels and knocked the breath out of me.

For the longest time, I told no one any of this, until my Aunt Tootie.
I had driven to Covington, Kentucky. It had been 22 years, and I was
reconnecting with relatives I had not seen since I was five.

She owned a hair salon, a small wood-framed storefront. She can-
celled appointments, and we sat in styling chairs facing each other, rem-
iniscing and catching up. She asked about running. A cousin had told
her of my success.

I told her how running had gotten me in and through college. I said
the only part I hated about it was the wind. "I don't even like to walk
down the street when it's windy—"

"No." Her smile dissipated. "Seriously?"

I nodded and smiled weakly.

"I need to tell you something." She lit a cigarette and took a long drag.
"You don't know this, but you need to."

...

This is the beginning of a traumatic narrative, one told many times to
future teachers. I never referred to it as such, however. I prefaced it by
saying it is a true story. What I have told so far *is* true.

After I tell it, some students ask, "Did that really happen?" Others
smile and say, "That didn't happen." I shrug. I have nothing to add.

But *something* did happen, something that only in the telling became recognizable to me over time.

Naming the Unknown

Such is trauma and questions of what really happened and what did not, what one remembers, does not remember, or leaves unsaid. Caruth (1995) wrote, "to be traumatized is precisely to be possessed by an image or event.... The traumatized...carry an impossible history within them, or they become themselves the symptom of a history that they cannot actively possess" (pp. 4–6). Traumatic history cannot be narratively recreated with standard story grammar or realist temporal-spatial chronotopes of beginning, middle, and end. Traumatic experience relived "bears witness to a past that was never fully experienced as it occurred.... [It is] of an experience that is not fully owned" (Arva, 2011, p. 151).

Owned can be understood in a couple of ways. First, a traumatic experience is often so alien and shocking that the traumatized does not fully grasp what happened. The experience, even as it occurs, seems implausible. Second, finding language to name the experience can be impossible, then and later. Naming it can be disquieting, even harrowing—so little of it can be claimed through language. After having experienced something and involuntarily feeling and living out its repercussions every day, one cannot find the words that do justice to what happened, much less provide solace. Some other way of telling is needed.

Recognizing trauma for what it is, trauma studies scholars such as Arva (2011), Bortolussi (2010), and Takolander (2016) have sought ways of telling not beholden to realist temporal-spatial chronotopes. Arva called for an imaginative leap, or a *traumatic imagination*, that bypasses facts and moves beyond codes, signs, rules, and even language of temporal-spatial worlds we know. He identified magical realist imagery as the leap needed. This imagery "is an 'aesthetically and ethically adequate means of coping with a painful memory by *telling*—by bearing witness to it'" (p. 40). Similarly, to redefine magical realist imagery to account for its relationship to trauma, Bortolussi wrote that the implausibility of the magical reflects the traumatic, or that which in real life seems implausible, unreal, and unthinkable.

I Hate the Wind, Part 2

"I have to go way back for this to make sense," Aunt Tootie said.

"Before your mom and I were born, when your granddad was a boy, there was a huge storm—storm of the century they called it. The Ohio River overran its banks, wiping out everything. Old timers say we were under water for weeks biding time. When it finally receded, the only things left were muddy hills and broken homes...and the river, of course, but it had moved. It now *divided* Covington from Cincinnati."

She grimaced. "Anything of value ended up on the Cincinnati side. Us on the south bank were all but forgotten. It's been that way ever since."

"During the Depression and war, Dad, like a lot of people, crossed the river to work construction in Cincinnati," she said.

"Right before I was born, and your mom was three, our dad—your granddad—had an accident. One day, he was on some scaffolding six stories up and fell. He died two days later. No one knew what to tell your mom. Everyone thought she was too young to know. So, they told her a big wind took her dad on a journey."

Aunt Tootie laughed. "Stupid, huh?"

I took a deep breath, having a hunch where this was going.

"You can imagine the effect it had on your mom, being a little girl and all. She was horrified the wind took her daddy away. She couldn't comprehend it," Aunt Tootie said.

"And she became deathly afraid of the wind, Chris. She hated it. There were days she wouldn't go outside. And when she did, she was always grabbing onto something. She would go down the street grabbing fence posts, car mirrors, what have you—even people—making sure she had a hold before moving."

"We got used to it and let her be." Aunt Tootie laughed weakly and took a drag off a cigarette. "Yep, and then years later, she got pregnant with you, Chris. That changed everything." She exhaled and smiled. "Your mom was sooo happy when she learned she was pregnant. We all were." She leaned forward and patted my knee. "I mean, she was 16 and having a baby. That's a big deal."

Aunt Tootie saw my disbelief and shushed me with her hand. "You better believe it."

"So, what happened?"

"Your mom weighed 90 pounds wet, but she gained weight as you grew inside her. And you know what? She became more and more sure of herself. Before we knew it, she was going up and down the street showing off her bump. She wasn't afraid of the wind no more. It was like it never happened. And then at seven months, *you* became too much for her. The doctor put her in bed. Told her not to move until you were born. She sulked a bit but got over it. And then you were born."

I smiled, and Aunt Tootie winked at me.

"You were so beautiful, Chris," she said.

"We all wanted to take care of you, but your mom wouldn't have it. It was like none of us sisters knew what we were doing, although there already were six nieces and nephews running around the house. She had to do it all. Mind you, after two months she still hadn't left the house. She was getting her strength back.

Then one day she bundled you up and headed for the door. I asked where she was going. She said I should mind my own business. I pestered her to go and even followed her outside. I felt I had to go. She gave me the stink eye and said to keep my mouth shut and stay out of the way."

Re-Presenting the Past and Imagining the Future

Traumatic studies posit magical realism as more than a postcolonial genre of fantastical depictions of historical happenings—a literary ethnography of sorts. Instead, it "foregrounds the *implausibility* of the fictional world, thereby flaunting its rejection of the realist codes of mimesis and representation" (Bartolussi, 2010, p. 357). The fantastic, however, is not imposed on the real for effect but is revealed amidst the real. As Roh (1995) wrote, "mystery does not descend to the represented world, but rather hides and palpitates behind it" (p. 16), reflecting a larger reality. Thus, magical realism imagery "is not an escape from reality but an enhancement of a 'real' reality which tends to escape us— more often than not as a symptom of trauma" (Arva, 2011, p. 89).

The magic of magical realism imagery fills voids in existence by providing a construct to conceptualize unknown experiences as real. The imagery fosters traumatic narration, providing mediational means to name traumatic memory. The imagery manipulates imagination and emotions by injecting an ironic element into a narrative to create dialectical uncertainty that destabilizes and makes questionable what is real. It opens opportunities within a narrative for new truths or representations of reality.

Takolander (2016) wrote that the irony of magical realism imagery "demands a critical engagement with history as essential to reimagining futurity" (p. 96). Revealing new truths about one's experience is a first step toward reimagining and possibly healing. Hence, the goal of magical realist imagery is not to eliminate or rewrite history but to "precisely [permit] *history* to rise where *immediate understanding* may not" (Caruth, 1995, p. 11).

From this perspective, magical realist images are *felt reality*. The images do not so much represent reality as they *re*-present reality in a way designed to generate an emotive response, or to communicate what in real life is incommunicable or unspeakable. Thus, magical realism imagery serves as a true expression of trauma—"an auspicious formula for representing trauma" (Takolander & Langdon, 2017, p. 46). It is a real understanding of what impressionably happened that is graspable by the traumatized.

I Hate the Wind, Part 3

"'You know how Covington is laid out?' Aunt Tootie said. "Big hills rising up from the river?"

I nodded.

"We lived at the top of one of them a few blocks from here. You mom, you, and I came out the door that day and walked along the crest. After a few blocks, we turned north and below us was the river, maybe a quarter mile away, tucked between buildings. Cincinnati lay beyond it, like some Land of Oz. And beyond that dark, heavy clouds kind of hung there."

"We walked down the hill a couple of blocks, turned and went a few more blocks before turning again and heading back up. The whole time your mom's stopping and talking, stopping and talking—to everyone, neighbors, strangers. She's showing you off. It's 'Chris this, Chris that.' I could see she was getting tired."

"When we got back to the top, I asked if I could hold you. 'No,' she said. I kept asking; she kept saying no. In fact, the more I asked, the more determined she got. She walked right past our house. She was going around again!"

"At the next corner, I asked one last time, 'Can I carry Chris?' Your mom looked at me, hair blowing across her face. She had the saddest-looking eyes. She looked so tired."

"I can take him for a while," I said, expecting a big fat 'no.' But she nodded. "Just for a moment," she whispered.

Aunt Tootie, who had been staring at her lap, looked at me.

"I remember starting to turn the corner and looking down the hill and suddenly feeling very cold. The sky had gotten dark, like it was dusk. Debris was swirling around the street down by the river. People were holding their hats, skirts, what have you, and hanging on to things to keep from being blown over. I saw it coming."

She shook her head and hesitated.

"I reached for you, Chris." She held out her arms, showing me what she did.

"I wrapped my arms around you as I looked at your mom. She was looking at you, and in her eyes, I saw the clouds. I pulled you from her and stepped back around the corner. Your mom stood there, looking at you as I moved away. Your blanket blew up over your face as all that debris and garbage flew past. When I looked up, your mom was gone."

Aunt Tootie looked at me. "That's why you hate the wind, Chris."

Traumatic Narrative and Understanding

"Magical realist fiction," Arva (2011) wrote, "may be both an unconscious way of acting out trauma as well as a conscious struggle to work through it" (p. 32). Both are the case for me. Aunt Tootie's story is my story, my grappling with a traumatic experience of abandonment. When I began to tell it, I had not connected it to traumatic experience. I simply wanted to tell a story about myself, and the wind seemed the perfect foil. However, I did not know what the story's sensory impressions—the sounds, sights, and feel of the wind—meant or why those impressions were so readily relatable to my mother, whom I had not seen in years. The more I told the story, however, the more truthful it became.

As depicted in the story, I *have* always hated the wind even as I knew it played no role in my mother's struggles. Looking back, I realize, in our constant moving from one place to another and our finally leaving Covington for good when I was five, my mother abandoning me began precariously enough when I was a toddler. She left me at home alone for hours at a time. We were constantly in flight from intimacy as she refused to let anyone into our lives. She suffered the loss of her lover—my father—who wanted nothing to do with us. He died when I was two, decimating her last hope he loved her—he loved us. She never talked about him again and tacitly passed on to me a belief we were unworthy of others' love. For me, her final abandonment when I was ten confirmed what I felt but never named—until I proclaimed my hatred of the wind.

My working through all of this was heightened the three or four times per year I told the story. It was cathartic to turn unassimilated events across time into a narrative that rang true. I spoke the unspeakable and pieced together the unknown even as I did not yet know what was unspeakable and what was unknown. It gave me access to a "truth of historical experience where there was no simple access before" (Caruth, 1995, p. 6). In the end, the story was as real to me as any story I might tell about myself. It formed an understanding of who I was and am that transcended all other stories.

My traumatic narrative made me aware that there was so much I did not know or will never know about my mother and our family. Brockmeier and Carbaugh (2001), writing about narrative in general, said, "the very idea of human identity…is tied to the very notion of narrative and narrativity" (p. 15). Narrative is responsible for our sense of self but also for "our sense of…who others are, and how we are related" (p. 10). Zen Buddhist monk Thich Nhat Hanh (2013) wrote, "the suffering inside us contains the suffering of our fathers, our mothers, and our ancestors" (p. 28). The truth that arose from my story spanned generations. My trauma, no matter how singular it felt, was part of a larger web of history, community, and relationship with others. Confronting it required a purposeful revelatory exploration that carried me beyond myself to account for others' memories and experiences.

Magical realism, as traumatic narrative, provided a way to confront my past by opening up space in narrative structures to re-present what was deeply felt but unnamable for not only me but also for others. It provided me—and can provide others—a passageway to otherness, especially others' trauma. It not only can foster understanding; it can also affirm as true others' traumatic experiences. As narrative, trauma stories rendered as magical realism call out for empathetic allying. As an impetus for action, these narratives open us up to allyship and the potentiality of others and ourselves.

For me, magical realism provided a means of searching for and naming truth, not only for myself but also for my grandfather, my mother, and for the community in which I was born. It made it possible to understand their suffering and offer healing language for them as well as me. This is the potential of traumatic narratives cast as magical realism: they let us into others' experiences in ways hopeful and affirming. They allow us to say, yes, I believe you even if I can't fully understand, and I stand with you.

References

Arva, E. (2011). *The traumatic imagination: Histories of violence in magical realist fiction.* Cambria Press.

Bortolussi, M. (2010). Implausible worlds, ingenuous narrators, ironic authors: Toward a revised theory of magic realism. *Canadian Review of Comparative Literature, 30*(2), 349–370. https://journals.library.ualberta.ca/crcl/index.php/crcl/article/view/10674

Brockmeier, J., & Carbaugh, D. (2001). Introduction. In J. Brockmeier & D. Carbaugh (Eds.), *Narrative and identity* (pp. 1–22). Benjamins Publishing Company.

Caruth, C. (1995). *Trauma: Explorations in memory.* Johns Hopkins University Press.

Hanh, T. N. (2013). *The art of communicating.* HarperCollins.

Roh, F. (1995). Magic realism: Post-expressionism. In L. Parkinson Zamora & W. B. Faris (Eds.) *Magical realism: Theory, history, community* (pp. 15–30). Duke University Press.

Takolander, M. K. (2016). Theorizing irony and trauma in magical realism: Junot Díaz's *The brief wondrous life of Oscar Wao* and Alexis Wright's *The swan book. Ariel: A Review of International English Literature, 47*(3), 95–122. https://link-gale-com.ezproxy.depaul.edu/apps/doc/A460186117/LitRC?u=depaul&sid=LitRC&xid=025a7177

Takolander, M., & Langdon, J. (2017). Shifting the 'vantage point' to women: Reconceptualizing magical realism and trauma. *Critique: Studies in Contemporary Fiction, 58*(1), 41–52. doi: https://doi.org/10.1080/00111619.2016.1152227

11 It *Is* Contagious, Honey

Katherine C. Brown

In this chapter, I explore loss, grief, healing, and hope through the lens of *assemblage*, a concept that describes the movements of a dynamic system of interconnected elements (Deleuze & Guattari, 1987). Assemblages operate in the poststructural landscape beyond a view of reality that is static, definable, and easily predictable (Deleuze & Guattari, 1987; Jackson & Mazzei, 2012; Nordstrom, 2015). The movements of an assemblage are generated through vibrations that take hold, pick up speed, slow down, and move about along *lines of flight* (Deleuze & Guattari, 1987).

My mother created a garden that she and I tended together, which I continue to tend. The garden is an assemblage of nature that has become a healing mechanism for my grief, so I will explain the concept lines of flight in consideration of how this concept functions in the garden. A rhizomatic root system is a line of flight that forms multiple connections, sometimes becoming so entangled as to be seemingly impossible to untangle. A bee hums from one flower to the next, stops to rest, and then moves along to pollinate other spaces. A tuft of dog fur drifts down from the porch, alights in the garden and, upon being scooped up by a nest-building bird, is put into motion as it connects with the inhabitants of the nest, providing comfort and warmth. These are lines of flight, constantly forming connections among the elements of an assemblage.

I work through the intense grief of losing my mother to cancer in this garden landscape. I found that hope for healing comes through thinking and working through my grief as assemblage—a grief assemblage. Poulos (2014) wrote that therapeutically writing one's way through loss and grief can serve as "a bridge to hope" (p. 342). Similarly, I am gardening my way through grief and toward hope. By digging my hands into the warm soil of my mother's garden, I touch and am touched by all the elements inhabiting her garden and indeed, I come into contact with the very molecules of her earthly body. I put the wisdom she imparted to me into motion; as I work the soil, that wisdom flows, and I hear her voice, reminding me to *be gentle* with all these elements of Nature (and with myself).

This chapter is in the form of a conversation with my mother. In choosing this format, I follow Nordstrom (2013), who used photo-text to present a "continuous narrative of alternating pages of texts and photographs" (p. 316). This dialogue is interspersed with photographs of various artifacts related to my mother, our garden, and our relationship. The conversation that unfolds is a dialogue between two people, one dead and one living, thereby generating transgressive data that erupts along infinite lines of flight as we move about with dreams, emotions, memories, physical sensations, and haunted artifacts (Nordstrom, 2013; St. Pierre, 1997). The lines of flight constantly sweep us into strange new territories that strain against traditional conceptualizations of reality, thus collapsing the boundaries that supposedly separate my mother and me, the dead and the living, nature and culture, and anything that was previously thought of as "separate." In this conversation, then, we continually perform these movements that form a grief assemblage of fluctuations, undulations, varying speeds and temperatures, and rhythmic vibrations among infinite, interconnected elements, or *multiplicities* (Deleuze & Guattari, 1987; Jackson & Mazzei, 2012; Nordstrom, 2015).

Deleuze and Guattari (1987) describe multiplicities as packs, stating, "These multiplicities with heterogeneous terms, cofunctioning by contagion, enter certain *assemblages*" (p. 242). For example, I dig my hands into the warm soil of my mother's garden, touching and being touched by an underground rhizomatic root system that connects all of the flowers, herbs, and ferns that continue to grow there. My mother's molecules are all around and within us. I am constantly becoming contaminated with all of these multiplicities, and we work quite well together, as a pack. I am grieving-daughter-becoming-healing.

Delueze and Guattari (1987) explain how these multiplicities cross over a threshold, which works as a becoming between two or more (and often infinite) multiplicities. The threshold springs into motion when various multiplicities connect, vibrating along lines of flight that take off into unpredictable directions, forming endless connections all the way down to the molecular level. The threshold sometimes becomes excessive, and "*something new happens*" (Jackson & Mazzei, 2012, p. 6). Grief acts as a threshold when it becomes a dreadful space of pain and isolation. Therefore, crossing out of this threshold and into a space of healing is a movement of hope. Hope emerges into possibilities for continuing bonds (Stroebe & Schut, 1999) with the object of loss, which may best be accomplished through doing. Lines of flight lead to a fantastic array of options for doing grief differently, allowing for unfoldings of hope and empowerment as a grieving person becomes immersed in creative, therapeutic processes of healing.

This conversation with my mother works against the idea that death, life, nature, culture, grief, and healing can be structurally contained

Figure 11.1 Artifacts from Trudy Reed Brown's Grief Assemblage

and predicted. While our garden is a focal point of this work that we are doing, it's neither a beginning, nor an end. As my mother and I talk about, within, and all around the artifacts in this grief assemblage, the boundaries that supposedly separate my mother and me, the artifacts, and the specters that haunt them continually collapse, and we are constantly becoming the assemblage. Other characters inevitably move about in this conversation. Their "voices" are not always apparent as such; some of these characters hum, buzz, bark, crinkle, and crunch, while some do not emit sound yet nevertheless have quite a lot to say.

Rosemary for Remembrance or, Here We Are

Mom, I need you. I really haven't been doing very well ever since May 7, 2009.
I know, honey. I've been watching you…. I've *always* been with you.
Oh God. I'm so sorry. You've seen everything then.
Lambey-pie, I never left. Look up. What do you see?
I see the magnolia trees in our backyard moving and glittering with the breeze and the sunlight. I'm sitting at the desk where ….
…. I used to do my work from home. Now, look over
to your left.
OH! You noticed the assemblage (Deleuze & Guattari, 1987)!
Oh KK I love it! I am within and all around it, as are

you. I feel that we can never be separate from it, nor
would we want to be. Tell me more about how we have
been tending this garden assemblage, and how we will
continue to tend to it.
The assemblage operates rhizomatically: knotted, entangled....
.... endlessly establishing connections. Yes, I
know about rhizomes!
Every time we touch the garden, we contaminate it, for we are contagious, becoming together through contagion (Deleuze & Guattari,
1987).
Contagion?
Wait, hold on.
What is it about that word? What's happening?
We will get there. I mean to say, we've been there before, we'll be there
again, and we're already there. Or, herewe are.

Here we are.

(Said in unison, after deep sighs).

Yes, we can move about with the assemblage through plugging in to
its various movements (Jackson & Mazzei, 2012). Only through
shifting. Varying sensations of temperatures, speeds, eruptions of
innumerable lines of flight (Deleuze & Guattari, 1987). We cannot
function without plugging in to the garden, dogs, insects, plants,
even inanimate objects. Especially not the inanimate objects in
the form of haunted artifacts that we're working with here.
It sounds a lot like the process of gardening. This
process never ends, even in the winter, when gardens
appear to be dead. Where is this line of flight taking us
now, KK?
Here we are.

  (Said in unison, after deep sighs).

We are in your bedroom, in late Spring of 2009. The day is sunny, and
the Reverend has come to visit you, be … because ….
.... I am dying.
Yes, Mom. You are dying. I am already becoming a bereaved daughter.
The Reverend asks you about your life: until we arrive *here. Here we
are.*
Yes, I say, "Here we are." The Reverend has brought a
gift, a sprig of Rosemary, for remembrance.
We have kept this Rosemary over the years. Do you see, Mom?
Yes, KK, I feel it.
I feel … cold, dark, and shaky. As I watched you becoming sick, becom-
ing a dying mother, I felt so helpless. Mom ….
It's ok, Lambey-Pie, I'm here.

Figure 11.2 Detail Taken from Artifacts in Trudy Reed Brown's Grief Assemblage

The room in which a person is dying, on her deathbed, is in that space
     outside the crowded threshold, that space where pleadings for mir-
     acles, desperate whispers of hope for life eventually give way to
     long, anxious stares into a dying face and hot, desperate tears.

It *Is* Contagious, Honey or, of Despair and Dreams

I feel your tears, your desperation.
I tried to overcome my despair by *getting back to work*.
Well, how did that work?
It didn't work. I was gasping for breath and movement in a space that
     had become congested—the *threshold*—that which is a liminal
     space with multiple points of connection (Jackson & Mazzei,
     2012). Between life and death ...
You reached the excess with your grief, didn't you
honey? I saw it, near the end of my illness. I was sitting
on the side of the bed....
.... and I was standing next to you. Oh Mom, you were in misery. You were
     vomiting up all the blood and mucous that your body just couldn't
     handle anymore. That's what the hospice nurse said, that your body
     just couldn't take it anymore. I was holding that bright blue plastic bag
     for you. Oh Mom! I held the bag gingerly, and you said ....

Figure 11.3 Detail Taken from Artifacts in Trudy Reed Brown's Grief Assemblage

Don't worry, it's not contagious, honey.
But it *is* contagious Mom! Please don't think that I was afraid to touch
    your bodily fluids. You had just gotten so frail, and I felt that if I
    touched you too much, I would hurt you. I'm so sorry! Oh, Mom!
There, now, that's better, isn't it?
Yes, the image of you smiling, with the corgis, as Master Gardener, is
    infinitely more comforting.
I knew that you needed something to remind you
of me as happy and healthy in my earthly body. Isn't
it funny how all these pictures, all these memories, are
popping up around the house?
Yes, we've been enjoying them. What amazes me even more are your
    visits to me in my dreams.
And that's why I visited you last night. Now, tell me
more about dreams and hauntings.
That smile: that's how you looked last night! You're helping me out quite
    a bit with your visits, you know! How could I ever close that door on
    you? Doucet (2007) described a "gossamer wall" as a liminal space
    between a living person and a person who has died. Using this
    metaphor, the person who has died is "always present and pain-
    fully absent" (p. 74). There you are.
Don't you mean to say, there *we* are? And there we have
always already been? Or, *here we are, working together.*
Ah yes. So, as we are working together continuously, we are generating
    spectral data (Nordstrom, 2013).

Figure 11.4 Photograph of Trudy Reed Brown Taken from her Grief Assemblage

Our relationship generates this data as you continue to haunt me, and
  includes our dream visits. Our relationship continues to generate
  the assemblage.
That adorable little flower pot full of curiosities?
Yes. And all of the photographs, plants, knick-knacks ... these are usually called *artifacts* in research terminology, but I much prefer the
  term *curiosities*.
I will continue to haunt those curiosities!
So let us gaze at these curiosities, and let us see what happens as the gaze
  is returned. You (and Deleuze and Guattari (1987), and infinite
  others) ask what it means to love somebody, or what is this "nasty
  developmental infection called love" (Haraway, 2008, p. 16) that
  vibrates, heats up, and erupts along infinite lines of flight.

Becoming Nurturing, Becoming Healing

In that photograph of me on the sofa, Red gazes at Eve
as she gazes at me. And you were gazing at us as you took
that photograph, capturing this moment in time.
The infection of love still rages on in this arrested moment in time.
  Love often feels hot to me. As I gaze at this photograph, I feel

heat vibrating as movements in the assemblage. Infections, contaminations of the body, are hot and red, and I think that love is no different.

I can see, I can feel, the heat in this photograph, how the sun's rays are streaming through it. There are curiosities nesting by the picture that I know so well. Nesting, like a bird.

Yes, Mom, I have been assembling bits of dog fur from Eve and Red.

Kind of like how birds take bits of dog fur to help build their nests! How did you do that?

Before the dogs died, I gathered tufts of fur from them. Some of these tufts even came from your perch on that sofa in the photograph, a favorite resting spot for you after the day's work.

There was never any shortage of corgi fur in our home!

As there is never any shortage of hauntings here. I also found your hairbrush, from which I extracted a strand of your hair, Mom. I carefully placed your hair in the middle of the downy dog fur. From your knitting supply bag, I took a bit of red yarn and wrapped it around all this animal hair, nonhuman and human.

Red yarn, the color of infections, the color of love …

Contagion has been at work this entire time and continues to pulsate throughout the assemblage.

That reminds me of a heart beating….

…. a heart continually beating, pumping red blood throughout, an affective line of flight, pumping movement all around the assemblage.

Where are we going now with this line of flight, KK? I am becoming more and more curious.

Figure 11.5 Further Artifacts: Insects, Shells, and Pebbles

Memories are flooding, flooding, swirling about like water! You are
holding me now, a small child, in the river....

.... we are in the river in Arkansas, below the Star
Falls lookout, while the water flows around us....

.... through us, within us, all around us. It is both cool and warm; cool
from the river water, and warm from your skin....

.... and constantly, constantly flowing. Dancing.

Becoming mother and daughter, nature lovers, the molecules of our
skin becoming contaminated and contaminating the water
around us. I could never forget the way your skin feels, the way it
smells ...

The assemblage shifts yet again as I see you constantly becoming a small
awestruck child, caretaker of our garden, grieving daughter, a female
human animal, a member of the pack, striving for achievement as a
student and counselor, struggling for self-care, becoming healer and
healing ...

I am always awestruck by your teachings—you, the Great Mother—I am
an awestruck child. It is a summer of my childhood, when we went
to visit the Butterfly Lady, bringing back cocoons, some of which

Figure 11.6 Artifacts from Trudy Reed Brown's Grief Assemblage

hatched into plump, bright green caterpillars and evolved into Luna Moths. We nurtured them, and, in turn, they taught us so much.

Yes, KK. What did we learn?

They are all there, mattering in their own little ways. They all play a part. Here is a seashell from the ocean, holding a shell from the river, holding three little creatures that have died: a June Bug, a Bumblebee, and a Scarab Beetle. I've capitalized their "names" because their deaths are tiny tragedies to be mourned. Even the snails that once inhabited those shells, and have long since disintegrated, long before we found them together—remember, Mom? You taught me so well to respect these tiny things. You showed me how every garden needs them, in some way.

There is a humming, a vibration.

Yes, for these tiny creatures have done their fair share of nurturing our garden, as they have infected it through pollination, decay and decomposition, and renewal and rebirth of infinite becomings. See these plants here in the pot. They could not be possible without the molecules contaminating the assemblage. And so, becoming curious, reaching out to touch, to gaze and to be gazed at, to respect, to love… this is how I continue to tend to all these things and am simultaneously tended as a healing bereaved daughter, broken but not shattered.

References

Deleuze, G., & Guattari, F. (1987). *A thousand plateaus: Capitalism and schizophrenia.* (B. Massumi, Trans.). University of Minnesota Press. (Originally published 1980).

Doucet, A. (2007). "From her side of the gossamer walls(s)": Reflexivity and relational knowing. *Qualitative Sociology, 31,* 73–87. http://dx.doi.org/10.1007/s11133/007/9090/9

Haraway, D. J. (2008). *When species meet.* University of Minnesota Press.

Jackson, A. Y., & Mazzei, L. A. (2012). *Thinking with theory in qualitative research: Viewing data across multiple perspectives.* Routledge.

Nordstrom, S. N. (2013). A conversation about spectral data. *Cultural Studies, Critical Methodologies, 13*(4), 316–341. doi:. http://dx.doi.org/10.1177/1532708613487879

Nordstrom, S. N. (2015). A data assemblage. *International Review of Qualitative Research, 8*(2), 166–193. doi: http://dx.doi/org/10.1525/irqr.2015.8.2.166

Poulos, C. N. (2014). Writing a bridge to possibility. *International Review of Qualitative Research, 7*(3), 342–358. doi:. http://dx.doi.org/10.1525/irqr.2014.7.3.275

St. Pierre, E. A. (1997). Methodology in the fold and the irruption of transgressive data. *International Journal of Qualitative Studies in Education, 10*(2), 175–189. doi:. http://dx.doi.org/10.1080/095183997237278

Stroebe, M., & Schut, H. (1999). The dual process model of coping with bereavement: Rationale and description. *Death Studies, 23*(3), 197–224. doi: 10.1080/074811899201046.

Part III
Grieving for/with Students and Teachers

12 Hiding behind Closed Classroom Doors and Opening up Space for Sharing Grief

Mandie B. Dunn

Storying as research opens up spaces for both researchers and participants to listen to others' stories and be heard (Kinloch & San Pedro, 2014). Furthermore, scholars have argued that people come to make meaning of experiences through narrating experiences in story (Clandinin & Connelly, 2001; Van Manen, 2001). Many scholars have explored the silencing of stories as a means of erasure (e.g. Baker-Bell, Butler, & Johnson, 2017). Stories are silenced in particular when people are made to feel shame or guilt for their experiences. Brown (2012) describes shame as working like termites in a house: "it's hidden in the dark behind the walls" (p. 189). Thus, humanizing research works to bring projects into the light. Projects in humanization through storying offer possibilities for creating spaces for emotions to come into the light when teachers and researchers tell of their lived experiences. In this chapter, I show how teachers sharing their grieving stories with me helped me to make meaning from and heal from my own story of loss. In this chapter, the exchange of stories "between" (Kinloch & San Pedro, 2014) assured teachers with whom I worked and me that we were not alone, relieving us of guilt and shame that may have previously prevented us from healing or moving forward.

Vignette 1: Jerry

When I first meet Jerry, he strikes me as calm and kind. He doesn't seem harried at the end of the school day; his footsteps are even, his voice mild, his demeanor inviting. Once his middle school students have left for the day, we sit down to talk about his experience losing a student who was murdered. As Jerry tells me about speaking at the memorial services, our eyes meet occasionally. I see little creases around his eye line, the only sign that he's been teaching for almost 20 years. Jerry remembers trying to stay focused on the lesson with the empty chair looming in the space. He tells me about planting a tree with his class in memory of their friend. He explains that he was always looking for what he could do to help: calling students to tell them the news personally, being lenient with students on assignments, and kissing one student on top of her head to comfort her while she cried.

I remember being surprised by how little Jerry talked about his own feelings around the loss of his student. I told him then that I heard a lot in his story about what he was trying to do for students—the personal phone calls, the listening ear, the planting of the tree—but that I did not hear much about his own feelings. He said that he did feel sad, but it was his job to focus on the young people who were going through the experience. He assured me that he was never in danger of "breaking down" in front of students. In his story, I see Jerry carefully managing his emotions, both in response to his loss and in his restorying of that loss to me.

Managing Emotions as Emotional Labor

Hochschild (1983) described the work of managing emotions or regulating one's emotion to maintain the emotions of the client as *emotional labor*. In developing this concept, Hochschild (1983) studied flight attendants and argued that service professionals are more often engaged in jobs requiring invisible or unpaid labor, such as the managing of one's emotions. Building upon Hochschild's conceptualization, educational scholars have argued that teaching requires emotional labor (e.g. Zembylas, 2004). Many discourses about teaching suggest that teaching should be about students (Grumet, 1988; Hargreaves, 1998), and so teachers manage their emotions to serve the young people in the room. The work of building relationships with students intersects with rhetoric that suggests that teachers should always care for students first, thus rendering the teachers' role as one who prioritizes student needs.

I don't disagree that teachers should prioritize student needs, but this professional norm often positions teachers as under a moral imperative to enjoy their jobs because of their students, not because of money and certainly not because of their own emotions or comfort. I'm not arguing that students don't matter more than money, but sometimes it seems that teachers are stuck in a narrative where any ask or complaint on behalf of themselves can be equated with a lack of caring for their students.

In the Five Towns study, Lortie (1975) indeed found that teachers focused on *psychic rewards* in teaching, or rewards that come from building rapport with students over extrinsic rewards for teaching. Because teachers emphasized psychic rewards, teachers perceived their role as caring for students and diminishing any personal challenge or feeling that could potentially disrupt a student's experience in the classroom. Some teachers I have talked with describe this focus on caring for students as being "on," or hiding worries once one enters the school building for the day.

One interpretation then for why teachers hide emotions at work is to maintain a positive environment for students by prioritizing students' needs and emotions. Another interpretation put forth by Boler (1999) was that teachers control emotions to "preserve authority" over students (p. 139). Becoming emotional might be perceived as a loss of control. In both interpretations, teachers maintain a distance between themselves and students by attempting to control heavy emotions while at work with students.

Vignette 2: Tara

Tara, a 26-year veteran teacher of high school English, tells me about teaching the year that her mother died suddenly of a heart attack. She says she was "more private or closed off" that year, and she felt that she "was not sharing as much of [her]self in the classroom" because she was afraid of "losing it" or "crying uncontrollably." During this time, she had to "psyche [her]self up" for a particular chapter in *The House on Mango Street* called "Hairs." In this chapter, a daughter describes her mother's hair—"it smells like bread" (Cisneros, 1984, p. 7)—and describes the feeling of the warm spot left behind when her mother gets out of bed. Tara tells me she realized she would never feel the warm space left by her mother again. She explains that it "probably is a good thing that [she] was still in that first couple of weeks after her death actually, that sort of numbness" because she "could push [her]self through reading that chapter. She shares that she worried that she was "just gonna cry her whole way through that chapter" and she "had to do a lot of self-talk about how to do it." She describes how she "defaulted to business mode" and "focusing on the text."

Tara knew what it meant to hide something she was feeling. Like Jerry, she put students' needs above her own. Yet, Tara also felt guilty still because she knew grieving her mother's death strained her relationships with students even when she wasn't explicit with them about her grief. She wondered about what she should share with students and what she should hide.

Zembylas (2004) warned that when teachers "suppress certain emotions when communicating with colleagues and children" over extended periods of time, it "may be excessive and harmful" (p. 319). Similarly, Hochschild (1983) warned of the strains of repeated emotional labor because it requires "emotive dissonance, analogous to the principle of cognitive dissonance," and because "maintaining a difference between feeling and feigning over the long run leads to strain"

(p. 90). Hochschild (1983) explained that "when conditions estrange us from our face, they sometimes estrange us from feeling as well" (p. 90). Here, Hochschild suggested that the worker focuses on what feelings are being put on display or outwardly performed, perhaps on their face, and pointed to the danger present when the worker displays particular feelings by masking true feelings.

Indeed, Tara described to me how she would shift into teacher mode as soon as she entered the school building and begin sobbing as soon as she shut her car door to go home after school. Her effort to save face with her students and focus on the curriculum required energy as well as required her to suppress her feelings of grief. These feelings then spilled out when she left the school space for a private space in her car. When teachers cannot fully bring their stories into classroom spaces, where can they go?

Vignette 3: Mandie

A student uses the flyswatter to thwack the spot on the board that reads "metaphor."

My students are playing a review game. I read an example aloud, and they swat the matching literary element on the board. As the game proceeds, I hear one student complain that the example I've given could also be personification. Later, I overhear others grumble about the upcoming test to each other. They are overwhelmed because they also have a physics quiz the next day.

I feel like the students are needling me. This is the third time that I've gone through these examples today and I feel abnormally impatient. I think that I might yell.

I say, "I need to leave," and walk out. I burst into tears as soon as I cross the frame of the door. I tell myself to get it together, that I'm being ridiculous. I walk to the water fountain.

I'm still crying. My nasal passages swell.

I realize that I'm not going to stop crying, so I walk to my assistant principal's office. I apologize for my emotional state. I tell her that my uncle passed away and that I'm overwhelmed. I ask if she would go sit with my students for a few minutes while I gather myself. I'm not even —wasn't even —that close with my uncle. I feel guilty for getting upset.

Later I cross the threshold back into my classroom, red-faced and ashamed.

The truth is that I don't have a grieving experience like Jerry's or Tara's, or like the other teachers I've talked with as part of my study of teachers' experiences teaching while grieving. Teachers I've interviewed in my work have lost mothers, children, and students. Even though our experiences differ, I do understand something about the pressure we teachers might feel to maintain certain emotions in front of the classroom regardless of what might be going on in one's personal life.

I had wanted to be a teacher from an early age. I had started attending pre-school and was learning Spanish, so I brought home my worksheets, erased the answers, and forced my sister to complete them under my careful tutelage. I wore my mother's high heels for extra ethos.

Soon into my teaching career, though, I realized that there were many external expectations on teachers that compelled me to hide certain things from students, such as the death of my uncle and accompanying grief and exhaustion. My story is one of loss, too. I had wanted to be a teacher since I was 3 or 4 years old, but burnt out quickly, primarily because of hiding and because I was isolated and disconnected behind the closed door of my classroom.

When I talked with teachers such as Jerry and Tara, about their own challenges hiding emotions, their stories rang true to me. Their desire to put students' needs above their own resonated with me. Their feelings of shame and guilt when they weren't their best teaching selves reminded me of me.

The teachers in my project, including Jerry and Tara, have lost loved ones. But in our conversations, it became clear that losing a loved one also came with a loss of an idealized view of the teaching profession, because losing someone made them realize what parts of themselves, specifically their losses, didn't seem to belong inside walls of their classroom.

Our stories did not have to be the same, but sharing our stories with each other became a way for us to feel heard and understood.

Storying as Research

Scholars have argued that the reciprocal exchange of stories builds trusting spaces for storytellers, especially those who have been marginalized (e.g. Dutro & Bien; 2014; Pedro, 2017). Dutro and Bien (2014) argued for trauma-informed pedagogy that undertakes critical listening, where people listen to stories and then witness them, a process that requires mutual sharing. Part of witnessing, then, is for the listening party to engage in storying with the same vulnerability required of the storyteller (Brown, 2012; Pedro, 2017). These scholars speak to the power of storytelling as a two-way street: "the power of stories is not only in the telling, but also in having someone to hear their words" (Pedro, 2017, p. 105).

The opportunity to interview and listen to teachers opened up spaces for teachers to tell their stories and opened up space for me to tell my own story about teaching and heal some of the hurts I felt. My engagement with qualitative inquiry helped to validate some of the feelings I had when I left teaching, even years later. As a result, I feel less ashamed. I think of my own actions as less selfish and more symptomatic of schools as places where we are asked to check ourselves at the door.

The exchange of stories through research "*with* and *alongside* others" positioned my participants and me as part of a dialogic spiral in which researchers "meaningfully and openly collaborate with participants to learn about the complexities of human lives, the conditions under which people engage in teaching and learning, and the ways positions—e.g. as researcher vs. participant or teacher vs. student—can shift as relationships are fostered" (Kinloch & San Pedro, 2013, pp. 23–24). Indeed, sharing of myself was a key part of how I conceptualized conducting my project in humanizing ways. Sharing my story was in some ways the only way that I could be human with the teachers to whom I listened. I could not ask them to be vulnerable without being vulnerable myself.

When teachers feel they have to keep their classroom doors closed for fear that their feelings and emotions are not welcome within the walls of school, we as educational researchers and human beings lose opportunities to more fully understand teachers' experiences in school spaces. We lose opportunities to engage with others in the dialogic spiral and change ourselves. When stories remain silenced or are erased, we limit opportunities for moving forward.

The feelings of shame and guilt teachers feel about the challenges they face in teaching well during times of deep grieving happen because of two things: discourses about who teachers should be in classroom spaces and the silencing of teachers' stories. I suggest that teachers telling their stories as part of research is one possible space for listening and sharing that promotes healing and resilience. I also suggest that educational researchers must consider their ethical roles as listeners in research; researchers must seek to build relationships with participants built on trust and reciprocity of the sharing of experiences (Dutro & Bien, 2014).

Opening Doors

My study of teachers' grieving became a way for me to feel less alone because I was able to connect with teachers and because I realized that I'm not the only one who struggles with being "on" in the classroom, when being "on" means hiding something major that someone feels. The stories teachers and I shared with each other became part of a conversation with my burnt-out teacher self. The spaces between Jerry and Tara's story and mine became spaces of trust, transformation, and healing for me and, I hope, for my teacher friends.

As one example of how the teachers in my project built hope together, a few teachers, including Jerry, met to talk together after I concluded individual interviews. In that gathering, we brainstormed together about ways for building connections across teachers in buildings even when classroom doors are often closed from bell to bell. In his written reflection, Jerry wrote that he "liked being reminded of the shared struggle and responsibility that we have as teachers." The sense of community that we built as part of the study seemed to disrupt pervasive feelings of isolation.

Creating meaningful relationships ensures us that we are not alone as educators and builds our capacity for resilience, or for building each other up and through grief and loss.

References

Baker-Bell, A., Butler, T., & Johnson, L. (2017). The pain and the wounds: A call for critical race English education in the wake of racial violence. *English Education, 49*(2), 116–129, [Editorial]. Retrieved from http://www.ncte.org/journals/ee/issues/v49-2

Brown, C. B. (2012). *Daring greatly: How the courage to be vulnerable transforms the way we live, love, parent, and lead.* Gotham.

Boler, M. (1999). *Feeling Power.* Routledge.

Clandinin, D. J., & Connelly, F. M. (2001). *Narrative inquiry: Experience and story in qualitative research.* Jossey Bass.

Cisneros, S. (1984). *The house on Mango Street.* Random House.

Dutro, E., & Bien, A. C. (2014). Listening to the speaking wound: A trauma studies perspective on student positioning in schools. *American Educational Research Journal, 51*(1), 7–35. http://dx.doi.org/10.3102/0002831213503181

Grumet, M. (1988). *Bitter milk.* The University of Massachusetts Press.

Hargreaves, A. (1998). The emotional practice of teaching. *Teaching and Teacher Education, 14*(8), 835–854. doi: http://dx.doi.org/10.1016/S0742-051X(98)00025-0

Hochschild, A. R. (1983). *The managed heart: Commercialization of human feeling.* University of California Press.

Kinloch, V., & San Pedro, T. (2014). The space between listening and storying. In D. Paris & M. Winn (Eds.) *Humanizing research: Decolonizing qualitative inquiry with youth and communities.* Sage Publications.

Lortie, D. C. (1975). *Schoolteacher.* University of Chicago Press.

Pedro, S. (2017). "This stuff interests me:" Re-centering indigenous paradigms in colonizing school spaces. In Paris, D. & Alim, H.S. (Eds.), *Culturally sustaining pedagogies: Teaching and learning for justice in a changing world.* Teachers College Press.

Van Manen, M. (2001). *Researching lived experience.* Transcontinental Printing Inc.

Zembylas, M. (2004). Emotion metaphors and emotional labor in science teaching. *Science Education, 88*(3), 301–324. https://onlinelibrary.wiley.com/doi/abs/10.1002/sce.10116

13 Designing "Patterns" after Hurricane Sandy Uproots Structures

Josefa Pace

Ethnography does not separate language and culture and so the researcher is able to weave a rich pattern through "thick description" (Geertz, 1973). In addition, through ethnography, "we need to see social lives as containing many different kinds of meaningfulness, incarnate in different practices and forms, layered and overlapping, connecting us in complex ways" (Willis, 2000, p. 22). Having personally taught and lived in communities impacted by hurricanes and fires, the "supercomplexity" of these relationships considers how teachers and students engage with language and expression while also coping with catastrophe and loss.

This chapter will include narrative ethnography in the aftermath of Hurricane Sandy. The narrative illustrates my experience at a public college on Long Island in New York during my first semester as a full-time visiting professor during the Fall 2012 academic semester. These observations assisted with connections to theoretical understandings that were informed by lived experiences (Taylor, 2018a) and these observations reasserted the need to create transdisciplinary paths where academics approach grief and loss in their own lives and with their students. Considering Snyder's (1996) hope theory along with my ethnographic research, documenting the narratives of four Italian immigrant women (Pace, 2013) became inextricably connected to my experience during Hurricane Sandy; and these frameworks serve as models when understanding the sociolinguistic practices within communities and classrooms as teachers and students "work through" grief and loss (Neimeyer, 1999, p. 65).

Frameworks

In 2009, when I first learned of the term "supercomplexity," I was working with Dr. Denny Taylor, the Director of the International Center for Everybody's Child, at Hofstra University. Taylor conducted research in schools heavily impacted by trauma of war and natural devastation, e.g. Hurricane Katrina. In thinking about the challenging effects and considering existential philosophers like Greene (1995) and Calvino (1982), we enacted a transdisciplinary framework that could assist teachers, parents, students, and communities who dealt with catastrophe. We attended an ICSU (International Council for Science and International Social Science Council) Re-visioning Conference in 2010 in Paris. The delegates at Planet Under Pressure engaged in a global conversation. They explained:

> With the struggle for social and environmental sustainability, five areas were identified that could assist the issue: a. active engagement b. the participation of diverse social groups working together c. a focus on human well-being d. the development of political will e. ethical and principled global agreements. (Taylor, 2018a, p. 38)

We may consider this conversation a conceptual metaphor "when thinking about the combination of physical, biological and social sciences with humanities, including data from government, economic, and industrial sources and social media" (p. 32). Taylor (2018a) continued that the conversation provided transdisciplinary spaces that encourage situated engagement in research on human vulnerability and resiliency. In this way, resilience is described as "depending on the ecological dynamics as well as the organizational and institutional capacity to understand, manage, and respond to these dynamics" (ISSC & ICSU, 2010). These ideas were connected in non-linear ways, however, patterns emerged.

After completing my research and writing the narratives of the four women (Pace, 2013) during the hurricane, it was evident that the structure and ethos of classrooms and communities shifted. Change is an integral part of transdisciplinary research, and institutional frameworks should cross disciplinary paradigms (Taylor, 2018a). In addition, the message at ICSU coincided with Snyder's (1996) hope theory when considering avenues to fulfill goals. Students returning to school after homes were destroyed is an act of following pathways to hope (Sieben, 2018). Also, the strength shown by teachers, provides a space of familiarity and motivates students.

Hurricane Sandy: Narrative Ethnography

The following narrative section is excerpted from my dissertation for important context:

> On October 30, 2013 at 5:30 a.m., the morning after Hurricane Sandy, people trickled out from their homes with glances of fear and disbelief. Pumps were pushing water out of hoses linked to houses. Pumping would go on for days. Daylight came and went. The neighborhood was devastated.

The hurricane left us without power. Daylight arrived later and departed sooner. Sitting in one area of the house, with random sized candles as a source of light, was not a pastime. The resounding noise of generators beating was a regularity throughout the day. Policing at gas stations became a daily ritual as gas became scarce. Car lines were on the shoulders of main roads. People held red gasoline buckets. Many were turned away because the station did not have enough gas (Tyrell, 2012). And so, rations for gas began. The odd numbered license plates could get gas. I went in the evening and waited thirty minutes in line. I grew anxious approaching the gas pump. Eventually, no police would be in sight. Many people waited with the red gas buckets on a separate line. The station had a cash only policy.

When driving on main roads, stores were boarded up with wood or tape. Trees were completely uprooted on streets and some trees landed on houses. Select coffee shops were filled with communal wires. Power in the humane sense was leveled. It humbled us. It reminded us that we were fragile, and not invincible against mother nature. We all experienced an event that was relative to our lives.

We emotionally weathered a storm. We saw it. We felt it. We sympathized with the loss that some experienced. We saw the physical remnants left behind. We saw faces of those who will spend a significant amount of time picking up their pieces. I did not have power for eight days which was a modest outcome, as some lived in shelters since they would not be able to return to their homes. Now a week after the hurricane, they were predicting another storm. This time they said snow. There were still wires down with caution tape around them. My neighbor across the street had mounds of material–debris from his house covering the entire driveway.

It was also an election year. Despite the effects of the hurricane, spaces were set up to vote. After I voted, that night I returned to my house with a suitcase of work in the back seat of my car; it was my first semester teaching full-time at a state college, and I was completing my dissertation. As I was about to approach the doorway of my home, I was scared. I took out a flashlight that was in the car. I used the light as a guide when I walked from the car to the front door and into a dark, empty house. I strolled into silence with my red suitcase; entering complete darkness was unfamiliar and eerie. Sirens from down the street sounded once I was inside. I heard the siren when I tried to write in the afternoon. This afternoon there was a voice coming from the truck with the siren. The voice from the truck echoed.

There was food. At night, it was not the same siren—the night sirens continued to sound and no voices were heard. I found my way upstairs to my bed. I bundled myself in multiple layers of sweats and wrapped myself in a blanket. I thought it funny how involuntary habits formed. I was conditioned to reach for the light, but there was no light to turn off. The less time we stayed in my empty and unpowered house, the colder it became.

On November 8th, 2012, a nor'easter hit. I walked out of my office and could not find my car amongst the line of snow-covered cars in the parking lot. That day, I went to work early for supplied power, and after work, I roamed the parking lot with my suitcase. I had forgotten which car was mine because I was given a temporary rental since my car was taken by the flood. It looked like a winter wonderland. I drove home. A sign next to my neighbor's house read "*This Property is Condemned.*" No, it was not a Tennessee Williams's play. They had a mobile home next to their house with holiday lights hanging around it. This was not the only trailer on the block.

That night, at the kitchen table, my grandmother who grew up in occupied Italy during the WWII spoke of rations during the war. Meat was rationed during the war. She would be able to get one piece of meat every other Thursday. Her family would split the meat into three pieces. The pieces were not equal in size. Since there were three children in her family, her mother would split it among them. Her mother prioritized her children, and she would not have any (Pace, 2013, pp. 11–22).

Teachers as First Responders

During the Fall 2012 academic semester, New York was hit by Hurricane Sandy. "The federal government declared a public health emergency for New York in the aftermath" (Ricks, 2012). Throughout this time, I relied on close family for lodging. While dealing with these unexpected problems, strategizing how to organize the remaining five weeks of the semester was important so that students could complete their coursework. The campus was closed for almost a week. When classes resumed, I checked in with the students by having them share with me experiences of any personal loss as well as any concerns moving forward. They could respond orally or write me a note—as "grieving is an active process" (Neimeyer, 1999, p. 68). I wanted to gauge their mental and physical presence. On the first day back, a little more than half of the students returned. My students and I engaged in conversations about gas rations. Since I was teaching future teachers, we began class with an article written by Denny Taylor. This article exemplified teachers as first responders after catastrophic events and how schools change procedurally depending on the damage (Taylor, 2018b). This article's framework referred to the report on the aftermath of Hurricane Katrina as well as the ICEC philosophy (see Witte & Dail, Chapter 5, for more on Hurricane Katrina). This reading was not on the syllabus; however, it was relevant to include. Within my largest class, four students did not return to class after the storm. One student who lived in Long Beach,

NY, had significant property damage and asked for an incomplete. A central trait I try to instill in my students is adaptability (Snyder, 1996). By having the means to adapt to these events, the class was able to complete the semester, meeting the objectives of the course. Establishing structure and guidelines are essential when working with students but allowing for flexibility during catastrophe is critical when re-prioritizing goals to enable long-term success (Snyder, 1996).

Language Shifts

During Hurricane Sandy, sirens were used for multiple purposes. The image of the siren became a conceptual metaphor as it related to the context of the event. Sirens were heard as first responders were assisting those in need. Sirens were heard to distribute food. Some feared the sirens. In this sense, communication was more than understanding on the surface. These visuals placed emphasis on the absorption of an image through seeing and hearing it and feeling a connection (Damasio, 2010). Taylor (2018a) asserts that "language is embedded in human experience...language represents thoughts and feelings, and it is used to construct relationships" (p. 31). From a collective viewpoint, implementing frameworks of hope theory and acting as "facilitators of hope" (Sieben, 2018, p. 240), allowed for classroom practice and language to shift. Engaging students in dialogue supported their emotional and physical well-being and allowed for a multidisciplinary focus on life sustaining needs (Taylor, 2018a). After Hurricane Sandy, classroom goals were assessed so that students could complete the semester. Also, students were introduced to frameworks that could assist their teaching practices.

Conclusion

Writing the four women's stories (Pace, 2013) while also using writing as a mode of expression (Cixous, 1975) to understand the effects of Hurricane Sandy reasserts Noddings's (1991) claim that "stories invite us to come to know the world and our place in it" (p. 13). While the hurricane allowed for some warning, schools and homes were lost. It was in classrooms that a supportive space and "pathway" (Snyder, Rand, & Sigmon, 2002, p. 258) was offered so that students and myself could communicate and understand sensory and non-sensory experiences (Taylor, 2018a).

During Spring 2020, inviting stories and varying modalities within school structures reinforce the understanding of "supercomplexity" and transdisciplinary frameworks since most communities were impacted by the global pandemic. Throughout past and present crises, it is crucial to assess alternative learning environments when students are not physically in school. The learning environment is critical, and the constancy of attending school can provide students with security, especially when students' basic needs outside of schools are not always met (Taylor, 2018a). Attributes of patience and compassion should not appear as weaknesses when re-conceptualizing standards (Snyder et al., 2002). These characteristics are vital for all community partners as they come to interact with and support teachers and students during a period of unprecedented transition. Teachers and staff are immediate contacts when weathering storms. Their limits become tested, and lives are reconstructed personally and professionally (Neimeyer, 1999).

Within the past decade, it is apparent that teachers and educators are being called to have a greater role within schools and communities. When goals appear undetermined, implementing multiple frameworks can assist teachers, students, and communities to find pathways of hope and cope with natural disasters and ongoing crises (Snyder, 1996; ICSU & ISSU, 2010).

References

Calvino, I. (1982). *The uses of literature: Essays.* (W. Weaver, Trans.). Houghton Mifflin Harcourt.

Cixous, H. (1975). The laughing Medusa. In E. B. Freedman (Ed.), *The Essential Feminist Reader.* The Modern Library.

Damasio, A. (2010). *Self comes to mind: Constructing the conscious brain.* Pantheon Books.

Greene, M. (1995). *Releasing the imagination: Essays on education, the arts and social change.* Jossey-Bass.

Geertz, C. (1973). *The interpretation of cultures: Selected essays.* Basic Books.

ISSC and ICSU (2010). Earth System Science for Global Sustainability: The Grand Challenges Document. ISSC. Retrieved from https://science.science-mag.org/content/330/6006/916.full.pdf±html

Neimeyer, R. A. (1999). Narrative strategies in grief therapy. *Journal of Constructivist Psychology, 12*(1), 65–85. doi:. Retrieved from https://doi.org/10.1080/107205399266226

Noddings, N. (1991). Stories in dialogue: Caring and interpersonal reasoning. In C. Witherell & N. Noddings (Eds.), *Stories lives tell: Narrative and dialogue in education* (pp. 157–170.) Teachers College Press.

Pace, J. (2013). *Apri gli occhi e hai le cervello nel capo—Open your eyes and keep your brains in your head: Narrative Stories from Italian Immigrant Women—Pasqualina, Susan, Matilde, & Filomena* (Doctoral Dissertation).

Ricks, D. (2012, November 3). Health emergency declared. *Newsday: The Long Island Newspaper,* A22.

Sieben, N. (2018). *Writing hope strategies for writing success in secondary schools: A strengths-based approach to teach writing.* Brill/Sense Publishers.

Snyder, C. R. (1996). To hope, to lose, and hope again. *Journal of Personal and InterpersonalLoss, 1*(1),1–16.doi:.https://doi.org/10.1080/15325029608415455

Snyder, C. R., Rand, K. L., & Sigmon, D. R. (2002). Hope theory: A member of the positive psychology family. In C. R. Snyder & S. J. Lopez (Eds.), *Handbook of positive psychology* (pp. 257–276). Oxford University Press.

Taylor, D. (2018a). *From family literacy to earth system science: Denny Taylor's research on making the planet a child safe zone.* Garn Press.

Taylor, D. (2018b) Teachers as first responders in the aftermath of catastrophic events. Retrieved from https://static1.squarespace.com/static/5abc153cb1059858310b37e1/t/5b997a850e2e7257287d076f/1536785034949/Teachers+as+First+Responders+in+the+Aftermath+of+Catastrophic+Events.pdf

Tyrell, J. (2012, December 7). Concern over toll on children. *Newsday: The Long Island Newspaper,* A16.

Willis, P. (2000). *The ethnographic imagination.* Polity Press.

14 Grieving when Students Make the News

Two Teachers' Reflections

Stacia L. Long

The summer before starting my Ph.D., a former student was arrested for drug violations, evading arrest, and the kidnapping and sexual assault of multiple women. I learned of this through a colleague's social media post. I hadn't taught this student for three years or seen him in over a year, but I struggled with the idea that this engaging young person, a well-known student and athlete in our community, could have committed the crimes reported.

The reports didn't fit with my memory of the student in 10th grade English Language Arts (ELA): a boy who was quick to laugh and help out. Because I had moved away from my school community, I was unable to process this arrest with those who knew the student. I followed the story on the news and social media as I struggled to make sense of his actions and the portrayal of the school that I still considered my professional home.

After this experience, I became invested in exploring this kind of incident and how teachers make sense of it. I spoke with teachers at other schools and learned how common it is to need to make sense of how young adult students violate laws, at times perpetrating violent acts and sexual assaults. Like Dutro (2019), I wanted to better understand how news of a student's arrest for sexual violence "circulated in classrooms" and school communities (p. 21).

In this chapter, I relate narratives from Lora and Mike, two high school English teachers, who reflected on a sexual assault that took place in their school. They struggled to make sense of being faculty members at a school where a sex crime took place, in their personal responses to the incident and in the face of negative media coverage that painted their school in broad, harsh strokes. These sadly common experiences rarely include, in the broader narrative, insights into how teachers respond to the incidents and their effects, including community and media constructions of the school as dangerous and out of control. My interviews with Lora and Mike help illuminate how teachers engage with these situations and how their identities as teachers in their school are affected by the negativity surrounding the events.

Frameworks for Making Sense of Students' Arrest for Sexual Violence

Teachers experience complex emotions in the classroom (Liljestrom, Roulston, & deMarrais, 2007) through events like learning of a student's arrest for sexual assault and the attendant media coverage. Two strands of scholarship examine teachers confronted with such disconcerting news: (a) secondary trauma; and (b) hope, critical witnessing, and allyship.

Secondary Trauma

Maring and Koblinsky (2013) found that teachers were emotionally affected by the violence around their schools. Strong emotions, like those arising from learning about student violence, have "often been described as a private, psychological experience, as a painful event that an individual goes through but others cannot feel or fully understand" (Zembylas, 2008, p. 1). But traumatic events affect teachers and schools in communal ways. These responses emerge in response to a specific event and when incorporating attention to the event into instruction. These incidents can result in what Erikson (1976) calls *secondary* trauma, which Gill (2007) describes as "a blow to the social fabric of a community caused by inadequate response to an initial hazard event and/or inadequate responses to secondary hazards" such as media coverage "or public perceptions that inhibit timely community recovery and prolong stress and disruption" (p. 625). Secondary trauma can describe how a student's arrest for a violent act and attendant media coverage affect the school community and teachers' emotional responses.

Hope, Critical Witnessing, and Allyship

Snyder (2002; cf. Sieben, 2018) defines hope as "the perceived capability to derive pathways to desired goals, and motivate oneself via agency thinking to use those pathways" (p. 249). Sieben asserts that hope in this sense "provide[s] students [and teachers] with action steps and strategies for accomplishing goals that help balance systems of inequality" in ELA classrooms (pp. 3–4). To work toward hope, the teachers in this chapter engage in critical witnessing and allyship for and with their students.

Through their emotional responses, the teachers engaged in what Dutro (2019) calls *critical witnessing*. They advocated for their students and the school by critically analyzing deficit discourses surrounding them. These reflections produced opportunities to talk about trauma and the emotional impact of the news coverage of their school that led to attempts to change the image of their school.

This advocacy helped them serve as allies, who according to Shelton (2019) "take action and adopt values" that support students even when this work is "complex and even contradictory, because of various sociocultural factors and contextual power differentials that shape teachers' actions and agency to effect change" (p. 592). This definition also serves teachers seeking to support students through secondary trauma. Anzaldúa (2013) wrote that "becoming allies means helping each other heal" (p. 627). Although the teachers in this chapter may not have explicitly set out to ally with their students, they became allies in their respective approaches, changing deficit narratives about their school.

What Happened?

There are two high schools in University Town (all names of people and places are pseudonyms). Community conversation positions Town High School (THS) as more prestigious than River High School (RHS), which is perceived to be the stereotypical under-resourced school with attendance problems, inept faculty, drugs, theft, and violence. This reputation was amplified when reports of sexual violence that occurred at the school were published in the news two years prior.

The report shook RHS, the school district, and the larger town community when news broke that three male students had sexually assaulted a younger female student on campus during the school day. Community members, educators, and students were appalled that they found out three weeks after it was reported to school officials, and learned of it via the media rather than through school authorities. Teachers and students struggled with the negative perceptions of RHS that followed from the incident. The three male students were arrested and tried, news stories and social media commentators continued to discuss the event, the principal was fired, and the award-winning superintendent resigned.

Context

Mike self-identified as a White, cisgender, heterosexual male who had taught English and journalism for 12 years at RHS. Mike presented himself as unemotional and jaded, yet spoke persuasively about what he believes teachers can do. For instance, although he described himself as exhausted by the mandates imposed by high stakes accountability, they also galvanized him to stay in the field to counteract their adverse effects on students. Lora, a White cisgender, heterosexual woman had done her student teaching in Mike's department the semester that the sexual assault became news. Lora explained that her desire to support students through difficult experiences came from her mother, a teacher who modeled caring for students' emotional wellbeing.

Both teachers loved RHS and resisted the school's deficit perception, often based simply on the demographics of enrollment. Of 1490 students enrolled when news broke of the assault, 57% were Black, 25%

Hispanic, 14% White, and 3% Multi-racial; and 92% of students were on the free/reduced-price lunch plan (I am using demographic categories employed by the school). Lora and Mike described the students at RHS as engaged and community-oriented. Mike explained that students were "working their asses off" in that "they participate in everything." He argued that if someone worked at RHS "long enough, then you stop forming assumptions based on those things [negative labels ascribed to students], and you form them based on the actual conversations you have with the actual people." Both teachers hoped that the positive qualities they saw in the students would be reflected in the community conversations and news coverage.

Trauma of the News Coverage

Mike lamented that "it was very sad if you Google our school's name right now and do an image search. They're mug shots, right? And that's really sad and frustrating to me… and this is going to cloud people's judgment forever." Lora disdained "bad journalism" following the incident, because even in "an article about how RHS won the state track meet," news stories would say, "RHS, where the rape happened two years ago, won the state track meet," and news vans would arrive at the whiff of a crisis at RHS.

Mike was upset by these implications for his school's reputation as community members took up these negative reports. He described a woman who ran an affluent private school that actively perpetuated RHS's negative reputation whenever the event came up at townhalls or school events. Mike remembered how "she just really kept going at it, and at it, and at it. And I was like, 'you didn't even work in here.'" The news also affected the school's future enrollments. When Mike went to middle schools after the incident to garner interest in his journalism program, students said they wouldn't be attending RHS because their parents had made other arrangements. Even at RHS, there were "a lot of rumors that 'my mom's going to make me attend somewhere else in the next week.'" This negative perception infuriated Mike because, as he said, at THS, the other school, "it's the same….I know everyone that works there. It's the same shit, different school," minus the negative perceptions. Mike grieved the defamation from media coverage, implying that the reporting victimized the school community.

Lora also struggled with the difficult conversation about RHS in the media in her dual role as student and teacher. As a student teacher at RHS, she was expected "to help kids through these things that we [teachers] find it hard to navigate too. I think that's been my biggest challenge….It is really hard to lead some of these conversations when I'm still figuring it all out myself." At the university level, the members of her cohort, her field supervisor, and professors didn't understand how to talk with her about the incident. In both spaces and roles, Lora was expected to make sense of the news for others.

This obligation isolated her in the teacher education program, since she and RHS "became like the elephant in the room." Lora was asked if she wanted to leave RHS. She chose to stay despite the upheaval because this experience both "reaffirmed and made me question my beliefs...It reaffirmed the fact that I felt like I had a job to do here. But in terms of university support, I felt like nobody could relate because nobody had really dealt with it in their own teaching." This experience was a big part of her identity development as a teacher, so she felt she needed to remain at RHS where others understood her experience working toward the hope of changing the school's narrative.

Working with Students around the Sexual Assault

Processing the sexual assault and news coverage were not confined to Lora or Mike. Central to their narratives was how they talked about it with students as critical witnesses and allies. One of Mike's most vivid memories was when a student wrote him "the sweetest note" acknowledging Mike's stress and critical witnessing. He commented that "I'm not very emotional, but I teared up" when he received this note that illuminated the reciprocity between him and his students in allyship during this difficult time as they took care of one another.

Mike responded to students' emotional needs with an activity to help change the narrative around RHS. One day, when his students "looked tired and sad," Mike dropped what he had planned and told his students to "go do weird, goofy, happy crap and take photos" of themselves doing it. When they returned at the end of each class period, Mike instructed them to post the photos on social media with the school tagged "so that for maybe 24 hours when you browse through the internet, you won't see the three mugshots." Through this activity, Mike worked as an ally for hope as he supported students in changing the digital narrative about their school and its students.

Where Mike created space to move beyond the grief and trauma in seemingly small acts, Lora leaned in. Although she did rely on Mike for support, her mentor teacher wasn't present in the school during this period, so "it was up to [her] at that point to deal with it." Lora engaged in challenging conversations with her students about "sex, consent, that specific incident, of the rhetoric surrounding sex, of the rhetoric surrounding rape, of rape culture."

Lora talked about how in a new school two years later, she still consciously chose books about current events and justice issues that circulated in their community and consciousness. She explained, "I try to think about conversations that we need to have based on who my students are. And then like, 'oh! There's a book for that!'" Lora engaged in critical witnessing through crafting her instruction to respond to the incident in ways that valued students' abilities to engage in hard topics.

Attempts to Heal

Lora and Mike's stories reveal suffering in response to the sexual assault on campus and the secondary trauma of administrative mishandling and harmful media coverage. In interviews, they showed how these experiences shaped their professional lives as they moved toward healing. They did this work with their students even when hard, perhaps knowing that "the stakes for children, and for teachers, are higher in avoidance than they are in immersion" (Dutro, 2019, p. 11).

Although Lora is no longer at RHS, this event was a formative part of her story of becoming a teacher and shaped her professional identity. Lora reflected, "I am capable of taking on these kinds of problems and not cracking....I survived, and so it makes me feel good about when stuff happens now, well I already went through the hardest thing ever: my student teaching." She's drawn on the skills from her RHS experience while teaching in response to the deaths of students serving as a critical witness and ally to the students. Although she still feels the emotional weight of these tragedies, Lora explained that "I'm a lot better at realizing like, okay, these are the things that I need to do to take care of myself, so that I can take care of my students."

For Mike, healing from this event required letting go of the negative conversation about RHS. He explained that he doesn't "get sucked into" the gossip because "it's a negativity trap." For others in similar situations, he advised, "if there is such a traumatic thing [in the future], no matter what it causes for students or the adults or the community, calm down and listen more than talk." He also suggested that "you gotta make the kids happy," which is where he found meaning in allyship with students as they worked toward changing the narrative about RHS.

Conclusion

These teachers described emotional processing and multipurposed teaching: to make their own sense and help students through a difficult community event with literacy instruction. Although Mike and Lora remained in the community as teachers during the event and after, the experience was rife with secondary trauma stemming largely from the local news coverage of the event and administrative mishandling, updates on court proceedings, and the increased deficit narratives circulating about RHS. They shared their experiences in ways that demonstrate the need for and possibilities of responding to communal trauma with hope and allyship in their professional practice. "Caring and healing—as imperative foundations for literacy research and pedagogy—must be understood as part of the spaces, materials, and interactions of our work" (Garcia, 2018, p. 4).

The miasma of emotions in teaching has a strong impact on career decisions (Liljestrom et al., 2007). Though deeply rooted in the specific context of their community, Lora and Mike's stories demonstrate how there are complex emotions and secondary trauma in teaching that often go unacknowledged in research or school-based conversations. This oversight means that much of teachers' profoundly important experiences and identities may not be tended to, either in practice or in research. Teachers, like their students, need support when navigating incidents like those described by Lora and Mike.

References

Anzaldúa, G. E. (2013). Allies. In M. Adams, X. Zuniga, H. W. Hackman, C. R. Castañeda, & W. J. Blumfield (Eds.), *Readings for diversity and social justice: An anthology on racism, sexism, anti-Semitism, heterosexism, classism, and ableism* (3rd ed.). Routledge.

Dutro, E. (2019). *The vulnerable heart of literacy: Centering trauma as powerful pedagogy*. Teachers College Press.

Erikson, K. T. (1976). *Everything in its path: Destruction of community in the Buffalo Creek flood*. Simon and Schuster.

Garcia, A. (2018, December). *More than taking care: Literacies research within legacies of harm*. Scholars Speak Out: Journal of Language and Literacy Education. http://jolle.coe.uga.edu/wp-content/uploads/2018/12/SSO_December2018_Garcia.pdf

Gill, D. A. (2007). Secondary trauma or secondary disaster? Insights from Hurricane Katrina. *Sociological Spectrum, 27*(6), 613–632. doi: https://doi.org/10.1080/02732170701574941

Liljestrom, A., Roulston, K., & deMarrais, K. (2007). "There's no place for feeling like this in the workplace": Women teachers' anger in school settings. In P. Schutz, & R. Pekrun (Eds.), *Emotion in education* (pp. 267–284). Academic Press.

Maring, E. F., & Koblinsky, S. A. (2013). Teachers' challenges, strategies, and support needs in schools affected by community violence: A qualitative study. *Journal of School Health, 83*(6), 379–388. doi: https://doi.org/10.1111/josh.1204

Shelton, S. A. (2019). 'When I do "bad stuff," I make the most difference': Exploring doubt, demoralization, and contradictions in LGBTQIA + ally work. *International Journal of Qualitative Studies in Education, 32*(6), 591–605. doi: https://doi.org/10.1080/09518398.2019.1609117

Sieben, N. (2018). *Writing hope strategies for writing success in secondary schools: A strengths-based approach to teaching writing*. Brill | Sense Publishers.

Snyder, C. R. (2002). Hope theories: Rainbows in the mind. *Psychological Inquiry, 13*(4), 249–275. https://www.jstor.org/stable/1448867

Zembylas, M. (2008). Trauma, justice and the politics of emotion: The violence of sentimentality in education. *Discourse: Studies in the Cultural Politics of Education, 29*(1), 1–17. doi: https://doi.org/10.1080/01596300701801278

15 When a Teacher Lost a Student
A Narrative Pathway through Grief

Nick Thompson

At 8:20 AM, I gave a final exam to my high school seniors. By 8:45 AM, if any doctors had been present, they would have pronounced one of my students dead. My student, Ahmad, a pseudonym, had a congenital cardiac condition, and that was the day that his heart arrested. I have told this story many times in varying detail: first in a panic to the school nurse and administrators whom I begged to help me; next, to my gathering colleagues who came to comfort me; next, to the police; later, to my family; at their request, to the boy's parents; and almost a year later, I wrote a narrative of the memories from that day for myself. None of those retellings, even the bits that flash through my head as I type this, fully capture the experience, but the process of repeatedly narrating my experience has helped me heal (see Wolf-Prusan, Chapter 16, for more student death).

Storytelling has been at the core of my grieving process from the start. Each time, I revisited my pain, solidified some aspects of the experience, and questioned how I could have acted differently. Months after Ahmad's death, I entered a doctoral program, and I told the story to new colleagues. Even now, a few years past, I tell the story to student teachers whom I supervise and their mentors. Continuing to tell my story helps me to thrive despite residual pain, and I hope that it invites others to tell their stories of grief, so that they too may find narrative as a pathway through pain.

When a student dies, the school community goes into crisis. I have not met another teacher who has had a student die in their classroom. Likewise, most teachers I meet have dealt with the passing of a student. It is tragically normal. When a student dies, a life is cut short, and all the hope that is poured into them ceases to exist. The academy has written about pathways through grief for the students, but there is very little attention paid to teachers.

In this chapter, I will present my narrative journey through the grief. I wrote a personal narrative of the event with no audience in mind, I asked a colleague to interview me, so I could create a transcript of my oral telling, and I began using my story to complete coursework and make meaning of what I was studying. Using sociocultural theory and hope theory, I will discuss the needs, norms, and tensions that my stories revealed about my path towards healing. Finally, I will briefly discuss how the academy has attended to teachers' grief.

Hope Theory, Sociocultural Theory, and Narrative

Hope theory and sociocultural theory both come from the field of psychology. Snyder, Rand, and Sigmon (2018) argued that hope is made of goals, pathways, and agency: "Simply put, hopeful thought reflects the belief that one can find pathways to desired goals and become motivated to use those pathways" (p. 27). Sociocultural theorists argue that the development of the mind is goal-oriented, volitional, and socially situated (Vygotsky, 1987; Wertsch, 1991). Agency, goal orientation, and development are shared foci of the two theories of the mind. The concept of pathways from hope theory adds a sense of directionality to developmental focus of sociocultural theory. Sociocultural theory is useful for looking at a person's thinking, not as the act of an independent mind, but one that is situated historically, culturally, and socially.

Grief, as seen through hope theory and sociocultural theory, then, is a developmental process of how people create and act out pathways towards making meaning of their lives in the aftermath of the death. Bakhtin (1990) wrote that "It is only with the other that I have the possibility of experiencing the joy of meeting and abiding with him, the sorrow of parting and the grief of bereavement" (p. 105). Grief allows us to reflect on the nature of mortality and our place in the world. Neimeyer, Klass, and Dennis (2014) argued that people's ability to make meaning can have a significant impact on their ability to adapt to a loss, and the inability to do so can hinder them. They also argued that socialized narration is the tool we use to make meaning when we are "shaken by 'seismic' life events such as the death" (p. 489).

Watching Ahmad die shook me. Using a theory of hope to analyze my experience convinced me that narrative was my essential pathway through grief. Snyder, Rand, and Sigmon (2018) explained that agency in hope thinking "takes on special significance when people encounter impediments" (p. 28). My narratives revealed a discomfort with normalized grieving, and that rejection was an impediment to finding a pathway through grief. As an English teacher, I was comfortable with different genres, purposes, and audiences of storytelling, and that comfort gave me agency to use narrative as a pathway towards making meaning of my life in the wake of Ahmad's death.

Language is not solely the tool of English majors any more than observation belongs only to scientists. Language represents meaning and thought (Vygotsky, 1987; Wertsch, 1991), and people understand themselves through narrative (Bruner, 1990). Stories exhibit at least two functions of cognition: prior understandings and new meaning construction. Bruner (1986) claimed that narrative is one of two core human acts of making meaning, namely, "arguments convince one of their truth, stories of their lifelikeness" (p. 11). Bereavement is not a loss of truth, but a jarring reminder that life is ephemeral, and we can breathe life back into ourselves through narrative.

My role as a teacher and my disconnect from normal grieving practices were barriers to my healing, so I had to create an alternate pathway (Snyder, 2000). Language reveals individual thinking and shows social norms about "common sense" behavior and thinking (Bruner, 1990). Analyzing my stories helped me to better understand the nature of the friction between me and my community. My choice to narrate my grief was a turning point because I found a pathway that fit my need to tell my story outside of the grieving community. As Snyder (2000) has observed, a wave of positive thinking accompanied overcoming my barriers to healing.

Tensions in Grief

I prefer individual reflection to communal bereavement in times of grief. After the emergency phase of Ahmad's death, the other teachers, students, and staff gathered, and they offered each other and me support. I frequently created ways to be alone by ignoring phone calls, hiding myself in my classroom, and avoiding communal grief activities like the funeral. Since the deceased was a member of my school community, as a teacher, I could not escape completely.

In the wake of Ahmad's death, I also felt that I was expected to lead my students through grief, but I was unequipped to find my own pathway through grief, much less lead others in finding theirs. My role as caretaker impeded my ability to take care of myself, and that made me anxious (see Dunn, Chapter 12, for more on teachers, anxiety, and grief). My anxiety was compounded by the tensions between my personal grief practices and those of my community.

Solitary vs. Communal Grieving

Growing up, I learned to grieve through social and cultural activities. I attended funerals—typically framed by Christianity—I visited grieving neighbors with my mother who brought casseroles, and I listened as people shared stories of their loss, etc. Neimeyer (1999) described the narratives that people create while dealing with bereavement as "a complex process of adaptation to a changed reality, a process that is at the same time immensely personal, intricately relational, and inevitably cultural" (p. 66). The older I got, the more I retreated inwards during bereavement, and I only participated in group grieving as a duty.

My identity as an atheist and the close tie of religion to mourning was also part of my disconnect from my community. It is sometimes difficult to admit my atheism because some people question my morals. Most people in America identify as religious: 70.6% Christian and 5.9% Other (Jewish, Muslim, Hindu, Buddhist, etc.). While 22% of people identify as being unaffiliated with a particular religion, only about 3% of Americans identify as Atheist (Pew Research Center, 2019). I do not have negative emotions towards religions or religious people, but the infusion of religion in acts of mourning added to my isolation.

In my oral telling of the story during the interview, I said this—the dashes represent pauses in my speech:

> I deal with death by—by removing myself from anything and everything connected with it. Also, I know that I get very annoyed at the way that other people deal with death. I don't—I don't like— what I don't like—I don't like when people get together. I don't like hearing them cry over what they experience and share fun stories remembering the deceased's life. I don't like religious representations of death. I don't like that the tropes: "he's in a better place," or "he lived a good life," or—I don't like the things that seem to go along with grieving.

People left me alone when I attended gatherings, helped with memorials, or participated in other acts of communal grieving. However, when I behaved in ways that were resistant to typical grieving, the community became concerned. Since I was in the room when Ahmad died, people reached out to me often. Snyder (1996) pointed out that it is normal for goal blockages to result in negative feelings. The difference between those who have hope and those who lack it is their willingness and ability to construct alternative paths (Snyder, 2000). I was caught between wanting to be left alone which garnered unwelcome attention or grieving communally, and I needed an alternative pathway.

The above text from my oral telling shows that my sadness and anxiety grew from normal grieving practices, and I couldn't make progress towards healing. Snyder, Rand, and Sigmon (2018) wrote that they and others found that a lack of progress towards goals causes negative emotions and reduces well-being. My avoidance behaviors were failed attempts at making meaning of my loss and caused pain. There was also a tension between my role as a caretaker that is inherent in being a teacher and my need to take care of myself.

Self-care vs. Caretaker

The expertise that put me in charge of my classrooms came from my teaching experience and training. Snyder (2000) wrote that "goal-directed thinking almost inevitably arises in the context of other people who teach hope" (p. 523). I knew how to push my students towards learning goals, but not grief-management goals. I often felt unprepared to cope with my own grief while being responsible for helping others.

The first narrative genre that I used to explore my grief was creative nonfiction. I wrote about an interaction that I had with a student as we sat in a room next to the one where Ahmad was getting emergency medical attention:

"You weren't mean. Don't worry. You're a sweet girl, and you didn't do anything wrong," I said, and I thought about how I had failed to hide my annoyance with him.

Students and teachers often conflicted with Ahmad. Before the EMTs (emergency medical technician) even took him from my classroom, guilt began to plague us. I shared my students' regret but felt forced to hide it in order to take care of them, closing down a pathway of shared experience. Had it not been for my role as a caretaker, I might have seen and pursued our shared pain. Looking at my three narrative accounts revealed that I behaved like this repeatedly.

In my attempt to be dutiful in taking care of my students, I felt forced to ignore my own grieving. If constructing pathways is integral to hope thought as Snyder, Rand, and Sigmon (2018) argued, then focusing on students' needs can be an impediment to creating pathways because it is distracting from one's own needs. A lack of pathways also pushes against agency. What is required, according to Snyder (2000) is resiliency. I sought audiences outside of the school community which helped me through some of my grief while allowing me to avoid the community who shared my bereavement.

A year later, I was a doctoral student and no longer in a caretaker role. I first made meaning of Ahmad's death through creative nonfiction. I focused on my grief needs though writing. Hope theorists argue that finding alternative pathways when presented with impediments is an important behavior for hopeful thinking (Snyder 2000; Snyder et al., 2018). Stories of grieving are often shared, so focusing on others can be productive, but the student-teacher relationship is not inherently reciprocal in that the burden of care is clearly (and correctly) placed on the teacher.

A Narrative Pathway

I was Ahmad's teacher. It was my duty to help him move forward in his life, but I was helpless in the moment of his death. I had grieved for students before, but this time was amplified by witnessing and responding to his emergency.

Finding a pathway through grief requires understanding the new world and one's place in it. That kind of thinking requires reflection, and a community's shared experience can be an integral part to gaining perspective of one's self. Bakhtin called the ability to see the individual and their environment as one a *transgredient perspective*. He outlined two main limitations to gaining a transgredient perspective: first, is that a person cannot see themselves wholly in context; second, people are never in a finished state of being. We need the perspective of others because they more readily see our context and development. The tensions that I felt in grief isolated me when I needed others' perspective.

Language is socially situated (Vygotsky, 1987) as it is learned from others and it is reactive since it is constructed in anticipation of an audience (Bakhtin, 1986) even when that audience is one's self. Storytelling became my pathway through grief when I felt isolated. Narrative can "guide one's experience of current happenings, as well as one's understanding of what may happen" (Snyder, 2000, p. 2768). It helped to provide me with a modicum of a transgredient perspective. The passage of time between each telling allowed me to see my experience in context through hindsight, so I saw my past-self developing and gained hope for my future-self on that trajectory.

Writing and re-reading my creative nonfiction piece helped me identify negative language and thinking to identify barriers (Snyder, 2000). I moved past them by changing the way I told the story. The interview gave me a transcript of my oral storytelling. I considered the elements and style of my story, and it gave me enough separation from my feelings that I could see my role in the events, and I became more hopeful. Incorporating my story into my academic writing created a meaning-making relationship between new, difficult concepts and the old bereavement wounds.

By looking across my different narrative genre pieces, I saw consistencies, inconsistencies, and development of meaning-making. The consistencies suggested deeply held beliefs like my belief that I could not have changed the outcome of the medical emergency. Inconsistencies between the narratives suggested tensions that I had not addressed. For example, I was inconsistent about my level of guilt about causing Ahmad's heart attack, and I oscillated between feeling culpable and absolved. Apart from guilt, my other emotions progressed. Earlier tellings were stunted, but the interview added reflection that was absent from my written accounts. I was forging a pathway towards the "reaffirmation, repair, or replacement of the basic plot and theme" of my story as a teacher (Neimeyer et al., 2014, p. 489).

Attention from the Academy

When I began considering my experience as a possible research topic, I conducted a literature review of research about educators' experience with grief from the death of students.

Of the 370 results that I got from my initial search, only 14 abstracts fit my criteria. This suggests a lack of attention from the academy about teachers' experiences with grieving about students' deaths. There is a significant body of research examining the way that teachers can facilitate students' experiences with grief. However, very little work has examined teachers' experiences. Of the 14 articles, only four dealt directly with educators' bereavement of a student. It is worthwhile for the field to consider the effect and experience of teachers in the event of a student death, so that a purposeful conversation can build towards an understanding of how schools can take care of caretakers during times of grief.

References

Bakhtin, M. (1986). The problem of speech genres. In C. Emerson & M. Holquist (Eds.) & V. McGee (Trans.), *Speech genres and other late essays*. University of Texas Press.

Bruner, J. S. (1986). *Actual minds, possible worlds*. Harvard University Press.

Bruner, J. S. (1990). *Acts of meaning*. Harvard University Press.

Neimeyer, R. A. (1999). Narrative strategies in grief therapy. *Journal of Constructivist Psychology*, *12*(1), 65–85. doi: https://doi.org/10.1080/107205399266226

Neimeyer, R. A., Klass, D., & Dennis, M. R. (2014). A social constructionist account of grief: Loss and the narration of meaning. *Death Studies*, *38*(8), 485–498. https://www.tandfonline.com/doi/abs/10.1080/07481187.2014.913454?journalCode=udst20

Pew Research Center. (2019). *Religious Landscape Study*. https://www.pewforum.org/religious-landscape-study

Snyder (1996). To hope, to lose, and hope again. *Journal of Personal and Interpersonal Loss*, *1*(1), 1–16. doi: https://doi.org/10.1080/15325029608415455

Snyder, C. R. (2000). *Handbook of hope: Theory, measures, & applications [Kindle book]*. Academic Press.

Snyder, C. R., Rand, K. L., & Sigmon, D. R. (2018). Hope theory: A member of the positive psychology family. In M. W. Gallagher & S. J. Lopez (Eds.), *The Oxford handbook of hope* (pp. 27–44). Oxford University Press.

Vygotsky, L. S. (1934/1987). *Thinking and speech*. In R Rieber & (Ed.), N. Minick (Trans.), *Collected works* (Vol. 1, 39–285). Plenum.

Wertsch, J. (1991). *Voices of the mind a sociocultural approach to mediated action*. Harvard University Press.

16 Grief as the Pathway to Hope and Hope as the Pathway through Grief in the Teaching Profession

Leora Wolf-Prusan

In 2010, I sat in silence across from two high school teachers in Oakland, California, grappling with the news of another student death (see Thompson, Chapter 15, for more on student death). Behind us, the faces of students who had died in the last couple of years muraled the corridor walls. We were exhausted, at the brink of burnout, fatigued by colleague turnover, feeling under resourced and deeply unseen. With our commitment to the profession already tenuous, the question emerged: what happens to educators' already complicated access to hope when a student is killed, and how might the experience of a violent student death impact educators' experience of the teaching profession?

Death has the powerful capacity to be transformative and, in some ways, reformative (Gillies & Neimeyer, 2006), and violent death often causes us to reassess our purposes, senses of self, and worldviews (Armour, 2002; Bailey, Hannays-King, Clarke, Lester, & Velasco, 2013), leading the griever to integrate the death experience into new ways of seeing themselves and the world (Ayers, 2015). Drawing from a larger mixed-methods study (Wolf-Prusan, 2014) that examined the factors that contribute to educator coping and resilience in the event of student violent death, this chapter explores the grief and hope experiences of public high school teachers, all of whom self-identified as having experienced death of at least one student due to off-campus-gang-related gun violence (see Dunn, Chapter 12, for more on students and violence).

In an era in which more education settings are adopting trauma-informed and healing-centered approaches to teaching and learning (Ginwright, 2018), the positive student-teacher relationship has re-emerged as a primary protective factor for student and school resilience (Hughes, Cavell, & Wilson, 2001; Jennings, & Greenberg, 2009; Klem et al., 2005), a student's sense of belonging at school and connectedness (Jose, Ryan, & Pryor, 2012; Gehlbach et al., 2016), and is one of three foundational elements to successful student learning outcomes (Hall & Souers, 2019). If the educator-student relationship is a primary factor for students' success and resilience, what happens to the educator when another person in the relationship—the student—dies?

For many educators working in school contexts that demand educators grapple with the potential of their students dying due to gun violence, hope becomes a tool to intervene fatalism, passivity, or the general sense that nothing will change and their students' lifespan is predetermined. Nolan and Stitzlein (2011) define hope as a way of living tied to specific contexts that evoke reflection and action in effort to navigate the realities of a particular condition. In this case, school cultures that experience student violent death. The hope that we and other educators have to take on is neither escapist ("nothing will happen to me or my students") nor rooted in saviorism ("I can save these students and rescue them"), both of which are steeped our own racism and classism. Instead, hope is necessary not as a pathway to get over something, but, instead, a pathway for educators to go in. "Griefed" hope requires us to reflect, connect, and become grounded in the reality that because of social determinants of violence, students will be killed ("pragmatic hope" in Nolan and Stitzlen's terms), death is chaotic and difficult, and student-grief is unique, disenfranchised, and an unacknowledged part of the teaching practice (Rowling, 1995; Doka, 1989, 2002).

Ginwright (2016) identifies hope as a central healing ingredient for educators working in schools embedded in community violence; grief provokes educators to contend with the social structures, policies, and systems that create the probability of their predominantly students of color dying violently. An active, contemplative, and radical practice, hope allows educators to confront their grief, the conditions that created their grief, and invites educators to re-engage with their profession with renewed meaning and purpose. Hope isn't something we use to get out of grief; hope is the very practice we wrestle with to confront the despair, face our complicity, commit to change, and access fuel to sustain in the profession (Nolan & Stitzlein, 2011). Hope, in the context of student death and grief, can transform the educator in five ways: relying, returning, reforming, reimagining, and redefining.

Relying on Students for Vicarious Hope and Healing

Educators access hope and then healing through inspiration and support from current students. Three teachers described their current students as motivators for helping them after a student's death; as one teacher explained, if students could imagine other possibilities beyond death, she could too. After feeling out of control and strained after the death of her student, Jocelyn found hope in her current students' work: by investing in the surviving students' learning, the despair from student loss decentered and the focusing on her present students re-centered her focus and commitment to teaching. For Jocelyn, it was her students who supported her to proceed through her grief: "As an adult, I don't like to lean on kids for my support," she explained, "but oddly, sometimes when they would come to me and want to talk about it, sometimes that was helpful for me." Joanna relied on her students for vicarious regulation. Educators who previously saw themselves as the dominant member in the student-teacher relationship found that grief reoriented the power dynamics in the relationship: the students become the agents of hope for their teachers.

Returning to the Original Why?

After a student's homicide, educators self-reported changes in how they related to their students and in their approaches to teaching: they shifted from focusing on standards and achievement to social emotional competencies in order to build relationships with their students. In reflecting on the effects of a violent death of a student, teachers found themselves self-modifying to become more relational in their interactions with current students, returning to the original "why" they originally entered teaching.

Three teachers spoke directly about shifting from being achievement focused as teaching professionals (i.e., with an emphasis on standardized tests, academic performance, etc.) to becoming socio-emotionally focused. At the time of the interview, Bill had experienced over 20 student gang gun-related deaths and while stressed and burned out from chaotic school conditions, he shared that his students' deaths reminded him of why he had entered the teaching profession in the first place: relationships. Describing the impact of his students' death, Bill shared that each death reminded him that:

> I didn't become a teacher to teach people how to put a period at the end of a sentence or what a noun is...I became a teacher to make a difference in people's lives on a deeper level. The more I invest in standards and curricula and agendas and readings, the more I will burn out...[when my student died] I remembered that it's about the human connection.

While it may not be the only event that can resurface hope for teachers, a student death can and often re-humanizes the educator-student relationship. Grief after violent student death can evoke a return to their pre-burned-out selves, evoking inspiration and a re-hoping.

Reforming Pedagogical Practice

When asked how experiencing the grief from student violent death impacted their approach to teaching, nine out of sixteen teachers said their relationships with their current students changed, becoming more caring for students they perceived as belonging to or were affiliated with gangs. When discussing the impact of how one of his student's deaths impacted his teaching, Josef began to cry. "I'm a lot nicer to them," he sighed. "I'm a lot nicer to them, because it's so fleeting. It takes so little time, like the next day [a student is] gone. And I can't control that. The only thing I can control is how they feel here." Here, hope and grief couple and reform Josef's pedagogical practice from punitive, assumptive, and detached to empathetic. "That's the biggest change between then [before his first student was killed] and now," he further explained.

> Back then I would call out a stupid gang member and say, 'Get your stupid stuff, and blah blah blah.' But you know what that did? For the most part, they'd stop coming. That's all it did. It pushed them away. I just reinforced what they already felt. And now I don't do that anymore.

Similarly, when Valentino's student was shot, he found himself approaching current students with more compassion and understanding. "You just realize how much you really want to make every moment count in the classroom. Even if it's not teaching, it can be just a conversation, the most important part of teaching is just listening to the student because they have so much to say," he reflected. Student death can reform a teacher's way of living, altering habits of hopelessness to hopefulness.

Reimagining the Student as Whole

Attending students' funerals and memorials in the aftermath of a student death can evoke hope in teachers, broadening their understanding of the context of current and future students, which in turn broadened their ability to envision possibilities for their students beyond violence and grief. Teachers cited attending memorials or funerals for students as a significant catalyst in adopting socio-emotional competencies in their teaching practices. Through those events, they were exposed to the deceased students' lives beyond the classroom walls. Seven out of the 16 teachers from different school sites described a change after attending funerals and memorials in how they understood their students and the everyday realities of students' lives. Suddenly, teachers became intimately connected to their students' family, friends, and community.

After his student's funeral, Bill shared:

> I could see people's reactions to [the killed student] and how much he meant to them. Could just see how much love there was there for him, you know...So you know seeing that reality...I guess it changed my worldview of the deep impact people can have on each other, even though they're not really aware of it...Some of his buddies, his gang-banger buddies from the street, they were just bawling. They just loved him so much.

Bill's colleague Jack had a similar experience after this student's funeral: "It really let me see under the surface of students. There are people that care about them, there are people that love them. They've had a background." Bill and Jack were exposed to who students were beyond what they knew of them in the context of the school and the classrooms, often the first time they internalized the lives of their students outside of the classroom border.

Attending funerals and memorials invites educators to understand their students' worlds beyond the classroom and the preconceptions who they thought their students were. The possibility that students' lives are multidimensional, educators expand their understanding of students: grief widens educators' paradigms, widening their hope principles and practice.

Redefining the Teacher as a Collective Hope Leader

In the aftermath of student violent death, educators often redefined their role conceptualization during and after violent student deaths. When teachers who previously may not have seen themselves as school site leaders, or community leaders, stepped into roles and created healing experiences that served not only themselves as individuals but also the collective, they began exhibiting collective hope leadership. They became more attuned to the needs of other community members, led the school community in response, healing, and often became agents of change in ways previously unactuated.

Teachers' new and now heightened awareness of the contexts of their students' lives and the realities of community violence influenced them to redefine their approach to teaching. Steve, for example, offered his experience helping his school navigate student violent death aftermath. "Ultimately it comes down to having a leader who understands staff and student needs. You need to have a leader who will step forward and step up and serve as a liaison," he explained. "I've done that role—the liaison between the teachers, administration, and the students. A clearinghouse so to speak...You need someone to be a clearinghouse. You need a way to get through the grief." Steve, a classroom teacher, became that clearinghouse not only for his own grief navigation but also for the whole school's healing. He had an active role in one of his student's funerals at the request of his principal: "[My student's] execution resulted in me having a very different place in that community." His leadership in arranging and leading portions of the service not only helped his own process but also led him to subsequently take on new leadership roles. After one funeral, the retaliating gang asked to meet with him. At Steve's former school, where he had experienced three student homicides, he and the student leadership created altars, wrote plays about community violence, and much more. Through those conversations and the collective act of creating a memorial space, he and his community were able "to think about it, talk about it, cry about it, express the grief about it.…I think what has to happen is that it needs to be marked somehow. It needs to be memorialized. It cannot be glossed over." Memorializing became a collective act and one that redefined Steve's role from classroom teacher to community leader.

Teachers became collective hope leaders through activism (e.g., teachers advocating for community health and against gun violence). Teachers became collective hope leaders when they became school site grief peer supporters (e.g., starting teacher led grief circles and organizing resources for teachers' mental health and healing). Teachers became collective hope leaders when they stewarded funerals, commemoration and memorialization (e.g., working with the school community to recognize the students' death through a mural, planting ceremony, *velario*, or other ceremonies). By redefining their roles for their own healing purposes (in contrast to a district or other actor imposing teacher role definition), teachers accessed a sense of control, contribution, connection, and hope.

Closing

Student death demands educators to make meaning of the context of their own lives, the lives of their students, and the context and conditions of their school community. The grief involved therein demands that educators transform, to challenge and contend with their pedagogical practice. Hope is often positioned a pathway for meaning making and grief healing; here, it is that *and* the reverse: educators' experience of grief following a student violent death becomes the gateway for tending to their hope in their professional and personal commitment to the practice. Through five transformation patterns; relying, returning, reforming, reimagining, and redefining, student violent death can deeply impact the student-teacher and the teacher-self relationship. Bill, Steve, and Diana shared that they were able to return to their original sense of professional purpose, regenerate, and become even more committed to the practice. Jack, Jocelyn, and Adam reformed their approach to the teaching practice, and Steve redefined his role from classroom teacher to school site leader and community activist.

The voiced grief narratives, in this study, raise these questions and more: How might we get to a place where teachers don't have to experience a violent student death to remember the very reason they entered the profession in the first place—the student? How might we cultivate access to meaningful leadership for teachers that doesn't need to emerge from traumatic loss? And, how might we create school systems and conditions that cultivate teachers to see the whole human behind the student without attending a funeral?

The conditions that generate students' violent, gun-related deaths are not vacuous. These conditions require individual, communal, and social challenge to unjust contexts. Grief can transform the educator, thrusting them into new and, sometimes, old ways of being, thinking, believing, and belonging in their profession and practice. Hope, when meaningful, grounded, and rooted in facing reality, helps us as educators to continue through and against such conditions of our lives and the lives of our students.

References

Armour, M. P. (2006). Meaning Making for Survivors of Violent Death. *Violent Death*, 101–121.

Ayers, R. (2015). *An empty seat in class: Teaching and learning after the death of a student*. Teachers College Press.

Bailey, A., Hannays-King, C., Clarke, J., Lester, E., & Velasco, D. (2013). Black mothers' cognitive process of finding meaning and building resilience after loss of a child to gun violence. *British Journal of Social Work, 43*(2), 336–354.

Doka, K. (1989). *Disenfranchised grief: Recognizing hidden sorrow*. Lexington Press.

Doka, K. (2002). Disenfranchised grief. In Kenneth J. Doka (Ed.), *Living with grief: Loss in later life* (pp. 159–168). The Hospice Foundation of America.

Gehlbach, H., Brinkworth, M. E., King, A. M., Hsu, L. M., McIntyre, J., & Rogers, T. (2016). Creating birds of similar feathers: Leveraging similarity to improve teacher-student relationships and academic achievement. *Journal of Educational Psychology, 108*(3), 342.

Gillies, J., & Neimeyer, R. A. (2006). Loss, grief, and the search for significance: Toward a model of meaning reconstruction in bereavement. *Journal of Constructivist Psychology, 19*(1), 31–65. http://dx.doi.org/doi:10.1080/10720530500311182

Ginwright, S. A. (2016). *Hope and healing in urban education: How urban activists and teachers are reclaiming matters of the heart*. Routledge.

Ginwright, S. (2018). The future of healing: Shifting from trauma informed care to healing centered engagement. Occasional Paper. Retrieved from http://www.shawnginwright.com/shawns-blog/the-future-of-healing-shifting-from-trauma-informed-care-to-healing-centered-engagement-1

Hughes, J. N., Cavell, T. A., & Wilson, V. (2001). Further support for the developmental significance of the quality of the teacher-student relationship. *Journal of School Psychology, 39*(4), 289–301.

Jennings, P. A., & Greenberg, M. T. (2009). The prosocial classroom: Teacher social and emotional competence in relation to student and classroom outcomes. *Review of Educational Research, 79*(1), 491–525.

Jose, P. E., Ryan, N., & Pryor, J. (2012). Does social connectedness promote a greater sense of wellbeing in adolescence over time? *Journal of Research on Adolescence, 22*, 235–251.

Klem, A. M., & Connell, J. P. (2004). Relationships matter: Linking teacher support to student engagement and achievement. *Journal of School Health, 74*(7), 262–273.

Nolan, C., & Stitzlein, S. M. (2011). Meaningful hope for teachers in times of high anxiety and low morale. *Democracy and Education, 19*(1), Article 2.

Rowling, L. (1995). The disenfranchised grief of teachers. *OMEGA – Journal of Death and Dying, 31*(4), 317–329.

Souers, K., & Hall, P. A. (2019). *Relationship, responsibility, and regulation: Trauma-invested practices for fostering resilient learners*. ASCD.

Wolf-Prusan, L. (2014). *Urban high school teachers' cognitive appraisal and response to student violent death (gun- gang related) (doctoral dissertation)*. University of California.

17 How Experiences with Student Grief Inform Our Practice

Teaching Teachers to Navigate Healing Processes

Katie Rybakova, Katahdin Cook Whitt and Christina Christie

Introduction

Because most educators have not been formally trained in counseling or social work, leveraging the professional knowledge of trained counselors can help educators humanize grief and support students as they heal. Educators' experiences serve as powerful portrayals of how to overcome grief with learners, and thus this chapter revolves around our own stories of individuals who worked through their grief in our classrooms. The first author is a teacher educator, the second author is an educational consultant, and the third author is a trained social worker; our narratives can inform the ways that we teach about humanizing grief and healing processes to preservice and practicing teachers.

Student Grief in the College Classroom: Katie's Experiences

The opportunity to teach Young Adult Literature (YAL) with preservice teachers permitted exploring a text as a mirror (Bishop, 1990) to oneself as people and future teachers. The texts ranged in scope, context, and lexile, and included controversial YAL such as *Speak* (Anderson, 2011) and *Looking for Alaska* (Green, 2005).

This narrative is about the time I encountered a student who herself went through the tragedy portrayed in *Speak*. In my syllabi, I always include a statement about the controversial topics covered in the course and student sensitivity to those topics. After the syllabus review, I ask students via exit ticket if they have any concerns. While I do not ask for them to share their experiences, they often do. Because I know in advance about a student's grief and experiences, I try carefully to shield them where appropriate. This time I didn't know. Throughout the book discussion on *Speak*, the student stayed ominously quiet throughout discussions, eyes glazed over and out of focus. I asked her if she was okay, and when the response was "yeah," didn't think more of it other than just to keep an extra eye on her as we started the next book.

Counselor's Corner

The student's affect exemplifies being overcome by the primal brain and experiencing the survival instinct of fight, flight, or freeze. Whether she was frozen in her re-triggering, or she had the urge for flight but found enough self-control to not leave the classroom and instead dissociated to cope for the time being, the student was overwhelmed by her trauma. Her in-class presentation and choice to not come to the teacher while the book was being discussed indicates that any connection to her grief at that time interfered with her vertical brain integration and the ability to use analytical brain skills such as self-understanding, emotional regulation, and communication (Seigel & Payne Bryson, 2011).

About midway through the next novel, she asked to speak with me and revealed that she had been raped. I sat down with Lily (all names are pseudonyms) and listened intently as she described her trauma. I'd like to think that I kept a poker face, but my insides were breaking. No, she didn't want to report it to the police (it was reported to administration due to mandated reporting requirements). No, she hadn't told her parents yet. No, she didn't want to see anyone, just wanted me to know that the book we had just read had really hurt to read but also helped her heal. She didn't submit a critical analysis of the text because she had stopped and started several times, deleting each word as she typed out "I was raped too." It was too hard, she said, but she perceived a sense of strength as she found her own parallels to the main character. To this day, I remember thinking to myself, "I will never again assume that someone who is so happy and outspoken has nothing to hide."

Counselor's Corner

A teacher may feel unsuccessful after a conversation similar to the one had with Lily. Lily declined all offers of further action to address her grief and her academic work remained incomplete. However, the process of listening to a student and being fully present in their experience and emotions is often more powerful than any attempt to fix a perceived problem. According to interpersonal neurobiology, the brain has plasticity and therefore is always able to change, and human brains are extremely social (Siegel, 2012). Compassionate interpersonal communication (CIC) leads to increased brain integration and continued movement toward healthier functioning. CIC is grounded in empathy, which means Katie worked to understand not just the words being said but also the emotion behind the words. When a teacher attunes not only to the facts a student shares but also the emotion fueling the shared information, the student "feels felt." Simply by listening with empathy, the teacher may help the student connect to their own grief without becoming overwhelmed, which allows the student to maintain access to their logical brain regions and move forward in the healing process (Siegel, 2015).

I continued to invite Lily to come and talk to me about books and teaching. I didn't bring it up again unless she did herself. About a month later, we started discussing the books we read as a whole. I reminded the preservice teachers that they might never know who experienced what in their lives, and a preface to the books' controversial topics was essential. This sparked another debate—many students suggested that exposing the story's general plot ruined the "bam" factor of the text. A preface seemed like a spoiler.

Counselor's Corner

Providing advanced warning if there will be reading that involves sensitive topics can be an effective option. Educators can provide the book title and general category of sensitive material without disclosing explicit details for those who want to avoid spoilers. Communicating this information ahead of time and inviting students to talk with the teacher if they have concerns about reading and/or discussing the book sends the message that the teacher honors the students as individuals with their own histories, values their personal experiences, and is open to mutual discussion that will support students' whole-brain growth and development.

I share this story with the intent to showcase that a.) sometimes, an effective strategy includes simply listening to students and b.) we can never assume that students in our classes have never experienced the traumas present in the books we read. Books are mirrors, and sometimes those mirrors give students the opportunity to see themselves and their trauma clearly for the first time. Allyship and hope begin with the teacher's acknowledgement of the potential for grief and trauma in all students.

Experiences with Student Grief in a Secondary Science Classroom: Kate's Experiences

I became a science teacher because I love the practice of *doing* science and the disciplined nature of a content area that values data, evidence, and models. As a teacher, I have a history of being uncomfortable and squirmy with emotion-laden topics or situations. I care deeply for my students but I struggle to talk about emotions and feelings. I am much more comfortable talking about evidence, data, and models when I feel confused or overwhelmed. Such is the case with grief. Grief is confusing, overwhelming, and inherently doesn't make sense. As with any other phenomenon, our next step as scientists is to ask "how?" and "why?" and then to look to the data. In the case of my students' experiences with grief, though, my focus has always been on understanding the "how?" and "why?" of the cause of the grief—e.g. cancer—and not necessarily the grief itself.

Counselor's Corner

Through the lens of interpersonal neurobiology, learning is not viewed as taking place in a vacuum; it occurs within the context of relationships. Human connection affects neural integration of all brain activity including emotional regulation, attention, communication, and memory. This relational impact on the brain is most significant during childhood, adolescence, and young adulthood (Siegel, 2012). Teachers are more effective if they are comfortable connecting emotionally with students. Presenting subject content confidentially is important, but teachers who can tune into and feel comfortable talking about students' emotional selves will take their students' learning to the next level.

Several years ago, I collaborated with an English Language Arts (ELA) teacher to develop an integrated unit on cancer. In my biology class, students sought to figure out an answer to the question, "How can a seemingly healthy cell start dividing uncontrollably?" In ELA class, students engaged with the question, "What is the experience of cancer patients and their loved ones?" Through this collaboration, my students investigated cellular division, protein synthesis, and other cellular processes in biology, while the same students in my colleague's ELA class read *My Sister's Keeper* (Picoult, 2004) and *The Fault in Our Stars* (Green, 2012). Across both courses, students wrote multi-genre journals from multiple perspectives—the patient, loved ones, a doctor—to document the course of an individual's battle with cancer. Prior to implementing the unit, I knew that a unit focusing on cancer would bring up feelings of grief and uncertainty for many students. I felt a sense of relief, however, in knowing that in science we could focus on the evidence, the data, and the models. I could engage students in a unit designed to figure out the cell processes involved with cancer—a really interesting scientific phenomenon—while avoiding the touchy-feely discussions that I felt ill-equipped to handle. While teaching this unit, I felt that the ELA teacher was better equipped to handle the emotionally driven content. But in retrospect, it was a false assumption to feel that because the ELA teacher worked often with texts that elicit emotion that she'd somehow be more responsible for this approach—though neither of us were formally trained to leverage professional knowledge about grief.

Counselor's Corner

Every teacher will have their own moment in the classroom when they realize emotions cannot be kept separate from academics. From preservice teachers to seasoned professionals, educators at all experience levels can embrace the benefits of developing interpersonal skills to confidently navigate students' emotional needs, and self-reflection is fundamental to this learning process. The teacher should reflect upon how they experience, express, and process their own emotions; this is challenging yet necessary work that will facilitate their ability to support a student through a similar process when emotion-laden topics surface.

As anticipated, many of my students had a loved one who had battled cancer. When I first introduced the unit, Sara immediately approached me after class to let me know that her father had been diagnosed with brain cancer only two weeks prior. I didn't find out until close to the end of the unit about a second student, Jerome, whose grandmother and primary caretaker was battling lung cancer. Interestingly, both students seemed to handle engaging in the cancer unit in very different ways. Sara, who was typically very involved in class, did not say much throughout the unit and rarely engaged in small or large group discussions. Jerome, on the other hand, who rarely spoke in class, started asking question after question about the behavior of cancerous cells and treatment approaches. When it came to writing their journals, both Sara and Jerome struggled with writing some of the more emotional pieces. They struggled to get started, likely because writing about cancer was so fresh and emotionally charged. So, I encouraged them to start by writing about the facts. And, they did. They wrote detailed descriptions about how cells become cancerous, how cancer spreads, and how a variety of treatment options work. Both Sara and Jerome brought in names of chemotherapy drugs to investigate how they work. They brought in third-hand reports from the doctors so that they could "translate" the doctors' words into something comprehensible.

As I was teaching the unit, I felt mixed emotions. On the one hand, I thought that helping Sara and Jerome make sense of the science behind cancer might have helped them feel a sense of control when their worlds were otherwise out of control. Understanding the terminology and being able to explain the "how?" and "why?" of the disease processes can give people something to understand, something to control, and something to talk about. On the other hand, I worried that by allowing Sara and Jerome to focus *only* on the science of the disease, I was somehow enabling them to avoid engaging in the necessary feelings of grief and subsequent healing process. In some ways, I worried that I was dehumanizing the experience by focusing only on the cells, mechanisms, and treatments rather than complicated human emotions—the very concept I was relieved to focus on initially. I wondered, was I pushing the complicated human emotions away because I wasn't equipped to handle them?

It wasn't until this past year that my approach with Sara and Jerome during the cancer unit began to make a little more sense. About two years ago, I lost a cousin to a very aggressive form of cancer. After reaching what we believed to be the most difficult time in the grieving process, my family was hit again by a second diagnosis. Only a few weeks into the grieving process, my cousin's sister was diagnosed with a very similar aggressive cancer. As this chapter was being written, cancer took her life. My family has been living in the world of confusion and uncertainty that Sara and Jerome were living in during the cancer unit. Just as Sara and Jerome could only write about the science behind cancer, the conversations in my family centered on treatment plans, statistics, data, and mechanisms of action. Perhaps, this was because it was the only thing that gave us a sense of control in an unimaginable situation. Perhaps, this was because we couldn't yet allow ourselves to fully feel all of the complicated emotions we needed to feel. And perhaps, this was because the statistics, data, and science were the only things that we could bring ourselves to talk about.

In reflecting on my experience with my cousins and with Sara and Jerome in the cancer unit, I wonder if focusing on the things we *can* explain may be an important first step in the grieving process. I worry, though, that we may become stuck in the explainable, without ever allowing ourselves to sit with our emotions and process them. Perhaps, we sometimes need a gentle nudge to push beyond our initial explanations to dive deeper into processing our grief.

Counselor's Corner

Teachers should not be afraid to ask a student questions if the student appears to be struggling. Teachers will typically never regret reaching out to a student, even if the student declines to engage, but may regret remaining silent. Understanding professional limitations and boundaries is necessary; teachers do not have all the answers, and it is necessary to know the available resources for students upon conversation. If an unfamiliar topic is brought up, or a need is identified that the teacher cannot meet, the teacher can help the student find a more qualified support. Connecting with the student and offering to be a partner on their grief journey is what is most important. Teachers do not have to become grief experts before supporting students emotionally. When teachers navigate their own personal grief, this too informs their work and communication with students; it humanizes the experience.

Exploring Grief with Preservice Teachers

As we explored our different experiences as teachers working with grief, we realized that we never were taught how to approach these situations explicitly. We recognize the importance of doing so. While learning the procedures related to grief, such as reporting requirements, is important, preservice and inservice teachers are rarely equipped with skills that humanize grief. We realized that our experiences with student grief in the classroom might have been empathetic and supportive, but not necessarily healing. Our major takeaways were:

- make space for students to talk about their trauma, even if they don't necessarily bring it up themselves;
- sit in the discomfort; allow for the feeling of emotion without the rush to fix these emotions;
- be confident enough to ask the hard questions and invite expression, and to consider the role of the teacher as a guide and partner in various emotional processes;

- recognize that healing and processing grief, much like a content area, requires its own set of skills that students may not have yet. Teachers may not have these skills yet either;
- because teaching does not occur in a vacuum, emotion and empathy are part of the teaching process—this means that teachers should take care of themselves to prevent empathy burnout.

Hope can be a state of mind—it can also be a trait (Snyder et al., 2003). We should encourage hope through allyship in both our students and ourselves. In working with preservice teachers and inservice teachers, we encourage discussion about humanizing grief, helping students heal, and sharing narratives, however difficult they may be. One of the ways to begin processing grief is to first share the burden of it with others.

References

Anderson, L. H. (2011). *Speak*. SquareFish.

Bishop, R. S. (1990). Mirrors, windows, and sliding glass doors. *The Ohio State Perspective*, *6*(3). https://scenicregional.org/wp-content/uploads/2017/08/Mirrors-Windows-and-Sliding-Glass-Doors.pdf

Green, J. (2005). *Looking for Alaska*. Penguin Group.

Green, J. (2012). *The fault in our stars*. Penguin Group.

Picoult, J. (2004). *My sister's keeper: A novel*. Washington Square Press.

Siegel, D. J. (2010). *Mindsight: The new science of personal transformation*. Random House.

Siegel, D. J. (2012). *The developing mind: How relationships and the brain interact to shape who we are* (2nd ed.). The Guilford Press.

Siegel, D. J. (2015). *Brainstorm: The power and purpose of the teenage brain*. Penguin Group.

Siegel, D. J., & Payne Bryson, T. (2011). *The whole-brain child: 12 revolutionary strategies to nurture your child's developing mind*. Bantam Books.

Snyder, C. R., Shane, J. L., Shorey, H. S., Rand, K. L., & Feldman, D. B. (2003). Hope theory, measurements, and applications to school psychology. *School Psychology Quarterly*, *18*(2), 122–139.

Part IV

Finding Hope through Activism

18 My Father's Keeper

Pathway to Grief-Inspired Activism

Ericka Roland

As I dialed the number to the local newspaper, reality set in that my Father was gone. He'd been murdered and was gone forever. In 2017, Palm Beach County had over one hundred homicides as a result of gun violence, and my Father was among that number. Less than 24 hours later, the local newspaper had published an article about his murder, comprised mostly of my Father's mugshot and criminal background spanning 30 years. The article read more like a criminal rap sheet than a call for information to solve a murder. Policies that supported the "War on Drugs" that disproportionately targeted Black men, including my Father, meant he was over-policed and had little chance of staying out of the judicial system. As I read the article, I was devastated—anger rested in my chest, sadness welled up in my throat, and my thoughts raced, thinking about my Father's final moments. I picked up the phone and dialed the number to the newspaper reporter.

For as long as I can remember, the media has portrayed Black people in my community in dehumanizing ways. The local media depicts Black people's deaths as deserved by criminalizing and demonizing Black bodies in ways not done with White victims (Dukes & Gaither, 2017). In my experience, this criminalization includes local newspapers publishing Black victims' arrest records and mugshots, even when they are irrelevant to the causes of death. Even in death, Black bodies remain socially and politically inscribed with sets of meanings that reinforce racism, leaving mourners to deal with racial injustices and their grief simultaneously.

In this chapter, I illuminate the omnipresence of oppression in the lives, deaths, and grief of Black people, and how such oppression led to my grief-inspired activism as a pathway to hope. To do so, I first process a conversation with a local reporter about the newspaper article on my Father's murder using Sharpe's (2016) wake work theory. I focus on this incident because it forced me not only to acknowledge death and welcome grief but also to be responsible for proving my Father's humanity beyond his past. Then, I address how my grief manifested and resulted in grief-inspired activism (Al'Uqdah & Adomako, 2018). I consider the critical role that grief played in my journey from mourner to social justice advocate during my doctoral experience. Finally, connecting wake work theory and grief-inspired activism, I end with a discussion on hope that is evident through my scholarly work as a means of resistance and liberation. Throughout this chapter, I write Father with a capital F to honor my Father and signify his importance to me.

Like waves in the ocean, my grief ebbs and flows sometimes. As I write this narrative, I am working through my grief, and academic writing has been a safe space where I ride these waves of grief emotionally and intellectually. As a result, my emotions are present throughout this piece, but I also retreat to intellectual framing as an act of self-preservation and public performance of grief.

Breaking News: Palm Beach Man Dies After Being Shot

The shrill rings were interrupted by a lady's soft voice. "Hello, how can I help you?" Based on a Google search of the reporter who wrote the article on my Father, she appeared to be a White woman, so I prepared myself to perform respectability. According to Cooper (2017), respectability is a performance done by Black people to distance themselves from stereotypical aspects connected to our community. Smith (2014) argued convincingly that respectability politics denies Black rage as the result of oppression. Therefore, I swallowed my tears and exhaled my anger to match the pleasantries she offered me. More importantly, I wanted her to hear my pain clearly, without the stigma of being a stereotypical angry Black woman.

In a calm demure voice, I introduced myself and explained my kinship to John Roland. Perhaps, I thought, providing my relationship might give me more legitimacy to question the reporter about how she went about doing her job. I explained, "I would like to give more information on my Father so that his criminal record is not in the article, and I will also provide you with a better picture. I'm not sure why his mugshot and record were used." As I exhaled, she quickly responds "Oh yes, please tell me about him." I voiced to her how my Father should be portrayed as a loving man who had a smile that could brighten anyone's day. At that moment, I was drowning in a sense of responsibility to prove my Father's humanity and serve as his protector.

Drawing from Sharpe's (2016) wake work, I think through the racial stereotypes used in the media to depict Black people, especially Black men, as criminals who deserved violent deaths. Sharpe conceptualizes *wake work* as an analytical tool to explore the notion of living with and in constant racist subjection, and the mournful wear of the constancy of the ongoing Black trauma process. Being put in a position to prove my Father's humanity connects to Sharpe's notion of Black death being predictable and normative, which is grounded in anti-Blackness. Thus, leaving my family and me to mourn and remember my Father's life in the "wake" of racism that "occurs at the level of a structure that constitutes the Black as the constitutive outside" (Sharpe, 2016, p. 28).

As the conversation continued, the reporter started to ask questions about where the murder occurred and my Father's relationship with others. I angrily responded, "I don't know anything, and neither do you. That is why you published his mugshot and record." I continued,

"Can you explain to me why this was the information you used, when it has no connection to his murder?" She tried to explain that his record and mugshots are public records and the use of these documents is a common practice among reporters; Dukes and Gaither (2017) confirm this media practice of depicting racial minorities as criminals or perpetrators in relation to violent deaths.

Trying to hold back my anger, I explained to her that he had turned his life around and had not been in trouble for years. I worried that my Father's murder case would never be solved because this article provided a narrative that suggested that perhaps he had deserved such a violent death. Then I asked, "What would you have done if he didn't have a record?" Her silence and lack of answers infuriated me more. Not only did I feel that my Father's life and death were insignificant, but now my grief had become public. The public expression of grief from racially marginalized groups transforms into social and political mourning, with the aim of addressing social oppression, thus requiring the mourner to perform grief that is accessible to all and denying them a sense of privacy (Al'Uqdah & Adomako, 2018). Tears gathered in my eyes, anger apparent in my shaky voice, and my thoughts filled with ways to tell this reporter in a not-so-kind way about her lack of respect. Instead, I provided her a summary of what I wanted in the article, asked where I could email a picture, and told her how she could contact me if she had more questions. I felt an obligation to speak about the injustice of this article and rectify such a practice, although I would have preferred to sit with my Father's body for a private goodbye.

Under the big tree that shaded the driveway, my family discussed the media's constant negative portrayal of Black people in our community. As I listened in this moment, my heart ached for my loss. And, the aching amplified as I thought of my community and the constant manifestation of this type of media coverage—a concurrent tradition that accompanies death and violence. I wanted to fall to my knees and let my tears water the earth, but I stood planted like the roots of the tree, hoping that my bravery would mend my aching heart. My family expressed their gratitude with head nods of "this shit ain't right" and "thanks cuz." As the child, I had never imagined

I would need to protect my Father from the cruel world. From that point on, I became my Father's keeper, taking on the responsibilities to ensure he was respected in death, and racial injustices did not cloud the precious homegoing traditions in the Black community in the celebration of life. In taking this position, I often had to swallow my tears and stand with authority to remain conscious and vocal about racial injustices related to death and gun violence.

Pathway to Grief-Inspired Activism

A few months later, the same reporter called to get comments about the arrest of the man who killed my Father. The call threw me back into the waves of grief, but I had no more tears to shed. I gathered myself enough to be conscious of showing respect via the media to this Black man who had murdered my Father; he too had children who would now mourn the loss of their Father. Although different from a physical death, I understand that incarceration is still death. I wanted to offer a level of grace to this man's children that was not given to me. I realized that as children of Black men who had been taken away from us through violence and incarceration, we were living in a cycle of death and grief. I wanted to challenge how the media normalized death and grief of Black bodies and connected such trauma to the dehumanization of my community for both my Father and the Black man who had murdered him. During this time, I felt the urge to develop my sense of activism that vigorously demanded political and social change. But, where could I go to be part of an organized demand for change?

For a while, I felt like I was wandering aimlessly through life, grief was the vast ocean, and I was lost at sea with no rescue insight. Perhaps taking the position of my Father's keeper, it was him I wanted to save me with the words "Baby, I love you." That moment never came, causing the aching of my heart to become the aching of my soul. In the midst of grief, police reports were released and court hearings scheduled, leaving my soul openly wounded and unable to heal. However, as my Father's Keeper, I needed to hear this information to ensure the accuracy of reporting, and understand the process. Once again, being my Father's Keeper required me to step into spaces and roles that I did not want to fill.

The court hearings were too much to bear. My elegant rage could not be contained any longer as I felt my knees buckle and my soul cry out from the pain. I needed to find a way to be my Father's keeper while simultaneously healing. I thought of joining a local group on gun violence and racial injustice, or of supporting Black kids who had lost loved ones to violence and incarceration. My grief-inspired activism was to address racial injustices in relation to gun violence and death because no one deserves the treatment that my Father, family, and I endured during our painful loss. Al'Uqdah and Adomako (2018) posit that grief-inspired activism allows for a sense of agency, is empowering, and can affect social change. Although social justice activism can lead to healing and social support in grief, I felt silenced, for I could not support others while drowning in my own grief. During this time, I read about activism and social movements. Carruthers (2018) wrote about healing justice, which requires activists to radically enact self-care while intervening against generational trauma and violence.

During the time I was drowning in grief, I was working on my dissertation, which felt pointless given where I was in processing my pain. I tried to write, but I could only stare at the computer screen, unable to think in complex ways. I wanted to step away from school; however, my dissertation chair offered the possibilities for my work being a space where I could heal and enact agency and activism on my terms. I gave myself permission to relinquish my position as my Father's keeper and began to heal. Taking my cue from bell hooks (2013), "writing has enhanced our struggle to be self-defining it emerges as a narrative of resistance, as writing that enables us to experience both self-discovery and self-recovery" (p. 5). I embraced scholarly writing as a space that allowed me to grieve in private, while still participating in activism related to systems of oppression.

From Private to Public: Writing to Hope

In Sharpe's (2016) wake work, she calls for consciousness and praxis that imagine a resistance to anti-Blackness. Meanwhile, grief-inspired activism serves as an act of healing for an individual and community. Undergirding wake work theory and grief-inspired activism is the *hope* that social injustices can be addressed and we can live in a socially just world. Hope alone cannot achieve social liberation, but without hope, the struggle for justice becomes disheartening. Critical theorist Giroux (2004) provides insights into the importance of hope in social justice work. He writes, "we must see hope as part of a broader politics that acknowledges those social, economic, spiritual, and cultural conditions in the present that make certain kinds of agency and democratic politics possible" (p. 38). In other words, hope is the connection between social critique and transformation. Therefore, I write first to heal myself and then to join a collective of scholars in the resistance against domination and subordination. My hope serves as both therapeutic and mobilizing in the possibility of change.

My hope serves as a pedagogical and performative practice in my scholarly writing that becomes a way of engaging with social injustices in every life, while enabling others to learn and develop as social agents.

Thus, my experiences and positionalities shape my work as responses to the circumstances that move my private expression to public declarations. I write to heal myself, which includes scribbling my sense of becoming around being a critical scholar. I affectionately name this writing my "soul work," where I can be honest, reflective, and emotional about my pathways and the community that support and inspire me along the way. This soul work gives me hope to write with and for others, and it moves beyond my individual experiences to exposing systemic injustices.

In my scholarly writing, I focus on critical educational leadership development, with the hope developing leadership that will reimagine education. I write to enact freedom-dreaming that imagines liberation for all people through innovative methods, which includes formal and informal social justice education. Although the development of leadership to challenge racial injustices does not ensure the enactment of such practice, I argue education is a starting place to uncover the realities of oppression and dream of the possibilities. Therefore, my writing is my activism that identifies spaces where we as a collective can grapple with injustices and social justice, enact healing justice, and cultivate a radical imagination. I unapologetically write about oppression and privilege with hopes of transformative change that dismantles socially unjust systems and promotes liberation.

As my Father's picture adorns remembering pamphlets to urge the end to gun violence in my community, grief floods my heart, and I retake my position as his keeper. However, as I seek healing to hope through writing, my posture of my Father's keeper changes to be less stoic and more fluent, which allows for an opening to dialogue around racial injustices and all injustices in various spaces. I know it will take time for healing of grief and social injustice, but hope reminds me to ride the waves, for the waves become easier to conquer and inspire others on this journey for transformative change. Through the murder of my Father, I experienced immense grief; the newspaper article gave me a responsibility to prove my Father's humanity; grief-inspired activism granted me permission to heal; and hope is subversive in my writing, offering the possibility for change.

References

Al'Uqdah, S., & Adomako, F. (2018). From mourning to action: African American women's grief, pain, and activism. *Journal of Loss and Trauma, 23*(2), 91–98. doi: https://doi.org/10.1080/15325024.2017.1393373

Carruthers, C. (2018). *Unapologetic: A Black, queer, and feminist mandate for radical movements.* Beacon Press.

Cooper, B. C. (2017). *Beyond respectability: The intellectual thought of race women.* University of Illinois Press.

Dukes, K. N., & Gaither, S. E. (2017). Black racial stereotypes and victim blaming: Implications for media coverage and criminal proceedings in cases of police violence against racial and ethnic minorities. *Journal of Social Issues, 73*(4), 789–807. Retrieved from https://spssi.onlinelibrary.wiley.com/doi/full/10.1111/josi.12248

Giroux, H. A. (2004). When hope is subversive. *Tikkun, 19*(6), 38–39.

hooks, b. (2013). *Remembered rapture: The writer at work.* Henry Holt.

Sharpe, C. E. (2016). *In the wake: On blackness and being.* Duke University Press.

Smith, M. (2014). Affect and respectability politics. *Theory & Event, 17*(3). https://www.muse.jhu.edu/article/559376

19 When the Music Changes, so Does the Dance

Critical Racial Events as Told through a Narrative Inquiry Beat

Kara M. Taylor

EVAN: I was 14. I was heading up the stairs when I saw two white boys walking towards me. They were conversing with one another and I wanted to get upstairs without interacting with them. I overheard one of them say, "I hate, I want to kill them all." I assumed that they may not have seen me walking by when they made their remark. So, I stopped and looked one of them in the eye and he said, "Yeah, I am talking about you."

Two years ago, I began studying the culturally relevant pedagogical practices of three elementary school teachers in grades K-12. One of the teacher participants, Evan, an African American, recounted this traumatic, yet shaping incident of the first time he was called a *nigger*. His journey to become a 3rd grade teacher was framed around a deeply personal commitment to create safe spaces to validate and sustain the students of color he served (Paris & Alim, 2014). Unbeknownst to me, being granted permission to enter and access Evan's life world would initiate a concurrent journey for me of identifying and grappling with my own trauma. Conducting this study allowed me to interrogate experiences with my father, and how my experiences with my father shaped my pursuit of equitable educational outcomes.

KARA: My teacher offered to drive me to school because she lived down the block. She pulled up for the first time finding my dad dumping our stuff out the window in the front yard while calling us names. I ran to the car, so my teacher wouldn't see what happened, even everyone could see.

This chapter documents the (unforeseen) synergies of growing up Black, with a recognition that racism is endemic to American life, and the experiential knowledge of people of color and our communities of origin are needed to examine society (Crenshaw et al., 1993). Drawing on narrative inquiry (Clandinin & Connelly, 2000), Evan and I developed a cipher through which we tracked individual and mutual understandings of how we processed our grief. An allyship was built between us based on shared beliefs of hope for new equitable outcomes of schooling. My research questions were: how do written and spoken reflections illuminate issues of race, class, and/or gender along with how does self-reflection on critical incidents regarding racialized events influence one's work in education?

Review of Literature: Teacher Narratives

Teacher narratives have the power to support teachers as they examine the knowledge, perspectives, understandings, and experiences that guide their classroom work (Johnson & Golombek, 2002). This chapter turns attention to formative experiences that significantly impact a teacher's practice. Critical event narrative analysis (Webster & Mertova, 2007) serves as a means to examine society and culture regarding race and class.

Teacher narratives tell "stories of teachers' professional development within their own professional worlds" (Johnson & Golombek, 2002, p. 6). For example, Kramp (1995) found that teachers' awareness of personal stories, particularly of present and past selves, can lead to changes in future selves. Also, Kong (2017), an in-service teacher, traced her evolving conceptualizations of interactive teaching and the mediational means through which her questioning patterns fostered student participation.

Reflection affords teachers opportunities to work through problems of practice, providing a pathway to process the stress and emotions that emerge from the complex, multi-faceted work of teaching (Jalongo et al., 1995). McCabe (2002) suggests that through storying, a productive dialogue is initiated, encompassing strategies and possible solutions for addressing teachers' common problems.

Narrative reflection is effective when it is specific, honest, and grounded in events teachers deem important to their identity (Clandinin & Connelly, 2000). Dewey (1933) argued that reflecting on experiences allows teachers to remember that their lives are narratives, composites of critical incidents and experiences. A critical incident can be defined as a vividly remembered unanticipated event that occurs during/outside class or during a teacher's career (Howard, 2003). Events become critical through conscious reflection, and the process can unearth teachers' new understandings of their practice (Richards & Farrell, 2005). Such critical events must be addressed because they contribute to a teacher's identity and sense of self (Neimeyer, 1999).

Teachers' critical incident narratives may consequently lean into grief. Processing critical incidents that one has experienced within or beyond the walls of the classroom brings the potential to promote recovery because the grieving process allows individuals opportunities to return to themselves pre-loss (Wortman & Silver, 1987). During this reflecting and narrating, teachers become meaning makers—weaving together narratives that give significance to salient plots in their lives and issues that impact society (Neimeyer, 1998). Teachers are empowered to be *authors* over the narratives of their lives, shattering prescribed oppressive narratives imposed on them by others in society (Monk, Winslade, Crocket, & Epston, 1997).

Howard (2003) argues that one's worldview, comprised of both past- and present-lived experiences, shapes the act of teaching. A teacher's instructional practice is fueled by attitudes, biases, and understandings developed from those experiences; which are always entangled in issues related to race, class, and gender (Dutro & Moran, 2003). Within schools, teachers are rarely afforded opportunities to engage in this critically engaged self-reflection to interrogate how personal experiences inform epistemological stances and propel pedagogical decision-making (Mushin, 2001). This critical reflection by teachers can create allyship (activism for the purpose of liberation and support) among teachers (Brown & Ostrove, 2013).

Data Collection and Analysis

This work is drawn from a larger case study examining culturally relevant (Ladson-Billings, 2001) literacy instruction and assessment practices of three urban teachers. This chapter focuses on my interactions with Evan, a 26-year-old African-American third- and fourth-grade teacher. During the study, Evan was teaching in a predominantly black school in a large urban city. Evan self-identified as the "Jay Z" of teaching— working with his students around activism to dismantle the oppressive aspects of schooling. He viewed each school year as an "album," marking moments of artistry in time for both him and his students. Evan openly shared his stories, expressing how influential they were in shaping his teacher identity, and created a generative space where I was compelled to do the same.

This study draws primarily from two semi-structured, in person interviews regarding a narrative artifact Evan authored during the study. In this three-page written narrative entitled "King Salmon," Evan responded to a prompt asking what brought him to critical teaching. The interview focused on Evan reading his artifact and engaging in a dialogue about the criticality of this narrative to his teaching and identity. In the initial dialogue with Evan, he posed a series of questions, which inspired me to craft a similar artifact, "Writing to Heal," where I examined my journey to critical teaching and scholarship. These stories serve as a *telling case* (Mitchell, 1984), discussing how the grief of a teacher can be funneled into hope. This hope is defined as our ability to be agentive players in our healing and initiate civic change through teaching (Snyder, 1996).

Findings

The findings section is organized around three themes found across the data: confronting trauma and/or grief, beginning the process of wounded healing, and interrogating the world around you through critical incident analysis. Excerpts of our narratives are woven into the findings to strike a chord at the intersectional experiences of growing up Black and growing into our roles as educators.

Confronting Trauma/Grief by Narrative Stories of Critical Events

EVAN: I dashed up the stairs to my teacher's classroom. I kept thinking about what they were going to do to me and who would be able to protect me. I got to my teacher's door. It was locked, leaving me vulnerable in the hallway. I sat on that floor with my heart beating fast and with fear residing in my mind. There was no teacher to speak with, no Black counselor, not even a Black friend in whom I could confide and share this experience—I lived in fear. I had learned that no mask or chameleon skin would protect me from racist thoughts.

The trauma that Evan carried over the first time he was called a *nigger* by white classmates after moving to Arizona at the age of 14 was palpable. After telling this story, he said, "I will never forget the fear it caused because I never felt that way before. I felt alone." This event gave Evan hyper-awareness of being Black in a predominantly white place. In this moment—being a freshman in a new city, Evan was subjected to attitudes that were pervasive yet unfamiliar. As he said, "you read about this kind of racism in books, but when you live it, the experience is much different." The task of writing and reflecting about this trauma shifted Evan's outlook on the nature of his fear and resurrected the grief he felt about the event that he had suppressed. Telling his story had less to do with the details of the encounter and more with how being called a *nigger* impacted Evan's life. The telling marked the moment Evan wanted to become a teacher.

KARA: I knew my teacher knew but understood why words were never spoken about it… I can't say I blamed my father for the words he said and the lashes [hits] he gave because he too was a prisoner. He enacted aggression and strength Black men exhibit instead of addressing the stigma of mental health help. My father never had a present father because my grandfather was trapped in bottles of alcohol. And, in turn, he trapped me and my family inside a box of profane words, intimidation and fear.

Being granted "authorship" of my narrative with my father allowed me to become agentive in the process of meaning reconstruction of an event that I was actively invested in (Neimeyer, 1998). This authorship and power gave me the ability to add hope of liberation/change for myself and in my teaching within my narrative. I took a step back, and reflected on the irrational actions of my father, viewing the formative childhood experiences from an adult lens. The processing of grief and trauma is contextually bound, and experienced differently according to markers such as race, class, or gender. Gaining agency through [re]writing is another quality or strength that hope gives us access to understandings of self and the world. Social norms within the Black community resist openly discussing psychological trauma and seeking out help, resulting in maladaptive coping behaviors (Polanco-Roman, Danies, & Anglin, 2016). My father always told me to "suck it up." This made me feel that I was supposed to fold my feelings into myself, which led to a pattern of detachment. With Evan, I found a way to write about the issues I had with my father as a young child and face the trauma and challenge traditional and longstanding paradigms associated with research.

Interrogating Critical Incidents through Narrative Writing

EVAN: My first days of high school in Arizona made me painfully aware of what it means to be a young Black boy in America. I needed to learn to navigate this space for my preservation and myself because no one at my school was going to do the work for me.

KARA: I realized that being hurt causes you to hurt other people, because that is all you know.

By reflecting on these events, we created a space to initiate the process of healing. Marc Lamont Hill (2009) describes this communal act of bearing scars, grief, and suffering through stories for the purpose of relief and release as wounded healing. Evan kept this event to himself until his narrative artifact because he was ashamed of how he would look. The task motivated Evan to articulate authentic feelings so he could interrogate the event and its influence on his present. Similarly, the act of reflection allowed me to come to understand a new counter narrative to my trauma.

Our narratives also allowed us to interrogate the world. The explicit racism Evan encountered prompted a critical awakening to (c)overt racism; it opened Evan's eyes to the concept "new racism" and how it is enacted in public spaces, e.g., school. Being called a *nigger* became the overt racism, while his teachers' collective silence and unwillingness to support Evan was a covert way that racism took shape. We both realized that identity- and self-preservation as people of color should be prioritized, and extended to our work with students.

Discussion & Implications

EVAN: This experience birthed a deeper longing to know myself so that I could be someone others could look to in a time of trouble. To be the Black man who would tell the Black boy that it is okay to cry and be scared and to run for dear life. Also, tell them that they are not the only ones who live in between two worlds. I want to be the teacher who I could have run to that day when those well-dressed jackals called me a *nigger*.

Our collective experiences highlight the importance of addressing traumas—as individuals and as educators teaching across contexts. Narrative tasks like these provide opportunities to confront grief and trauma and reach for fuller expressions of our individual and collective humanities. Our narratives provide evidence that introspective work can confront pain in productive ways. With the current sociopolitical context, it becomes necessary to cultivate opportunities for critical reflection on constructs such as race, ethnicity, gender, sexuality, class, and religion.

Our narratives highlight the potential of critical reflection through narrative writing in surfacing the motivations and epistemological commitments of the teacher. For example, Evan's narratives worked to explain his desire to create activist spaces and a more equitable world. He channeled his fear into empathy for his students and the realities they're grappling with in their own lives. Sharing my hurt, in growing up with an abusive father trapped by the stigma of black aggression camouflaged as strength created a generative healing space. As Evan said, "all of us hurt, and it looks different for each one of us, but when do we learn to overcome and get past that hurt in healthy ways?" Though our stories were different, our joint enterprises became intertwined by which we both gained greater access to understanding the process of wounded healing—a necessity for emancipatory visions of schooling.

Finally, this work suggests a new vision for research, and a shift from doing research on communities to doing research *with* participants. Evan exhibiting vulnerability challenged me to think through my journey with grief and trauma blurred the lines between researcher and researched in ways that humanized our interactions, while providing mutually beneficial outcomes. When personal stories change to include hopeful outlooks, new possibilities become attainable.

References

Brown, K. T., & Ostrove, J. M. (2013). What does it mean to be an ally? The perception of allies from the perspective of people of color. *Journal of Applied Social _____Psychology, 43*(11), 2211–2222. Retrieved from https://onlinelibrary.wiley.com/doi/abs/10.1111/jasp.12172

Clandinin, D. J., & Connelly, F. M. (2000). *Narrative inquiry: Experience and story in qualitative research.* Jossey-Bass.

Dewey, J. (1933). *How we think: A restatement of the relation of reflective thinking to the educative process* (vol. 8). DC Heath and Company.

Dutro, E., & Moran, C. (2003). Rethinking English language instruction: An architectural approach. In G.G. Garcia (Ed.), *English learners: Reaching the highest level of English literacy,* (pp. 227–258), International Reading Association.

Hill, M. L. (2009). *Wounded healing: Forming a storytelling community in hip-hop lit. _____Teachers College Record, 111*(1), 248–293. _____http://www.tcrecord.org/Content.asp?ContentId=15215

Howard, T. C. (2003). Culturally relevant pedagogy: Ingredients for critical teacher reflection. *Theory into Practice,* 42(3), 195–202. http://www.jstor.org/stable/1477420

Jalongo, M. R., Isenberg, J. P., & Gerbracht, G. (1995). *Teachers' stories: From personal narrative to professional insight.* Jossey-Bass.

Johnson, K. E., & Golombek, P. R. (2002). *Teachers' narrative inquiry as professional development.* Cambridge University Press.

Kong, M. (2017). "You speak English, no?": The expectations and experiences of Asian in-service teachers of English in Australia. *The English Teacher,* 44(1), 10. _____http://journals.melta.org.my/index.php/tet/article/view/218/118

Kramp, M. K. (1995). Narrative, self-assessment, and the habit of _____reflection. *Assessment Update,* 7(1), 10–13.

Ladson-Billings, G. (2001). *Crossing over to Canaan: The journey of new teachers in diverse classrooms.* Jossey-Bass.

McCabe, A. (2002). A wellspring for development. In J. Edge (Ed.), *Continuing professional development* (pp. 82–96), IATEFL Publications.

Monk, G. E., Winslade, J. E., Crocket, K. E., & Epston, D. E. (1997). *Narrative therapy in practice: The archaeology of hope.* Jossey-Bass.

Mitchell, J. (1984). Typicality and the case study. In R. Ellen (Ed.), *Ethnographic research: A guide to general conduct* (pp. 237–241), Academic Press.

Mushin, I. (2001). *Evidentiality and epistemological stance: Narrative retelling* (Vol. 87). John Benjamins Publishing.

Neimeyer, R. A. (1999). Narrative strategies in grief therapy. *Journal of Constructivist Psychology, 12*(1), 65–85. doi: https://doi.org/10.1080/107205399266226.

Paris, D., & Alim, H. S. (2014). What are we seeking to sustain through culturally sustaining pedagogy? A loving critique forward. *Harvard Educational Review, 84*(1), 85–100. doi: https://doi.org/10.17763/haer.84.1.982l873k2ht16m77.

Polanco-Roman, L., Danies, A., & Anglin, D. M. (2016). Racial discrimination as race-based trauma, coping strategies, and dissociative symptoms among emerging adults. *Psychological Trauma: Theory, Research, Practice, and Policy, 8*(5), 609–17.

Richards, J. C., & Farrell, T. S. C. (2005). *Professional development for language teachers.* Cambridge University Press.

Snyder, C. R. (1996). To hope, to lose, and hope again. *Journal of Personal and Interpersonal Loss, 1,* 1–16, https://doi.org/10.1080/15325029608415455

Webster, L. (1998). *A story of instructional research and simulation in aviation (air traffic control).* [unpublished PhD thesis]. Monash University, Melbourne, Australia.

Wortman, C. B., & Silver, R. C. (1987). Coping with irrevocable loss. In G. R. VandenBos & B. K. Bryant (Eds.), *Master lectures series. Cataclysms, crises, and catastrophes: Psychology in action* (pp. 185–235). American Psychological Association.

20 Homeless Adolescents, Grief, and Advocacy for Others

Hope for the Future

Kate Shands Haq

Young people who are homeless or runaway encounter barriers that include poor nutrition, unsafe living conditions, drug and alcohol abuse, physical and psychological violence, transportation difficulties, academic gaps, and difficulty maintaining friendships (Milner, 2013). Considering civic opportunities for young adults in marginalized communities are not often available (Ginwright, 2010), I co-created a youth activist/empowerment club with young adults and other caring professionals at a homeless drop-in center.

While some researchers (MacGillivray, Ardell, & Curwen, 2010; Noll & Watkins, 2003) have explored literacy connections with homeless families and young children, few have looked at adolescent homeless and runaway youth in terms of literacy practices. As a critical literacy scholar, my goal was to gain a fuller, more nuanced understanding of the intersection of literacies, critical consciousness building, civic engagement, and homeless urban youth aged 16–23 in the northeastern city of Westside.

The club and the research it engendered was designed to counteract deficit narratives of Black urban youth who frequent a homeless and runaway resource center, to adopt one of hope, where "hopeful thought reflects the belief that one can find pathways to desired goals and become motivated to use those pathways" (Snyder, Rand, & Sigmon, 2002, p. 257). Hopefulness was driven by dialogic discussion of texts, exploration of participants' sophisticated range of literary consumption, and the performance and celebration of the innovative nature of their literary works. Club sessions included discussions on power differentials, police brutality, violence, transportation and housing problems, Black history, intersectionality, everyday racism, xenophobia, and bigotry. Participants were not only challenged to think critically about justice issues and the ways they had personally been impacted but were also encouraged to read their world critically (Freire, 1983) and question the dominant neoliberal "boot straps" narrative found in media and literature around homelessness (Jacobs, 2014; Rogers & Marshall, 2012; Rogers, Winters, Perry, & LaMonde, 2015).

This chapter explores one finding from this study. By focusing on ways participants physically positioned themselves as agentive in helping peers navigate their complex and stressful living situations, the chapter aids readers in gaining a better understanding of resiliency, hope, and allyship young people generated in support of each other, even when it appeared they had little to offer. The young adults who participated in this work lived with grief as a constant. As a long-time teacher, I knew that nearly 35 million children in America have experienced at least one type of trauma (Kwong & Hayes, 2017). At the drop-in center, young people had often suffered a series of losses, so grief was embedded in our daily interactions, stories we connected with, and those told to each other.

In order to get the club started, it was necessary for me to build relationships with youth who frequented the Scope Resource Center for Homeless and Runaway Youth (SRC) over a period of months, proving myself to be a trusted adult before inviting participants into the club and research. This chapter employs narrative to tell stories of youth resilience, creative problem solving, and the shared, advancing hope (Snyder, 1996) that permeated the SRC and inspired adults, like myself, who were lucky enough to befriend these young people.

Methodology

This work draws upon positioning theory (McVee, Silvestri, Barrett, & Haq, 2018) and narrative inquiry and explores adolescent practices culturally situated in an urban setting across multiple spaces throughout 2017. As part of larger Vygotskian sociocultural theory, positioning theory allows a close look at how interactions occur, for "how one positions oneself—or is positioned by others—occurs in and through discourse, both verbal and nonverbal, and at the local, institutional, and societal levels" (Glazier, 2009, p. 827). Positionings can best be examined through narrative and are often vehicles behind the stories themselves (Wortham, 2000; 2001). This study adopts a critical lens as developed and situated within critical literacy theory and pedagogy espoused by Freire, Giroux, hooks, and others. Through this lens, positioning acts can be viewed as contributions to the development of personhood (Davies & Harre, 1990) as well as used to investigate societal influences linked to that development, such as homelessness.

Emphasis was placed on narrative participant experiences (Cruz, 2013) and the building of critical consciousness. A liberatory framework (Shor & Freire, 1987) was used with facilitated peer discussion of contemporary critical texts such as *Citizen* by Rankine (2014), *The Hate U Give* by Thomas (2017), *All American Boys* by Reynolds and Kiely (2015), the lyrics of Tupac Shakur, poetry, playwriting, prose, video, and social media.

Club curriculum was co-constructed with participants encompassing a range of topics and shared experiences. Voluntary participants included ten young people of color between ages 16 and 23, interested in exploring power dynamics through youth activism. These young people were accessing services offered at the SRC such as rapid rehousing, career counseling, and reproductive health services. Pseudonyms were used for participants and locations have been de-identified.

Data Sources and Analysis

I collected audio-and-video-recorded sessions, interview and focus group data, photos, and artifacts. Narrative-inquiry techniques of examining stories from texts as well as participants' stories and the ongoing story of the club itself indicated data units to be bounded by vignettes. Data reduction began through vignette identification. Vignettes were initially identified through the following steps: a) viewing video to identify stories told by participants, accompanied by analytic note taking for retrieval purposes; b) tagging stories told on video in their corresponding audio data base and transcribing each story; and c) member checking with participants to ensure a co-construction of narrative. This collaborative work contributed to participants' critical consciousness building through the research process. Vignettes were bounded by turns of talk and evidence that the narrator "actively and agentively" (Bamberg, 2004b, p. 136) positioned themselves in talk and action in the larger discourse at play during the session.

The club participated in a variety of events throughout the city including guest speakers from the Westside activist community, field trips to Black history sites, protests, government-sponsored meetings, theater and open-mic forums, and shared meals. One such event is the basis for this chapter. The annual Youth Point-in-Time Count (PIT) of 2017 was run by a county-wide task force, designed to count homeless youth in one 24-hour period. Club participants worked as allies and took on pivotal roles contacting young people in need of services prior to, during, and after this event. While the PIT counts are required by the federal government, they have mostly relied on shelter data in the past, omitting youth who may be couch surfing, living in unsafe spaces, or on the run (Auerswald, Lin, Petry, & Hyatt, 2013). Since discussions at the SRC often included the need for an overnight shelter for youth ages 17–24 in Westside (Bowen et al., 2016), the task force, with help of dedicated young people, worked to build a case to begin to gather funding. This federal funding was contingent on results of the PIT.

Youth Outreach and Allyship Generate Hope

On the late October afternoon of the 2017 PIT, energy was palpable as green and silver balloons bobbed in the breeze and hip-hop music from the DJ drew people in the SRC gate from all directions. Outreach volunteers, including club members, along with other SRC clients and case managers, were at strategic locations around the city asking youth to complete the survey. Following completion of the survey, young people were directed to the SRC for pizza, swag bags, informational tabling, and a chance at the cap raffle.

This one-day event required a great deal of planning and dialogue leading up to it. Many club sessions prior to the PIT included discussions like the one below, where Tarra, a dedicated case manager, encouraged youth leadership and participation,

TARRA: 50% of our referrals come from you guys, telling your friends. To find all the youth out there that might benefit from the SRC or just any of the stuff we offer, anyone who has couch surfed, the way we find them is through you guys. So, we're really going to be putting the pressure on you all getting the survey out.

LOUISE: I swear I tell people [about the SRC]. Even when you all have been pissing me off, I tell them, go to Scope Resource Center, they help you. I don't like them right now but I'll see you there later.

ALL: [laugh]

TARRA: We need to find out how many youths are really out there couch surfing because that is how we tell the government we need money for those youths.

MALIK: I got one of my brothers now couch surfing at my place.

Club participants often joyfully reminisced about the previous year's PIT as they planned for the upcoming event. Participants were fully engaged in supporting and advocating for others, sometimes within their own spaces and communities. For instance, Jayde often told of her role in church as one of support and advocacy for troubled teens. Data reflect many instances of youth housing others in the way Malik described.

The PIT included physical, embodied outreach that occurred over 24 hours, but many SRC youth were doing outreach in their own communities daily. This combination of questioning power structures like homelessness, combined with acting to help others, embodied hope and resiliency. The concept of resiliency as a dynamic system that allows for successful adaptation to traumatic events (Masten, 2014) underscores strength young people at the SRC exhibited when faced with adverse daily grief-filled occurrences, such as job loss and housing instability. Their capacity to put such problems aside to help others develop resources to combat the risks (Yates, Tyrell, & Masten, 2015) involved in living without a stable home embodied hopeful action.

Allyship as Youth Civic Engagement

In the week leading up to the PIT, BJ and Raymond, both study participants, joined SCR adults in a press conference with local media, designed to raise awareness of local homeless and runaway youth, the

PIT survey, and its related activities. Raymond spoke eloquently and personally of the effects of homelessness and life on the streets for himself and other youth, saying, "You could find any of us in the streets. You might've walked past somebody that might be homeless. You might have seen me and not even known that I'm homeless." BJ spoke directly to the press in the room, resisting the accepted narrative that lumps all homeless people together with the same needs, pleading:

> People don't realize that youth homelessness is totally different than adult homelessness. Just imagine being 16 or 18 years old wondering how to call the shelter or hotlines. How do you answer the questions that they're asking? What benefits do you get? How do you get to a shelter? How do you get help trying to find an apartment or a permanent home? How do you get to school? How do you eat? How do we survive as minors?

As teens who have been homeless, their personal stories were powerful and important. The bravery and resiliency exhibited by these individuals was an incredibly powerful and unselfish act. Positioning themselves at risk of rejection by peers, their families, and the community-at-large to raise awareness of youth homelessness and question Westside's commitment to the health and safety of their young citizens cemented their allyship to each other, their peers, and to their hope in creating societal change.

Youth outreach went far beyond a single press conference and news story. Members of the club worked together to brainstorm and revise the homeless youth survey questions, effectively helping design the survey. They set up event pages on social media, helped design fliers, such as the de-identified one shown below as Figure 20.1, and plastered them around the city to raise awareness in advance of the PIT.

Interestingly, throughout the planning and enacting phases of the PIT, club members continued to draw connections during our sessions between their struggles and the texts we explored. For instance, our discussions of microaggressions uncovered in Rankine's *Citizen* resulted in the sharing of personal stories steeped in racist policies and acts participants had endured and continued to question. The hopefulness of youth mixed with critical questioning worked to strengthen our collective resolve to act against such grief-inducing pain. Data collected paints a picture of youth outreach and personal sharing of grief narratives to support each other and to effect change.

PIT results indicated that approximately 12,834 youth took the survey county-wide, with 217 youth signifying they were engaged in couch surfing. One hundred fifteen youth identified as living in a shelter, with 80 in transitional housing. Fifty-seven young people indicated home was in a motel, with 107 living in places not meant for human habitation. This

Pseudonym	Age	Race	Gender	Education Complete
Angel Harris	17	Black	woman	high school graduate
Mackenzie Noelles	18	Latina	woman	high school graduate
Jayde Williams	19	Black	woman	one year of college
Brunhilda Jones (BJ)	19	Black	woman	one year of college
Natalie Rome	19	Black	woman	grade 11
Zamora Newton	22	Black	woman	one year of college
Jared Rath	18	Black	man	grade 9
James Morgan	23	Black	man	high school graduate
Starr Shakur	16	Black	woman	grade 10 (currently in high sc
Kalial Wagner	17	Black	man	grade 11
Malik Thompson	21	Black	man	Undisclosed
Louise Garvey	21	Black	woman	grade 10

Figure 20.1 Study Participants' Demographics

information, gathered primarily by youth for youth because of participant positioning as community activists within their city, was used to
procure additional funding for young people struggling with housing
issues across the county.

Conclusion

In this chapter, I have lifted a small portion of youth homeless-related
discussions, critical consciousness-building interactions, allyship, and
positions participants inhabited or resisted. I contend that through this
event and other shared experiences, young people involved became
more knowledgeable about ways they are positioned within their community and ways they may act to resist negative aspects of that positioning and instead position themselves as resilient people with actionable
hopes for the future.

These young people and thousands of others across the United
States live in the moral space that acknowledges youth homelessness
and racialized outcomes are wrong, while policies and power structures
perpetuate that space. This small place-based study gives us hope and
shows how young people demonstrated pathways to allyship with each
other and questioned power structures in their quest for sustainable,
honorable lives in their city. Study participants agentively positioned
themselves to question and resist social structures that perpetuate grief
and oppression and collaborated to make hope filled change.

References

Auerswald, C., Lin, J., Petry, L., & Hyatt, S. (2013). *Hidden in plain sight: An assessment of youth inclusion in point-in-time counts of California's unsheltered homeless population.* CA State Library. Retrieved from https://www.homelesshub.ca/resource/hidden-plain-sight-assessment-youth-inclusion-point-time-counts-california%E2%80%99s-unsheltered

Bamberg, M. (2004b). Positioning with Davie Hogan–Stories, tellings, and identities. In C. Daiute, & C. Lightfoot (Eds.), *Narrative analysis: Studying the development of individuals in society* (pp. 135–157). Sage.

Bowen, E., Savino, R., Miller, B., Zuchlewski, D., Ma, K., & Slocum, C. (2016). Homelessness among young adults in Buffalo: A research report highlighting youth voices. Retrieved from https://digitalcommons.ilr.cornell.edu/cgi/viewcontent.cgi?article=1003&context=buffalocommons

Cruz, C. (2013). LGBTQ street youth doing resistance in infrapolitical worlds. In Tuck, E., & Yang, K. W. (Eds.). *Youth resistance research and theories of change.* (pp. 209–217). Routledge.

Davies, B., & Harre, R. (1990). Positioning: The discursive production of selves. *Journal for the Theory of Social Behaviour, 20*(1), 43–63. https://onlinelibrary.wiley.com/doi/10.1111/j.1468-5914.1990.tb00174.x

Freire, P. (1983). The importance of the act of reading. *Journal of Education, 165*(1), 5–11. https://doi.org/10.1177%2F002205748316500103

Ginwright, S. A. (2010). *Black youth rising: Activism and radical healing in urban America.* Teachers College Press.

Glazier, J. A. (2009). The challenge of repositioning: Teacher learning in the company of others. *Teaching and Teacher Education, 25*(6), 826–834. https://www.sciencedirect.com/science/article/abs/pii/S0742051X08002047

Jacobs, M. M. (2014). Literacy, education, and inequality: Assimilation and resistance narratives from families residing at a homeless shelter. *Critical Questions in Education, 5*(3), 172–188. Retrieved from https://files.eric.ed.gov/fulltext/EJ1046708.pdf

Kwong, T. Y., & Hayes, D. K. (2017). Adverse family experiences and flourishing amongst children ages 6–17 years: 2011/12 National Survey of Children's Health. *Child Abuse & Neglect, 70,* 240–246. Retrieved from https://www.ncbi.nlm.nih.gov/pmc/articles/PMC5600852/

MacGillivray, L., Ardell, A. L., & Curwen, M. S. (2010). Supporting the literacy development of children living in homeless shelters. *The Reading Teacher, 63*(5), 384–392. Retrieved from https://ila.onlinelibrary.wiley.com/doi/abs/10.1598/RT.63.5.4

Masten, A. S. (2014). Global perspectives on resilience in children and youth. *Child Development, 85*(1), 6–20. Retrieved from https://srcd.onlinelibrary.wiley.com/doi/10.1111/cdev.12205

McVee, M. B., Silvestri, K. N., Barrett, N., & Haq, K. S. (2018). Positioning theory. In D. E. Alvermann, N. J. Unrau, M. Sailors, & R. B. Ruddell (Eds.), *Theoretical models and processes of literacy* (7th ed.). Routledge.

Milner, H. R. (2013). Analyzing poverty, learning, and teaching through a critical race theory lens. *Review of Research in Education, 37*(1), 1–53. Retrieved from https://journals.sagepub.com/doi/abs/10.3102/0091732x12459720

Noll, E., & Watkins, R. (2003). The impact of homelessness on children's literacy experiences. *The Reading Teacher, 57*(4), 362–371. Retrieved from https://www.jstor.org/stable/20205371?seq=1

Rankine, C. (2014). *Citizen: An American lyric.* Graywolf Press.

Reynolds, J., & Kiely, B. (2015). *All American boys.* Simon and Schuster.

Rogers, T., & Marshall, E. (2012). On the road: Examining self-representation and discourses of homelessness in young adult texts. *Journal of Adolescent & Adult Literacy, 55*(8), 725–733. Retrieved from https://ila.onlinelibrary.wiley.com/doi/abs/10.1002/JAAL.00087

Rogers, T., Winters, K. L., Perry, M., & LaMonde, A. M. (2015).*Youth, critical literacies, and civic engagement: Arts, media, and literacy in the lives of adolescents.* Routledge.

Shor, I., & Freire, P. (1987). *A pedagogy for liberation.* Bergin and Garvey.

Snyder, C. R. (1996). To hope, to lose, and hope again.*Journal of Personal and Interpersonal Loss, 1*(1), 1–16. doi: https://doi.org/10.1080/15325029608415455

Snyder, C. R., Rand, K. L., & Sigmon, D. R. (2002). Hope theory: A member of the positive psychology family. In Snyder, C. R. & Lopez, S. J. (Eds.), *Handbook of positive psychology* (pp. 257–276). Oxford University Press.

Thomas, A. (2017). *The hate u give.* Balzer & Bray.

Wortham, S. E. (2000). Interactional positioning and narrative self-construction. *Narrative Inquiry, 10*(1), 157–184.

Wortham, S. (2001). *Narratives in action: A strategy for research and analysis.* Teachers College Press.

Yates, T. M., Tyrell, F. A., & Masten, A. S. (2015). Resilience theory and the practice of positive psychology from individuals to societies. In Joseph, S. (Ed) *Positive psychology in practice: Promoting human flourishing in work, health, education, and everyday life,* (pp. 773–788). Wiley & Sons.

21 Visualizing Hope

Digital Storytelling with Refugee-background Children

Toby Emert

The complex dynamics of human immigration are a characteristic feature of the modern world (Hyland, 2015, para. 4), and issues related to migration may, ultimately, define the global trends of the early 21st century. Drawing distinctions between "political migrants (those trying to escape persecution) and economic immigrants (those moving from poverty) is difficult but important because international law treats these two categories of people differently" (Dragostinova, 2016, para. 10). Of the world's 68 million people forcibly displaced due to war, persecution, and natural catastrophes, as many as one-third are refugees—people who, according to the United Nations High Commissioner for Refugees, have a well-founded fear of returning to their homelands because of the threat of violence. Refugees may also be stateless because of discriminatory practices that deny national citizenship based on ethnicity, race, and religion, for example, and they may lack access to basic rights, such as education, healthcare, and employment. This chapter focuses on the educational needs of the children of political migrants who have sought official refugee status, a designation that allows them to request asylum in a host country where they receive legal protection and assistance. Most requests are denied, but a tiny subgroup of refugees is granted asylum and the hope of a new life in an adopted country.

Before being granted refugee status, many displaced families spend months—or, perhaps, years—in resettlement camps, where survival is the key concern and human services such as quality schooling are difficult to secure. When refugee-background children arrive in the United States, for example, it is likely that their formal education has been interrupted, and it is also likely that learning experiences they had in a resettlement camp were spotty and substandard. Furthermore, American public schools typically have no formal framework to integrate refugee-background children (Lerner, 2012, p. 9). Learners are often placed in age-appropriate classrooms and offered language support, but school communities are underprepared to attend to the wealth of needs. Refugee-background students are not usually offered the kind of language-acquisition or social support that would allow them to meet academic expectations, and they are often targets of harassment, which can lead them to underestimate their abilities and lose faith in the promise of education. They need opportunities to thrive in classroom settings, demonstrate what they know, and feel invested in schooling and hopeful about their potential to succeed academically.

Raising Expectations

Description of the Context

The United States has, until recently, been hospitable to refugees, accepting more asylum seekers than any other nation (Cepla, 2018, para. 4). Refugees have been resettled in all 50 states, but a few states consistently rank among the top destinations. Georgia is one of those states, and the community of Clarkston in DeKalb County serves as a national relocation center for newcomers. Over the last 15 years, more than 20,000 refugees have relocated from war-ravaged countries across the globe to this once sleepy town a few miles east of Atlanta. The challenges of integrating the newcomers have, at times, been overwhelming for the community.

As a faculty member working on issues of literacy and social justice in a college located near Clarkston, I have been involved in initiatives that address the learning needs of refugee-background children: academic summer camps, after-school tutoring, multi-generational literacy classes, and the development of curricula for local educational agencies. In this chapter, however, I discuss a multi-year research project with middle school girls that focused on English language acquisition and building academic confidence using digital storytelling (DST). This initiative began as a collaboration between Agnes Scott College's Department of Education and a local intervention program for refugee families that focuses on supporting young women. The program recruits cohorts of 12–18 girls each year to participate in an immersive academic experience that offers instruction in traditional content—science, math, social studies, and language arts—and provides extracurricular support for the students and their families. The primary objective of the program is to prepare the students for successful entry into a local public high school. Because Agnes Scott College is a liberal arts women's institution, the initiative provided an opportunity for the middle school girls to develop a mentor relationship with college-age women, who served as allies, as well as an opportunity to attend an academic program on a college campus. We saw these aspects of the project as important in helping the middle schoolers envision possibilities for their educational futures.

The partnership began in 2011, shortly after the founding of the middle school program. The research project took place from 2011 to 2016 and involved an eight-week experiential workshop that met once a week during the spring semester on the college campus. During sessions, the children worked with me and a selected group of undergraduates to share autobiographical stories, translate those stories digitally using film editing software, and present their projects to an audience of peers, teachers, and interested community partners. The students were consistently successful in moving through the phases of the project, which is not an insignificant accomplishment, given their emerging English and the lack of familiarity with digital tools. The emphasis of the research, however, was on their development of academic confidence, or what social learning theorist Albert Bandura terms self-efficacy—the belief in one's "ability to successfully accomplish something" (Hayden, 2013, p. 15). Bandura suggested that students with a limited sense of self-efficacy are less likely to persevere because they don't believe they can succeed, but those with strong self-beliefs are more likely to demonstrate resilience. For refugee-background learners who have experienced interrupted formal educational experiences, opportunities to succeed at a complex learning task are critical.

Description of the Curriculum

The Digital Storytelling (DST)—which "integrates the traditional art of oral storytelling with the technology available in the twenty-first century classroom" (Abdelmageed & El-Naggar, 2018, p. 278)—served as the central assignment for the project because it invites engagement, promotes visual understanding, and reinforces language acquisition, especially the development of vocabulary (Emert, 2013). It also inspires a sense of achievement for learners, partially because the creation of the story requires concept-development, continuous planning, writing, speaking, editing, audience awareness, and technical skill, and the process is iterative (Barber, 2016). Students have opportunities to rethink and rework their stories to refine them. As typically used for educational purposes, digital stories tend to take one of three forms: (a) personal narratives, (b) information or instruction, or (c) examinations of historical events (Robin, 2006).

For the project with the middle schoolers, we focused on the development of personal narratives, asking the students to first share a story about their lives orally in a story circle and then, later, helping them translate the story through a series of steps that led to the final product. The sharing allowed us to gauge the students' comfort with speaking in English and allowed them choice in selecting a story for the project. The college facilitators modeled the assignment by telling a story from their own lives, illustrating a range of possible topics—from learning to ride a horse to auditioning for a high school musical to getting a new kitten. The middle schoolers were not prohibited from sharing an immigration story, but most chose to tell a family story or recalled a memory from earlier in their lives.

We premised the lessons for the curriculum on Bandura's ideas that confidence can be generated through experiences that lead to mastery or through verbal persuasion and thinking about undertaking a new behavior (Pfitzner-Eden, 2016). Each two-hour lesson involved opportunities for the students to develop relationships with the facilitators, watch examples, receive feedback and coaching, and practice new skills—such as working within specific story frames for plot structure or learning about MovieMaker, the film editing software they used to create their digital stories. The lessons were also dovetailed to support the students' growth, with opportunities for review and skill-enhancement. It was important for the students to recognize their movement from neophyte to experienced storyteller and notice steps along the pathway that led to the goal of completing the assignment.

Reflection on their accomplishment provided evidence of the students' academic capacity and demonstrated for them that, though they were emerging speakers and writers of English, they could tackle a complex literacy task and, with appropriate support, achieve the objectives of the assignment. It was necessary for the students to recognize the shining moments (Hubbard & Power, 2012) in their learning experience. It's the recognition of perseverance in the face of an academic challenge that allows for the growth of confidence and a vision for what is possible. Snyder (2002) suggests that the characteristics of a hopeful disposition include the belief in one's ability to follow a path that leads to a goal. The frame for the curriculum was conceptualized to provide the students a belief in the possibilities of future academic success.

Reimagining a Story

Description of the Process

Writing the Stories. Sharing a personal story and revising it to fit the parameters of the DST project presented the middle schoolers with the opportunity to own the story they told and craft it for an audience in ways they chose. We understood that the students participating in the project likely had harrowing life stories, but, rather than asking them to revisit those stories—which is not an uncommon request for refugee-background learners (Colborne, 2015)—we asked them to select a moment or memory they wanted to talk about, and then we helped them reimagine the story as a visual text that spoke to an external audience.

To scaffold their success with the project, as we listened to the students' stories, we filmed them and then transcribed the recordings. Each of the middle schoolers worked with a facilitator to review her story and decide if it represented an idea she wanted to continue working

with. Then the students and the facilitators edited the stories to generate 12–14 strong sentences that could be illustrated in the filmmaking
segment of the workshop. The students wrote each sentence on a note
card and read it aloud to listen for sense errors—missing words, etc.
This style of revision honored the students' developing language skills,
as it allowed them to hear the sentences they had written; they were better able to notice possible edits, which they often overlooked when they
read the sentences silently. It also allowed us to individualize language
coaching. The students demonstrated diverse strengths as writers, and
they benefited from one-on-one instruction that pinpointed areas for
improvement. We also offered a mini-lesson on using strong verbs and
one on creating interesting titles, writing skills that all of the students
needed assistance with. After the mini-lessons, the students returned to
their note cards and identified the verbs in their sentences and asked
the question, "Do I know a stronger verb to use here?" Working with the
revised notecards, the students moved to the development of visuals to
illustrate their stories.

Generating Images for the Stories. We asked the students to create
images for their stories by developing *tableaux vivants* to accompany each
sentence and then taking a picture of the "illustration" with a digital
camera. A *tableau vivant* is a static image created by posing bodies to represent a scene or staged action. Asking the students to use their bodies
and the bodies of their peers and the facilitators to render their ideas
about the language they used to describe their experience was an effort
to help them remember the vocabulary they were using. The use of visual
and tactile methods of recall often improve students' capacity to remember words (Holden, 1999), and *tableaux vivants* can help extend com-
prehension (Gardner, 2011). We encouraged the students to visualize
the moments in their stories as scenes, just as writers and film directors
must, and express creativity as they demonstrated their understanding of how to translate their ideas for viewers. This aspect of the project required practice and, often, the students auditioned several ideas
before settling on a final image to photograph. Testing their ideas and
revising offered the students opportunities to demonstrate—for us and
for themselves—their capacity to be flexible and imaginative. Kim—a
pseudonym—for example, had told the group a story about a bicycle
accident she had when she lived in Myanmar. As she produced the visuals
for her story, she decided that her image of the wrecked bicycle needed
a background, so she drew one on the board in the classroom and then
positioned herself as the protagonist in the story within the background.
This kind of thinking about conveying ideas visually to an audience sur-
passed the expectations of the assignment; it showed Kim's creativity
and capacity to problem-solve, 21st-century skills not often prioritized
for newcomers in public schools, where the instructional emphasis is typically on remediation (Shapiro, 2011). The image-making allowed the

students to engage playfully with their compositions and further developed a sense of camaraderie and community in the workshop.

Translating the Stories Digitally. The middle schoolers were especially interested in the technical aspects of the DST workshop and were facile learners when we introduced them to MovieMaker. They were curious when we demonstrated how to import images, add text, select a soundtrack, and fine-tune their projects. The visual design of the software assisted them as they encountered vocabulary specific to the task. "Paste," "transition," "drag-and-drop," "import," "timeline," and "visual effects," for example, were words and phrases they learned during the instruction and that they began practicing, often using the program's icons as triggers when they struggled to remember the term. They also recognized their efforts, noting the difficulty of the project, as well as their sense of engagement. "I would tell them we are making video on the computer and it was fun," Kim offered when asked what she might tell a friend about her experience of participating in the project. When we asked her what she had learned, she said, "I learned making videos on the computer is hard and it takes some time." Kim's focus on both the effort and the enjoyment is a reflection of the project's aims—to invite the students to undertake a sophisticated multimodal assignment that would challenge *and* engage them. The capacity to persevere when faced with a difficult educational task signals confidence and a disposition of hope and possibility, important traits for all learners, but critical traits for refugee-background learners whose schooling performances often do not reflect what they may be capable of achieving.

Conclusion

Adolescents' emerging beliefs about their identities as learners influence their sense of self-worth and reinforce the development of academic confidence—a characteristic that allows them to tackle complex assignments and persist. Refugee-background learners benefit from educational activities that invite them to demonstrate skills they bring to the classroom, build on those skills, and then expand their repertoire. Multimodal assignments, such as DST, engage students in language play and creative problem solving and, when scaffolded sensitively, illustrate their capacity to tackle a demanding project. Over the six years that we conducted the DST workshop, we consistently witnessed the students' growth in interpersonal communication, their willingness to work hard even when presented with unfamiliar academic expectations, and their adeptness for translating traditional stories to a digital format. Their achievements routinely exceeded the expectations of their teachers, and, most importantly, the students noted their own learning, which we asked them to discuss at the culminating premiere event for each spring's workshop.

Refugee-background learners need allies within the educational system who recognize their potential and challenge them to thrive within a culture that may misperceive their needs and their gifts. They need learning opportunities that cultivate resilience, confidence, and, ultimately, hope for the future as they build the story of a new life in an adopted country.

References

Abdelmageed, M., & El-Naggar, Z. (2018). Digital storytelling enhances students' speaking skills at Zewail University of Science and Technology in Egypt. In E. Langran & J. Borup (Eds.), *Proceedings of Society for Information Technology & Teacher Education International Conference 2018* (pp. 278–287). Association for the Advancement of Computing in Education. Retrieved from https://www.learntechlib.org/primary/p/182537/

Barber, J. F. (2016). Digital storytelling: New opportunities for humanities scholarship and pedagogy. *Cogent Arts & Humanities, 3*(1), 1–14. doi: https://doi.org/10.1080/23311983.2016.1181037

Cepla, Z. (2018, May 14). *Fact sheet: U.S. refugee resettlement.* National Immigration Forum. Retrieved from https://immigrationforum.org/article/fact-sheet-u-s-refugee-resettlement/

Colborne, M. (2015). Syrian refugees' mental health is top priority. *CMAJ: Canadian Medical Association Journal, 187*(18), 1347 doi: https://doi.org/10.1503/cmaj.109-5183

Dragostinova, T. (2016). Refugees or immigrants: The migration crisis in Europe in historical perspective. *Origins: Current Events in Historical Perspective 9*(4). Retrieved from http://origins.osu.edu/article/refugees-or-immigrants-migration-crisis-europe-historical-perspective

Emert, T. (2013). "The transpoemations project": Digital storytelling, contemporary poetry, and refugee boys. *Intercultural Education, 24*(4), 355–365. doi: https://doi.org/10.1080/14675986.2013.809245

Gardner, H. (2011). *Frames of mind: The theory of multiple intelligences.* Basic Books.

Hayden, J. (2013). *Health behavior theory* (2nd ed.). Jones and Bartlett Learning.

Holden, W. (1999). Learning to learn: 15 vocabulary acquisition activities. *Modern English Teacher 8*(2): 42–47. Retrieved from https://files.eric.ed.gov/fulltext/ED450589.pdf

Hubbard, R. S., & Power, B. M. (2012). *Living the questions: A guide for teacher-researchers* (2nd ed.). Stenhouse Publishers.

Hyland, S. (2015). *Hacer América* and the American dream: Global migration and the Americas. *Origins: Current Events in Historical Perspective, 8*(8). Retrieved from http://origins.osu.edu/article/hacer-am-rica-and-american-dream-global-migration-and-americas

Lerner, A. B. (2012). The educational resettlement of refugee children: Examining several theoretical approaches. *Multicultural Education, 20*(1), 9–14. Retrieved from https://files.eric.ed.gov/fulltext/EJ1014867.pdf

Pfitzner-Eden, F. (2016). Why do I feel more confident? Bandura's sources predict preservice teachers' latent changes in teacher self-efficacy. *Frontiers in Psychology, 7*, 1–16. https://doi.org/10.3389/fpsyg.2016.01486

Robin, B. (2006). The educational uses of digital storytelling. In C. Crawford, R. Carlsen, K. McFerrin, J. Price, R. Weber & D. Willis (Eds.), *Proceedings of Society for Information Technology & Teacher Education International Conference 2006* (pp. 709–716). Association for the Advancement of Computing in Education. Retrieved from https://www.learntechlib.org/primary/p/22129/

Shapiro, S. (2011). Stuck in the remedial rut: Confronting resistance to ESL curriculum reform. *Journal of Basic Writing 30*(2), 24–52. Retrieved from https://files.eric.ed.gov/fulltext/EJ988209.pdf

Snyder, C. (2002). Hope theory: Rainbows in the mind. *Psychological Inquiry, 13*(4), 249–275. Retrieved from www.jstor.org/stable/1448867

22 Conclusion

Hope as an Ally to Grieving and Healing

Nicole Sieben and Stephanie Anne Shelton

When we consider our losses, both individually and collectively, we know that we must also consider the contexts within and through which they exist. We also know that though circumstances change and sometimes evolve, losses may not. They may, but this—the promise of change— is not an absolute or a required condition of grief. Recognizing the uniqueness of grief processes, we affirm that none of these chapters is meant to be prescriptive or formulaic for finding hope. Instead, we aim for this work to be *transcriptive*—to have transfer and application across contexts in many forms. While we see hope in these pages, we know that this hope is not naive and is evolving and intangible in many ways. However, the goal of this book is to make our collective navigation of hope tangible and recognizable, at least to some degree, to help those who are grieving to feel seen, heard, affirmed, and companioned in their quests for hope and healing.

Because finding hope in grieving can be about asking critical questions, for which we do not necessarily have any answers, we conclude this collection by reminding readers of two lingering inquiries that have become constant quests for us as we journey through hope as allies. As a reminder, we began this collection by inviting readers to consider two questions while exploring the chapters:

1 *How will I know when I've found hope in my grief? (What does this hope look like?)* and
2 *What are my pathways of hoping and grieving that will help me survive? (What allyship do I need to move me forward and through my grief?)*

These questions may not have been answered in whole or even in part for all readers, but we suggest that the *quest* for answers, reasons, or evidence can be a process or pathway to hope in and of itself. For us, and for many academics, it has often been in the searching that we have (been) found.

In this collection, we have witnessed the hoping, healing, and grieving of 29 scholars across multiple intersectional domains in higher education. Through multidisciplinary and transdisciplinary frameworks, authors allow us glimpses into ways of approaching, examining, interrogating, understanding, navigating, and theorizing the processes of grieving. Though sometimes work in academia can be siloed, grieving is not; it does not occur in a vacuum apart from certain aspects of our lives. As each chapter demonstrates, grief can happen over time, all at once, or in some combination of both, but always in concert with work-related and other life-related responsibilities that beg our attention despite our losses. Both grievers and academics, we see our work in academia as essential to surviving our grief and to finding hope through the messiness of it all. Our grief will likely always be there, but the pathways we travel as we navigate through can make all the difference in surviving our losses and thriving *despite* or even *because* of them.

When we began this book project, it was our hope to create an allyship in grieving with one another and for those in higher education (and beyond) looking for frameworks within which to think about grief. In witnessing these stories and examining these frameworks, we gain additional pathways to and through hope, with the understanding that none of these pathways is challenge-free. Each of these chapters has shown us that. Each author (or group of authors) has taken us through unique ways of hoping and grieving that can be taken up in various capacities using adaptations based on individual situations. Given the uniqueness of each person's grief journey, these chapters beg us to remember that being an ally in grief is hard, heart work. It means listening to one another's grief stories, hearing what each griever needs, and giving them the space to achieve those conditions. It can necessitate many other fluid processes as well. Too often, higher education does not provide that space or time for those in need of it to follow the hope pathways *towards* healing that would make a difference in surviving these devastating losses. Knowing that each loss requires a different set of pathways forward, through, or around the experienced pain, this collection provides a critical foreword and 22 chapters of thoughtful scholarship, hope-filled work, and intentional pathways from authors who have witnessed/experienced grief and have been willing to share frameworks and stories with our higher education community.

As grief scholar David Kessler (2020) shared recently in a virtual talk about grief with the National Council of Teachers of English (NCTE) Community of English teachers, "We have to attend to our grief. Our grief has a right to live," and we believe that this book provides a space for grief to live, and for hope to grow. Writing can provide one such pathway to travel towards hope; reading and witnessing others' stories can provide another. Discussing this work with others can create a space for movement to occur and for hope to build. When we read others' grief narratives, we give their grief "a right [and a space] to live," and we can open up a space for our own grief to be attended to as well. It is our hope that this book is able to do that for others, just as it has done for us.

In writing alongside, reading with, researching as, and collecting for these chapters, we have gained a companionship in grief that we both are grateful for as editors, educators, academics, and humans constantly in search of hope. Each chapter has given us glimpses into how hope can operate in our academic lives when we apply theory and practice to living and hoping amidst our grief. Just as Kessler (2020) has called on us to hold other people's grief as precious, we also hold our own grief as precious, and we hope others in higher education will do the same. As these chapters illustrate, grieving is not a shortcoming; it is a circumstance of life that all of us in higher education (will) face at some point. As academics, "We have to attend to our grief. Our grief has a right to live." In these pages, we give space and breath to the tragically beautiful dance that emerges as necessary between grief and hope, powerful partners in this journey of life that access the truest forms of our humanness.

Reference

Kessler, D. (2020). *A conversation about grief with author David Kessler*. NCTE.

Index